THROW OUT TWO HANDS

This edition, issued in 1964, is for members of The Companion Book Club, Borough Green, Sevenoaks, Kent, from which address particulars of membership may be obtained. The book is issued by arrangement with the original publishers, George Allen and Unwin Ltd.

Also by
ANTHONY SMITH

★

BLIND WHITE FISH IN PERSIA
SEA NEVER DRY
HIGH STREET AFRICA

*"Reading is an adventure with some of
the characteristics of the chase."*
HOLBROOK JACKSON

THROW OUT
TWO HANDS

★

ANTHONY SMITH

THE COMPANION BOOK CLUB
LONDON

DEDICATION

I wrote this book, but the expedition it describes would never have got off the ground had it not been for my companions and all those who helped us at every turn. So to those companions, in particular, and to all who helped in any way, this book is gratefully dedicated.

"I entirely agree with you about air balloons. I am tir'd of reading about them in the papers."

The Rt. Hon. Frederick Montagu in a letter
to Mrs Delany, October 22, 1784.

*Made and printed in Great Britain
for the Companion Book Club (Odhams Books Ltd.)
by Odhams (Watford) Limited,
Watford, Herts.*
S.1264.UC

CONTENTS

ILLUSTRATIONS

CHAPTER ONE

THE DREAM

I SAT down in the basket. There was just room to do this, and
it did grant some measure of relief. It was not particularly
comfortable, for the strange collection of shapes down there
made it unsuitable for real relaxation; but there are times
when a body simply has to sit down, however rough the
reception to it. This was one of them. I folded my knees as
best I could, inserted my feet into whatsoever niche seemed
vacant, and pressed my back into the rope behind me. The
basket stopped wobbling, and the whole world became as
silent as before. The top of my head was level with the
basket's rim, but I could see through that thick wicker weave
down to the ground over a mile below. Much of it was water,
for we were crossing a lake at the time, but there was also an
infinity of land stretching away, with cliff and plain, dust
and swamp, rolling hill and forest, all intermingling, all
leading one to the other until they became lost in the haze
and obscurity at the edge of the Earth. Within the protection
of the basket I looked at it all, and then closed my eyes. It
seemed safer like that, for the reason I sat down was not
because I was tired, but because I was terrified. I had never
before been quite so frightened.

Closing one's eyes is, of course, a fatuous act. Dangers do
not vanish by disregarding them; but they create less fear.
On that flight we had needed, and plainly would continue
to need, all our wits about us. We had half a sack of ballast
left in the balloon. We were 6,000 feet above a caustic lake,
and nearly 10,000 feet above sea-level. The wind had
virtually failed, and on all sides were the huge puffy giants
of thundercloud, the cumulo-nimbus of Africa. The balloon
itself was doing well, with its cords and toggles still in fine
trim, and its great orange and silver shape as resplendent as
ever; but the balloon and we were dependent upon the

atmosphere, and what it cooked up for us in the way of thermals, down-draughts, aerial waves and the rest of its turbulent manoeuvrings. A mile or so back we had been all but sucked into the dark lowering base of a thundercloud, and its cavernous rumbling was a sound none of us will forget. That particular danger was over; but, when the cross-wind had come from nowhere to sweep us out from that cloud, we had once again been bathed in sunlight. The physics of ballooning is such that we then rose even higher, and the lake grew further and further away. Hence, for nothing could be done, the great desire to sit down.

Involved with the empty sandbags, camera gear, instruments, rope, water-bottles, clothes, and film stock on which I distributed my weight—fairly evenly with one or two sharp exceptions—were the legs of my two companions. They were still standing up. Indeed, as balloon baskets have little roominess about them, they had no other choice. One man sitting down in a thing 3 feet 11 inches by 2 feet 11 inches tends to occupy the bulk of the available square footage, however contorted he may feel in his desire not to occupy it all. I had succeeded in tying myself into a passable imitation of a clove-hitch, and I half-opened my eyes again to look at things.

The legs belonged to Alan Root and Douglas Botting. Take Alan's first. They had short trousers on them, and ended in a pair of sandals. They were brown, not white, for he lived in East Africa, and spent little time in cities or towns. They were competent legs, but that right knee was shortly to cut itself on a piece of rock, and some blood was to dribble out of it. This was of no great consequence, for Alan's knees were always shortly to be cut by something or other. He and they had a great facility for damaging themselves, frequently. Douglas's legs were next to them. They seemed longer, although he was the same height, for they had long trousers on them. Despite the events of the previous weeks, these trousers still had a detectable crease, and the shoes at the bottom a visible shine. Both pairs of legs leant in their various ways against the furnishings of our basket,

8

as the owners rested their elbows on its rim, and peered down at the waters beneath.

Normally, these two kept themselves fully occupied with the business of photography. The changing of magazines, and of reels and lenses, and batteries, and cameras, and positions, is a time-consuming feature of the art, and the actual pressing of the button a relatively minor task. Up in a balloon, however, with the world constantly changing, with an elephant suddenly appearing from behind a tree, with a pink smear at the water's edge becoming the flight of a thousand flamingoes, any photographer is perpetually engaged. This is true when the balloon is satisfactorily near the ground, and when objects are well within camera range; but it fails to be so when the balloon leaps up a few thousand feet. Then, however long the focus of the lenses, however many millimetres they may be, even the biggest of elephants appearing round the smallest of trees is as nothing. Panoramic shots, encompassing the world, and taking in horizon after horizon, are all very well on occasion; but putting the camera steadily at infinity has its limits. From a high-flying balloon this is emphatically so. There is only a couple of feet of foreground and then nothing, nothing but air, until the land is reached and it stretches away towards its own particular brand of nothingness.

Consequently, Douglas and Alan were not busy for the time being. While I sat at their feet they instead occupied themselves estimating our chances for and against dropping into the lake. So long as we were maintaining height, there was a fair likelihood of our reaching some shore. Which shore did not matter greatly, for a balloon can land almost anywhere; but the thought of dropping into the lake itself was additional reason for disquiet. It is possible to descend on water, and then to float like a monstrous and ungainly sailing craft to land, but the 30 miles by 10 miles of lake then beneath us did not encourage the idea. Like many inland basins, with no exit to them, this accumulation of water had acted as a solvent for millennia. Such lakes frequently pick up salt, thereby becoming doubly buoyant, but Lake Manyara had picked up soda. Should we drop into

9

it there would be some miles of caustic water through which to swim. It would certainly attack our eyes first, and then our skin; but to what extent we could only guess, because naturally enough no one swam in it for long. I looked down at the lake through the wicker-work and saw it 6,000 feet below, with white streaks of soda stretching across its surface. I looked at the altimeter around my neck, but the needle had not moved since I had decided to sit down. So I too stayed where I was. Anyhow, there was still nothing to be done, until all the interacting forces of the atmosphere had planned what next to do with us.

Alan and Douglas, still staring down, assessed whether the small dot of a shadow was moving anywhere. It was certainly bouncing over the waves fast enough, but there was a minor storm down there, and the waves were whipping along from north-east to south-west. Was our movement actual, or only relative to those waves? I fingered the half-sack of sand ballast, all that remained to break our fall whether our landing was in the alkaline water or on the hard, dry ground surrounding it. The text books stipulate that at least 60 lb. of ballast should be in hand for every final descent, and more is necessary if the balloon is coming down from a great height. Well, we had 15 lb., and were undoubtedly high up. Nothing could be done about that now, except wait. And shut one's eyes. And pretend to relax, and wonder what on earth is going to happen.

Being up in a balloon like that, even with two companions so close at hand, induces a feeling of considerable loneliness. No one can do anything to help you. You are short of sand. No one can possibly give you more. You are too high, and above a burning lake. No one can move you elsewhere. We were without initiative in a situation we had created for ourselves. No one had ordered us to get into a balloon, to try and film the big game herds of Africa, to examine the potentialities of such a superb vantage point, and to commemorate the centenary of Jules Verne's first book, the one about exploration of the dark continent by balloon. We had wished to resuscitate the balloon for a modern purpose, and no one could help us while we were actively doing so. We were alone, and afraid, and yet the chain of events had been quite logical. On the other hand it had certainly not been easy to get into that particular circumstance.

You must understand, Mr Smith, that to fly a balloon you need a licence, said one. To take photographs you will need a commercial balloon pilot's licence as well. No, this firm cannot make a balloon for you, said another. Moreover, there are no spare hydrogen cylinders in East Africa. Undoubtedly, said a third, the animals will run from you as fast as their legs can carry them. The costs will be prohibitive. Think of the shipping alone! And the air-freight! And what are you going to do when you come down? Surely vultures will attack your balloon, even if you get one. And if it is possible to do this, why haven't others done it before? The authorities out there will be against it. If not, they should be. Why put other people to trouble? Why not just drop the whole idea?

With no doubt at all, many of those encountered in the expedition's planning had tried, valiantly, to put a stop to it. I still think it amazing that our economy survives in a changing world when so many pawns in its affairs consider it their duty to act as grit, whatsover the suggested move may be. If an idea comes up, it must be rebuffed. If a plan is put forward, then friction must react and impede its progress. "Well," says an employee of some miserable institution, after he has done all in his power to thwart, "if there's anything more I can do to help, you have only to let me know."

Such people, stiff and hard to bend, calcified and upright, are the backbone of any country. They are the enemy. They are there, to be bribed in some places, threatened in others, cajoled, bludgeoned, entreated, ingratiated or humiliated, until their own individual blockhouse of resistance has been overcome. Do nothing; and there is no problem. Suggest anything; and they rise up, in their hundreds. Had they won we would not have been grouped in the confines of that basket, however irrelevant such an act may seem to their everyday affairs.

They did not win because there are other people. There is

11

also a desperation which they engender, on occasion, in those who encounter them, and this gives strength to any cause. It was this frenzy, and those other individuals, who enabled everything to happen. A Belgian made a balloon in his attic. The Royal Dutch Aero Club gave me a licence. I learnt the art of lighter-than-air flying over the fields, the dikes, and trim towns of Holland. Money, of a sort, became available. Equipment, of all sorts, got into our hands. With regard, sir, to your request for petrol, for rope, for wind charts, for polyurethane, for a hydrogen purity meter, for a Tanganyika jack, for a flasher unit, or a Zanzibar flag, a statoscope, a variometer, a winch, lashings, life-jackets, emergency rations, a gyroscopic head, or what you will, the same will be delivered, by train, or plane, or hand, this week, or next week, sometime, or never.

An expedition by balloon is like any other. It involves far more than is initially imagined. Similarly, the original vision of flying with the wind proved to be equally faulty as soon as the expedition got off the ground. I had thought of us coasting, gently, silently, effortlessly, over the tracts of Africa. I had not dreamed for a moment of thunder-clouds, or snapping ropes, or the convulsions of a balloon when entrapped in a thermal. In other words, I had been monumentally wrong on a large number of vital aspects. I had produced talk, much talk, about the sensations of ballooning when still earthbound in Britain, and when knowing just a fraction more about it than the next man; but I had never spoken or thought of an occasion when I would slump into the bottom of the basket, close my eyes, and long for help.

For an hour or so that day we hovered above the lake. Occasionally one of us drank some water or ate a banana, but no banana-skins were thrown overboard because any lessening of weight would have sent us even higher. Earlier in the flight the canopy of balloon had shielded us from the sun, but as the day wore on the shade moved elsewhere, and the sun burnt its way to the three of us. Like ancient mariners stabbing their knives into the mast, we waited in the doldrums for events to take hold of us. Quite suddenly, they did.

The green pennant lifted itself into the air. At the same moment a breath of wind touched all our cheeks, and we began to move. We did not know where we were moving, for it is hard to judge when such a gust comes from nowhere. I looked at the altimeter. We were going down, at last, and decidedly so. Instead of hanging limp, the pennant was now flapping almost horizontally, and our dot of a shadow was heading purposefully for the lake's eastern shore. The wind had changed from 030 to 270, but what did that matter? I stood up at once, and stared down to see what piece of country lay in store for us.

The ballooning of my old imaginings was reasserting itself once more. I threw out a little of the precious sand so the descent would not be too rapid, and watched the approach of that soda-encrusted shore. With majestic ease we sailed over it. How ridiculous troubles seem once they are left behind! How insignificant, and unreal! The water changed into land with complete simplicity. Our shadow enlarged as the ground came up to meet us, and the dark lumps became trees, and the darker lumps were water-holes. Down there in the reeds was a bushbuck. Over there were two gazelles. And a bustard taking to the air. And a giraffe, standing aloof from the tree it nibbled at.

Down we went, and handful after handful of sand prevented our momentum building up. At 200 feet the tip of our trail-rope met the dusty earth, and dragged along behind us. As more and more of this rope reached the ground the balloon flattened out its downward course, and soon we were cruising along at tree-top height. This was as it should be, and quite miraculous. The wind was brisk, but not dangerous, and we floated along above everything at the comfortable speed of some 15 miles an hour. Birds flapped past as if in sympathy. Insects kept up their hissing chatter. More and more world appeared ahead of us. More and more animals were there. A huge tinkling herd of Masai cattle. And zebras. And gazelles. These danced about, and leapt a little, and then stopped. It was all entrancing, like being in love, when there is too much to take in, too much of beauty, too much of feeling a union with something else, of being absorbed in the wonder of all that is incomprehensible. The air was warm and perfect. The smells were good. The sights inexhaustible.

Alan and Douglas were now more than occupied. "Lyrical" they shouted at each other, and tried to capture one-tenth of the wonder going on around them. That word I was to hear many, many times, for it is an abbreviation, a technical term in the world of photography, which is used to describe anything that is lovely. Photographers must attempt to catch such sights, to be moved by them, and yet simultaneously to have their noses deep in the technical difficulties of capturing what they can. So they talk of lyricals, jauntily and without admitting that their souls are involved, for there is enough in trying to describe a scene on film without also attempting to tell it out loud. "Lyrical" Douglas and Alan said again to each other, as they stared through their respective eye-pieces; and indeed it was.

Of course, as is the nature of everything that goes up, even balloon flights have to come down, and to an end. It is advantageous if the inevitable can be mixed with the judicious, and if the balloon can be coerced to land near a road, for such prudence involves a great saving in effort afterwards. Sometimes, in Africa, this was impossible, and it seemed almost too much after crossing that lake that a road should appear, dead ahead. Yet it did, and it was tarmac. It was none other than the Great North Road, a thin ribbon of the twentieth century that runs from Africa's tip to toe.

I threw out more sand. Most gently, the gap between us and the ground decreased. The trees had gone, and the area ahead was of grass. Or at least, it looked like grass. "Fantastic" said Douglas, exercising his vocabulary. Alan gruntingly agreed through clenched lips, for he always chewed one limb of his spectacles when filming, and speech above the grunt-level was impossible. Yet it was an enthusiastic grunt, and so it should have been, for the world just then, and as we saw it, seemed near perfection. With a decrease in height between us and the ground, the grass changed from a visibly lush expanse to a few blades nobly

14

surviving between a liberal scattering of minor rocks, but a balloonist can only pick and choose his landing spot in the broadest sense of those words. After all, he has to achieve quite a lot without being too precise or finicky over his point of impact. He has to land a basket, a thing of wicker and nothing else, on any piece of ground that may come, with considerable speed, his way.

Yet there is nothing else, so far as I know, which can withstand the jolts and knocks that a basket is heir to without passing on too many of these indignities to the occupants. A balloon landing, defined by others as a controlled accident at the best of times, is a remarkable occurrence. At no time does it seem more remarkable than when it is about to happen. All three of the crew, or however many there may be, stand there, slightly hypnotically, as the ground slowly—or, probably, quickly—comes their way. The wicker is still sailing through the air, and all is peaceful, until it is obvious that it will soon be sailing no more. At this point, perhaps 10 feet above the ground, one man pulls the rip, a device for unleasing the trapped gas in the shortest possible time. It is while his hands are still pulling down this rope that the landing happens, and the basket gives out a tremendous creak of pain. It may creak more than once, if the landing is a bouncy one, but very shortly afterwards it will hit its final resting place.

If all goes well, the fabric of the balloon will land ahead of the basket, and will then lie empty on the ground, quivering slightly as the wind blows and ruckles its surface. The balloonists themselves will at this moment be lying on their side, in a ridiculous medley of legs and arms and sandbags and cameras, instruments, water bottles and much else besides. They will quiver in their own way, with laughter and relief, and instantly attempt disentanglement, an effort that will, equally instantly, be rebuffed, because every limb is involved in the knot. Only co-ordination is effective, and first impulses have to be quelled for unravelling to be achieved, for three people to become individual units once again. It is always a delirious moment, planting one's feet once more upon the ground when still glowing from the warmth of the flight. At that moment in time one is a king.

However, despite this brief introductory description of a particular flight, in which we were scared, then relieved and finally made gloriously happy in turn, our intention in going to Africa equipped with a balloon was not in pursuit of fear, relief and happiness. The motives were different, and obtuse. They hinged, for the main part, around the belief that a balloon might provide an excellent observation post for the study of animals. Aircraft had only become incorporated in the game wardens' lives in the previous decade and, although of great importance, their aero-engines did create a fantastic racket. No one knew how an animal would react to a balloon, and there was only one way to find out. On a previous trip through Africa, when I had been travelling by motor-bicycle, and had first heard of the balloon idea, every animal except one that I encountered had disappeared like a rocket towards the horizon. One creature that did not do so bounded along for some inexplicable reason by my side, and gave a hint of what it would be like travelling by balloon, and having all the wild life of Africa moving as silently below.

In short, as somebody had to try out the balloon idea, and as I had had more than my share of the sight of animals' backs disappearing with a flash of hooves and a flurry of dust, and as the motor-bicycle had made me warm to the notion of a silent, smooth and aerial voyage, it seemed thoroughly fitting that I should be the one to undertake the experiment. Besides, I argued, I had been a zoologist, and had once known how to fly. There was plainly a difference in method between an aeroplane and a balloon, but I had enjoyed being up in the air. Moreover, it seemed enormously sad that such a superb object of man's inventiveness had been allowed to die. In Britain the balloon had become extinct, and its revival was plainly due.

An extra point in the argument for examining the game herds with a balloon, an archaic and eccentric device belonging to an earlier century, was that its behaviour would inevitably put publicity their way. There are only a few spots in Africa where the game survive in something like

16

their original form, and in anything like their original numbers. These spots are being defended, vigorously, but it seems ridiculous that the defenders need all the help they can get to preserve one of the most fantastic legacies that have come our way. Think of half a million animals wandering through the wilds of, for instance, the Serengeti. And then remember that, if the course of events of the last few decades is allowed to infiltrate the area, those great herds will disappear. They would be gone, for good. Think of waking up, as you can in the reserves, and hearing the thunder of a thousand zebras as they gallop past your camp, or seeing tens of thousands of wildebeest, or watching the flight of half a million flamingoes, or the great skeins of just as many pelicans, and then imagine those areas of land and sky quite empty of such creation. This is not idle imagining. In the greater part of Africa this has already happened. Without doubt the remaining animal population is in danger. A few years of mismanagement, for whatever reason, be it shortage of the right ideas, or sympathy, or just money, and the vast game herds will vanish into the dust of the earth.

I found there were plenty of reasons for wanting to go to Africa with a balloon. Yet, in all such aims, there is only one reason that counts. When a climber says he wishes to go up a mountain because it is there, he is answering his questioners most effectively. A mountain exists. A man sees it. Thousands of men may see it, but in one of them something happens which dictates that the mountain is there to be climbed. He is then the victim of his own system, and has to climb that mountain. Why not fly over Africa by balloon, says something. It is there waiting for someone to do this. It would do good. Why not do it?

It was while I was vacillating in this way, dreaming of the idea, and yet fearful to start upon the preparations, that I met Douglas. We had known each other in the past, but happened to meet again at a friend's house near Godstone. I spoke of the idea, and he listened. And that is where the story really starts.

17

CHAPTER TWO

THE PREDECESSORS

THE Godstone conversation embraced all the fun of the idea, and happily faced none of the realities. Just think of being there in a balloon, we said. Think of anchoring above a forest. Think of trying to fish from a lake, or of being attached to a buoy and floating downstream. We thought, and laughed, and longed to be off. We thought of mooring for the night, and hearing all Africa down below; of stopping at some water-hole, and seeing all who came; of having the world at our feet, without even having to lift them to pass it by.

The next time I met Douglas he had by no means forgotten the idea. In fact, he had added to it by suggesting that the time was pleasantly ripe and 1962 a most excellent year in which to carry it out. Jules Verne's *Five Weeks in a Balloon*, written in 1862, had been his first venture into the amalgam of science and fiction he exploited so successfully. Moreover, its hero was an Englishman named Dr Samuel Fergusson who was not only brilliant in every way but sent back despatches of his ventures "to the *Daily Telegraph*, a penny paper with a circulation of 140,000 copies daily, which was not nearly enough to satisfy its millions of readers". Quite why Jules Verne had given this particular freelance role to the first character of his creation I do not know, but it suited me well enough for I too lived by writing on scientific subjects for the same journal. In other words, the bond between the fictitious adventure of 1862 and the factual idea of the present day already existed. Verne also described the doctor as being the most interesting and active correspondent of the paper. Be that as it may, it was plain that I should also follow in his aerial footsteps.

Besides, I agreed so precisely with many of his sentiments, and particularly when he sang a paean on behalf of his exploration by balloon. "If I'm too hot, I go up; if I'm cold, I come down. I come to a mountain, I fly over it; a precipice, I cross it; a river, I cross it; a storm, I rise above it; a torrent, I skim over it like a bird. I travel without fatigue, and halt without need of rest. I soar above the new cities. I fly with the swiftness of the storm; sometimes near the limit of the air, sometimes a hundred feet above the ground, with the map of Africa unwinding below my eyes in the greatest atlas of the world."

Having kindled my spark of an idea, Douglas then retired for the winter to Scotland. There was a two-fold purpose in his hibernation. Firstly, after meeting a friend who wanted his two otters looked after for the winter, and who was prepared to pay the keep of their keeper, he had agreed to otter-sit for the stipulated six months. Secondly, he wanted to write a book, and relished the possibilities of rent-free peace and quiet for such a time. The otters themselves had different ideas, and possessed the energy to distract a score of desk-obsessed novelists; but Douglas was not to know that in advance, and happily left for the Sound of Sleat. He left me to set the balloon ball rolling.

There was much to be done. Somehow or other, I had to learn about ballooning, and about balloons, and where to get one, and what to fill it with, and how to control it, and where the winds blew in Africa. I also had to decide where it was that I wanted to fly, who was likely to provide the necessary cash, how I should acquire additional members of the expedition. On such a brand new subject my ignorance was considerable, but I followed every lead I was given, and wrote to everyone I thought of who could supply either information or introductions or just further ideas of their own. I also read a lot about the old lighter-than-air days.

It was in 1783 that men first took to the air. In that same year balloons went up filled both with hot air and with hydrogen. Two years later a balloon was flown intentionally across the English Channel, and human beings gave full rein to their imagination as to how the air should be conquered most effectively. They also gave a fair amount of rein to their stupidity, and not everyone who went up deserved either to live or to achieve any degree of success. For instance, there were those who tried to combine the merits of hot air with the advantages of hydrogen, and they heated their gas bags with explosive success. A certain Madame Blanchard, whose husband had taken to ballooning, acquired a taste for giving firework displays from her own aerial gondola before the Emperor Napoleon and others. It is plainly wrong to sit back nearly two centuries later, and criticize her foolhardiness, but the inevitable did happen. Her hydrogen caught fire, and she landed briefly on a roof before being thrown fatally to the ground.

Catching fire was a common hazard those days for the men and women known as aeronauts, whether they indulged in pyrotechnics or not. The composite engravings which include miniatures of all the early balloon endeavours show how many of them ended in flames, for the artists always went to town in depicting the billows of smoke and the anguished moments of the craft and crew whose hydrogen had ignited, and let them down. In a way, it is more surprising that any of those pioneers survived rather than that many were killed. Their ignorance was colossal. The first hot-air balloon was deliberately filled with smoke from the burning of wet hay, and not with hot air of any other sort. Smoke was chosen because smoke was known to rise, and so the Montgolfier brothers went to great trouble to produce it. In other words, here were men exploring the physics of the air, making use of convection, and yet entertaining a fantastic notion that smoke possessed unique properties in this respect.

It was also strange that the first flight of normally earth-bound creatures was so misinterpreted. Man today puts chimpanzees into rockets before he entrusts himself, and eighteenth-century man did the same thing with his aerostatic devices. The first creatures to fly by human inventiveness were a lamb, a duck and a cock. All three were placed in a cage, and the cage went a few miles by balloon. Its three occupants were closely examined on their return to Earth, and diligent inspection revealed a fractured wing belonging to the cock. At once, it was publicly stated that the rigours of the atmosphere beyond the immediate surface area in which things lived were sufficient to cause even the breaking of bones. This supposition lasted for quite a time, and only later on did someone suggest that the lamb's clumsy feet were most probably the cause of the fracture. It was not only the pioneers who were occasionally wrong about certain fundamental aspects of their activities. The traditional public frequently believed the balloons to be works, not of courageous compatriots, but of the devil. An early landing near Paris was greeted by a crowd of peasants with pitch-forks who instantly destroyed the thing that had come down amongst them. An attempted take-off from Liverpool was thwarted by "the populace" for the very simple reason that, on allegedly religious grounds, they had torn the fabric into shreds.

In spite of rough handling at times, and various suicidal elements in the ballooning fraternity, the sport did take a hold. The Charlière type of balloon, named after Prof. Charles who favoured the use of light gases, gradually became dominant over the Montgolfière, named after the brothers Montgolfier, the hot-air men. Napoleon used them in several battles as observational aids, and prodigious plans were drawn up for invading England by balloon. Incident-ally, England did not contribute much at this stage of aerial transport. There was a Mr Lunardi, from the Italian Con-sulate in London, who made flights, but the people tired of him, and he was allowed to become sufficiently destitute to kill himself a few years after he had been the talk of the nation.

I read all that I could, and all that I had time for, during those early days of the expedition's planning. It was not a meaningless task, like a jet-pilot learning about the cross-bow, for the business of ballooning has hardly changed since it moved into its stride at the start of the nineteenth century. Everything relevant to those aeronauts was relevant to me. My hydrogen was to be just as inflammable as Mme Blanchard's, and it was up to me to profit from her experience. The only thing in doubt was whether my courage would be of a similar order.

Take Mr Simmons, for example. This American balloonist was giving shows a hundred years ago, and his press cuttings make anxious reading. "I left Milwaukee, and after two hours in a tremendous thunderstorm, at an altitude of 12,000 feet, descended into Lake Michigan, 25 miles out from land. Having no ballast left, I was compelled to cut away my car, and re-ascend by hanging onto the cords of my netting." He then went up to 9,000 feet, still hanging on the ropes, crossed the lake (120 miles), and arrived on land again with his hands "much cut by the cords" and in what he called "an exhausted state".

A couple of years later he took off from Peekshill in what must have been a hurricane. Record in the *Highland Democrat* has it that he landed 25 miles away after a 7-minute flight. Even allowing for a journalist's distortion, only a man with rubber bones could have withstood such a landing at one quarter of the reported speed. Plainly Mr Simmons was thus equipped, for the *Western Flying Post* of 1861 describes a flight from Hayle, Cornwall, in which he was "precipitated to the ground from a height of 100 feet, being only slightly injured".

The balloon's proudest hour came during the Siege of Paris in 1871. Exactly sixty-eight balloons left the city during the blockade. They carried about 400 lb. of mail each, a lot of carrier pigeons, and a very inexperienced collection of pilots. Only five balloonists were in Paris when the siege began, and so most of the escapers were having their maiden flights. A few landed in German-occupied territory, but most got to safety. A sailor, shouting as he left that he would make a flight the world would never forget, went much too far, and was drowned somewhere off the Plymouth shore. Every pilot had a tale to tell, but the tallest came from a crew of two who had found themselves when night had ended sailing over the North Sea. A lingering death in the freezing waters seemed certain, and they decided that a quick despatch was preferable. With the aid of the other, one man climbed up to set fire to the hydrogen; but he failed to spark it off. There was nothing to be done but throw the mail overboard when necessary, and hope for a miracle. The tall tale ended with a landing in Norway, and even the recovery of the lost letters by a fishing vessel. For this remarkable fluke the pilot was awarded a medal.

The pigeons which survived each flight were released to take back news into Paris. On their legs they carried microfilm of newspapers and letters. These were projected on to screens, copied, and then reprinted in the beleaguered city. The balloons could fly at a height where they were safe from the Prussian bullets, but the pigeons flew much lower. Many became pie for the Uhlans' pots. Each piece of pigeon post was strapped to thirty birds, with the hope that at least one would get through. For the citizens of Paris the departure of a balloon almost every other day was a most welcome occurrence. They flocked to watch each take-off, and they were extremely comforted by being kept in touch with the outside world. The balloon was in its heyday.

Towards the end of that century ballooning suddenly became the fashionable thing for men and women to do, or at least to have done—once. No longer was it the sport solely of adventurers who seemed, judging by their exploits, weary of life, but of modern society wishing to inject more into life. The Edwardians were fond of comfort, and they took all possible measures to make the balloon baskets an exciting extension of their living-rooms. The champagne popped, the crinolines fluttered and "Up in a balloon, boys" was a regular number at the Gaiety. Trottie True, the superb creation of Caryl Brahms and S. J. Simon, inevitably became involved, and was the first woman on record to be seduced when carried aloft beneath the soft gutta percha of a balloon. Sid was the balloonist, but he lost her in the end to a lord, partly because he spent too much time floating over Nine Elms gasworks, and partly because all the Trotties of that time had to get their lord.

Lighter-than-air flying suddenly took on a sterner aspect with the development of the dirigible. The advantage of being able to steer was, of course, considerable, and the Germans put great faith in it during the First World War. The word blimp comes from this period for, so the generally accepted story goes, the dirigibles were classified into A—

rigid and B—limp. Be that as it may, the rigids were the most exciting. Every flight they made was memorable. There was the first double Atlantic crossing, for example, which was accomplished by the R.34, an airship of British production.

Imagine that morning in the summer of 1919 when the 140 feet length of the R.34 was manhandled out of her shed at East Fortune, near Edinburgh. The five 275 h.p. engines were started, and at some 50 knots she nosed up the Firth of Forth on her way to America. There were 30 crew on board, 4,900 gallons of fuel, 3 tons of water ballast, and 80 gallons of drinking-water. In all, the load was slightly over 24 tons, including the weight of one stowaway determined not to miss the trip. It was four days before Nova Scotia was sighted; and, although the airspeed was then 36 knots, the groundspeed was nil. The landing party at New York assumed the airship would not reach them, and set off to an intermediate point. In the meantime, the wind relented, and half-way through the fifth day R.34 reached New York. Without a landing party to arrange things, one of the officers on board the airship elected to take charge. He parachuted to the ground, and a momentous trip was soon over.

It was partly the success of that voyage, and partly due to later voyages by British and foreign airships, that the principles of lighter-than-air flying were given their severest test. Two mammoth airships were built in Britain, one sponsored by industry known as R.100, and one by the Government known as R.101. They were housed in adjoining hangars near Bedford, and the rivalry of the two teams was immense. Unfortunately, the Government airship was ordered to proceed to India on her maiden voyage, and before she was fit for it. The great bulk of the R.101 took off from Cardington, dipped her nose twice over Bedford, either in salute or unavoidably, and set course for Karachi. Much of the voyage was accomplished at no more than 500 feet above the ground, and the catastrophe happened near Beauvais in France. It was not so much a matter of the airship flying into a hill, as a gently rising piece of ground of no great significance being too much for the over-loaded R.101, despite her 5 million cubic feet of hydrogen. Six crew men and no passengers survived.

The Government then ordered the scrapping of industry's R.100. The Japanese bought the metal for a song, and one girder remains in the old shed at Cardington. Lighter-than-air flying by dirigible in Britain was over, and the Hindenburg disaster a few years later in the United States hammered down the lid. The death knell meant that the competition between aircraft relying on the displacement of air for their lift and those making use of some form of aerofoil had ended. Three decades afterwards the story is still the same.

It was while I was learning this ancient but relevant history while visiting the old sheds at Cardington, while seeking out facts from the Royal Aircraft Establishment at Farnborough (whose telegraphic address is "Ballooning"), from the Royal Aero Club (which was founded by three people when up in a balloon), and from the Royal Aeronautical Society, that certain wires began to cross. They led me to Holland, to the Hague Balloon Club, and to Jan and Nini Boesman. I thenceforth wrote to them, expressing interest and asking how I could make a flight.

CHAPTER THREE

THE DIFFICULTIES

AN enthusiastic reply came back, telling me about their "privat balloon-haven, something like a midget London Airport", and bemoaning the fact that ballooning is a dying sport "because the balloons, the inflation, insurances, transports, etc. are rather expensive, and as there are coming each day more jets, it seems that the romantic balloon-flight comes to an end". A second letter informed me of their intention to fly in the forthcoming Birmingham Tulip Festival, and they said they might be able to find me a place. "We'll take good care of you during the flight, and you'll be a fine companion to show us the right way to make a romantic landing in a castle or at a garden party." I did not know of our chances of either type of landing in that area, but instantly accepted the possible offer, even though there were many months to go.

There was also much more to do about Africa. I wrote off to the East African Meteorological Office for facts about the wind. A most helpful plethora came back. Basically wind currents were from the north-east during the first three months of the year, and that was when we planned to go. In general, the wind force was not too strong, and 20 knots was a likely maximum to expect. The facts were comforting, but they generated optimism and Douglas and I agreed by post that Zanzibar should be our starting place. After all, according to the Met. Office, the January winds blew from 020, and have done since records began. Therefore, it would be possible to emulate Doctor Fergusson, Jules Verne's hero, a little further for he too started from that neighbourhood, as did virtually every explorer in the last century, and it would be a fine springboard for our own venture. How easy it is to have ideas when the actual planned event is more than a year away! How simple to look at those 30 miles of the Straits of Zanzibar, refer to the confidence of the Met. reports, and forget the possibility of contrary weather! We plumped for Zanzibar, and left it at that. One year later we were to be astounded at our immoderation.

The principal reason for the year's delay, which seemed excessively long at the start, but pitifully short towards its conclusion, was that I discovered it would definitely be necessary for me to acquire a balloonist's licence, contrary to my imaginings. There was a law to the fact. In fact, there was more than one law, and I became enmeshed with the Ministry of Aviation over forms S.A.(L)5, S.A.(L)1 and CA forms 541 and 601. There was even a department which knew how to deal with lighter-than-air licences.

"Do you mean to say that I have to make eight flights before I am allowed to fly a balloon by myself?"

"Yes," said the woman's voice. "Those are the regulations. Six training flights, one night flight, and one solo trip."

"That's going to cost the earth," I replied, coveting a hope that my leg was being pulled, and no such regulations existed. Unfortunately, the leg was quite unpulled, and the chilling voice began again.

"Will you be taking any photographs on your flights?"

"Of course, how else do you think we can pay for them?"

"In that case," she continued, "you will be conducting a business transaction and need a commercial balloon pilot's licence."

"What precisely does that entail?" I replied.

"Just let me see," came the freezing jauntiness once more.

"Oh yes, here it is. You need to make ten flights in addition to the eight training flights. You come under the heading of aerial work."

Something bubbled to the surface inside me.

"I don't care what I come under. Have you any idea how much eighteen flights cost? Have you any idea how we can achieve those flights, when no one has a balloon in this country? Do you realize that would set us back about £3,000, and where do you think that's coming from? Why, I could learn to fly a Boeing 707 for that!" And so forth. I had nothing more to say. Neither had she, for the time being, and the conversation ended.

A chain reaction followed of other similarly frustrating brick walls. The firm I thought most likely to make me a balloon refused to do so. They had sent up their representative to talk the matter over, a beautifully scented girl who had held her downy fur coat around her as if there was nothing on underneath, and who with her other hand made jerky notes of my requirements. I even visited the factory, drank gins and tonics with them, got given lunch and a calendar; but no one expressed interest in making us a balloon. They suggested other firms; but these others did not proffer even a calendar, let alone a downy, scented girl. What was a balloon expedition if it could not acquire for itself a balloon?

My office those days was something like Job's forecourt, and I sat there receiving ill tidings. The hydrogen cylinders were another worry. Fondly, I had imagined there would be no problem. Instead, there were no hydrogen cylinders, certainly none to spare in East Africa, and none I could discover in Britain. Yet we had to have them, and needed at least 200. I asked their price. I was told £45 each. (The sum on my plotting-paper came to £9,000.) "Who would make them?" I asked, as if that sum was at my instant command. "Oh, no one could make them for you, at least not this side of twelve months."

The problem of gas, so airily spoken of during that weekend at Godstone, also loomed hideously large as various messengers brought their bad news. A balloon has to be filled with a gas significantly lighter than the air which it displaces. There are not many such gases, with the only practical ones being hydrogen, helium, coal gas, and certain forms of natural gas. Helium was out of the question. Britain possessed none, and neither did East Africa. The United States had supplies, but guarded them zealously. Coal gas was found also to be out of the question. Natural gas, I discovered, did not exist out there. So it had to be hydrogen, even though I possessed no cylinders in which to have the stuff compressed. Moreover, there seemed to be no way to

28

replenish my non-existent cylinders once I had got them to East Africa. Various Indian firms expressed deep sincerity, deeper humility, and their deepest appreciation concerning my enquiry but, some three letters later, admitted their inability to produce anything like the amount of hydrogen I required. My balloon, I reckoned, needed 26,000 cubic feet of gas at each filling. The average daily production of hydrogen by those Indians to satisfy the fats and fatty oils of their refineries was generally about 500 cubic feet. It was plain our needs were of a different order.

It was also plain that the balloon safari, as it was being called, would founder most rapidly unless fate ceased smirking and began to smile on its endeavours. Progress to date elicited that I possessed no balloon, knew of no balloon-maker, had no licence, objected to the mummery of the Ministry of Aviation, saw no future in any gas but hydrogen, and could lay hands neither on cylinders nor the where-withal to fill them. I wrote to Douglas suggesting a meeting. As he could not leave his otters, it was up to me to drive the 600 miles to his particular lighthouse-keeper's cottage buried deep in the wintry Kyle of Lochalsh.

He had advised, through a crackling telephone line that seemed to be coming from Vladivostok, that I should get there before 3.30, when the fitful day changed once again into the darkness of night. Of course, with such a small speck of daytime to aim for, Anne and I arrived there late. We stopped the car opposite the pathway Douglas had described, and stepped out of cosy warmth into the dripping murk of a wet highland night. The stroll down to the cottage became a most ridiculous escapade. At first, we nursed fond ideas of keeping our shoes dry, then our feet, and finally anything above the knees. Working unsuccess-fully against these humble intentions were the gigantic holes, crevices and canyons left by the peat diggers. It was not like jerkily discovering one stair missing at the bottom of a flight of them, but of sailing effortlessly from one floor to the next without the trace of a stairway in between. Most remarkably it was always lovely and soft at the bottom, and no limb was ever hurt as we sorted them out again from the mud, the water holes and the great big tussocks of super-saturated grass which thrived tremendously in that aquatic environment. It was the sort of walk where you discussed, facetiously, whether the way you were treading was a path or an active river-bed. Later on, it became the sort of walk when you honestly did not know. We splashed down minor waterfalls, we splashed down larger ones. We walked into shrubs, all wet and dripping. We walked into trees which connived to pour water down our necks, as snowy trees do with snow. We walked, I am quite certain, into every obstacle on that 2-mile stretch between road and lighthouse cottage; but it mattered not a hoot. Besides, in the end we got there.

It was also a most ridiculous weekend, and one essentially indoors. Once in a while, when the clouds parted cautiously, and the Island of Skye appeared over the sound as a dank shape, we put on thigh-boots, we put on hats and macin-toshes, and walked. An otter always lolloped by our side, being entirely suited to such wetness, and not changing its undulating gait when it moved from water to land, and from land to water again. Down on the beach, while we collected cockles for the evening meal, the otter with us would cavort, and play, and chase things, and drown them, and toss them into the air, and prove itself inexhaustible of energy. When the soft drizzle had changed again to rain, and the rain to the torrents I shall always associate with that portion of Inverness-shire, we returned to the warmth of the cottage.

The cockles were for us, and while we ate our way through steaming bucketfuls, the otters effected similar justice on the eels and omelettes set down before them. It was in the drowsy haze of the last evening that the three of us talked again of balloons, and how the pressing array of obstacles could best be overcome. There is nothing so like a warm fire, and good talk, for the dissolution of problems. As always, the flickering light minimized them, and instead threw into strange perspective the new ideas that we had. Each novel scheme seemed brilliant in the warm and fitful shadows of that room.

For instance, we saw ourselves mooring the balloon on to the forest canopy. We saw ourselves camping there, watching the monkeys, and peering down at the world of normality 200 feet below. We thought more of anchoring our basket to a buoy, and then floating downstream. Provided the rope between buoy and basket was sufficiently long, we could even slide down waterfalls in an aerial kind of way.

"Why," said Douglas, "don't we ascend Kilimanjaro?"

"Why not?" I replied. "It's only 19,000 feet," and what is 19,000 feet when your toes are warm, and the cockles in your stomach are resting content?

"I believe," said Anne, "that elephants slide down the mountain when they want to get to some lower bit. You could film them."

We could indeed, and we would certainly make the most of such a magnificent sight, and sell it for thousands and thousands of pounds. On that night in the cottage we could do anything. Sliding elephants were child's play. So were shots taken over active volcanoes, and of lions chasing meat towed by our grapnel, and of lassooed animals (perhaps elephants, perhaps giraffes—we weren't going to be dogmatic) towing us happily for miles and miles. We even went so far as to make a list of "Special Features", and detailed them in a matter-of-fact way. 4. Catching Nile Perch, and filming struggle. 7. Proceeding at tree-top height up Mount Kilimanjaro, preferably to summit. 10. Discovering archaeological sites, made possible by slow-moving vantage point. And so forth. It was all so easy. As an addendum to the Special Features we did consider that "Some of these may prove impractical"; but we also wrote that other topics of equal interest will doubtless present themselves, and be more than sufficient compensation. It was a night of supreme confidence; and it was precisely what I had wanted after all those fatuous days of letting other people put obstacles in our way.

On the following morning, and before it was time to go, Douglas, Anne and I sat writing letters to every individual we had thought of during the weekend who deserved to be informed that a balloon expedition over eastern Africa was about to take place. Some of them may have been amazed at their desserts, when our letters came through the post; but we pursued every path we could, and therefore hounded everybody we could think of, for help comes from varied sources, either unexpectedly, or sought for diligently, and help was exactly what we needed. When the time came for Anne and me to leave Douglas to his novel and those otters, we strode out into the rain with a wodge of well-stamped supplications, and a quite unwarranted confidence in the complete lack of hindrances to our future enterprise. It was daylight then, and the path leading to the road was distinguishable from the peaty trenches on all sides; but, even so, it was a most aquatic exercise getting back to the sodden, glistening, rain-washed car.

Back in London there were many letters waiting for me. The Army, friendly but uselessly, offered to lend telescopes, compasses and radios provided we put down a deposit on those articles equal to their value. A balloon firm offered to sell, for twice the price we were prepared to pay, a balloon of the wrong sort about half the size of the one we needed. A chemical company, having made the necessary calculations on our behalf, concluded that the necessary hydrogen plant to be installed in Africa would cost £7,150 f.o.b. London. Heaven knows what it would cost in the middle of Tanganyika, let alone the fuel bills to follow! However, among the tedious letters was one from Jan Boesman, the Dutch balloonist, and that was sufficient counterweight. He had positively accepted me as a passenger for the Birmingham flight. The trip to a garden party or a castle was on. At last, I was to know what I was about. At long last, a trip in a balloon had come my way. There may have been other Birmingham Tulip Festivals, and Cannon Hill Park may have seen other resplendent occasions; but I looked forward to that particular April day with irritating impatience and urgent excitement. Not for one moment was I disillusioned by the events that followed on the tulip day when, eventually, it came.

Breakfast in the Serengeti
Joan and Alan to the left; Douglas and A.S. to the right

The Arab who wrote a poem, which was broadcast on
Zanzibar radio, in praise of the balloon

CHAPTER FOUR

THE FLIGHT TO WEDNESBURY

BEFORE the day arrived I received a weighty letter from the Boesmans. It was six pages of the official invitation to join the flight, and was headed: "TO UNKNOWN DESTINATION". Thereafter followed much information, including many hints for passengers. I read them diligently. "Although our balloonists have an experience of more than 300 flights, they are never 'uppish' about it, and only try and give you an opportunity to have an experience full of pleasant surprises, so that you will be in a position to 'sail on the clouds'. Even if the sky is overcast, or if it is raining in your place of residence, have no fear and go to the balloon ascent, for the ascent will take place even if it is raining. The balloonist has only to throw some ballast overboard to rise above the dull weather to put the tune 'You are my sunshine'. In this way you will really be 'away from the world' and also figuratively with your 'head in the clouds'. We wish you a pleasant experience in the balloon car."

After the exhortation were the many practical hints, of which I will quote just a few.

"Jewellery. Take as little with you as possible, as things easily get lost during the take-off, the flight or the descent.

"Luggage. Take with you as little as possible, at most some toilet articles, sun-glasses, sun-lotion, a strong pocket-knife, Michelin tourist maps, small torch, some bars of chocolate, perhaps a pair of socks and a shirt. Fasten your pocket-knife, fountain pen, etc., to a cord, so that they cannot fall overboard.

"Smoking. This is forbidden in the balloon car or near the balloon. For enthusiastic smokers the balloonist may make an intermediate landing to enable the inveterate smoker to disembark and enjoy a smoke at a hundred metres distance, whereupon the journey will be continued.

"Comfort. The balloon commander usually supplies peppermint and lemonade, which is served in a special balloon mug. It is a tradition that a passenger making a balloon trip for the first time brings a bottle of champagne for the balloon commander.

"Rights. After completion of your first voyage, you are entitled to be inaugurated in the Society of Illustrious Balloon Travellers, called Sic Itur Ad Astra. The balloon baptism and admission to the above society takes place in accordance with a special ceremony. If it occurs during or immediately after the trip, the champagne brought along by the passenger will be used for this purpose. If for some reason the passenger has been unable to obtain the champagne, the balloon commander will baptize him with chocolate milk.

"Duties. Each passenger will have to impress upon his mind the thought: I am nothing, and the balloon commander is everything. Any high-handed action with the balloon material is most strongly prohibited. Especially in dangerous circumstances, and during possible dragging of the balloon, when the commander needs the weight of each participant, it is a matter of honour for everyone to stay in the balloon car, and jumping out of the car prematurely will be considered as a contemptible and infamous act, which may endanger the lives of the other companions."

There then followed a word about insurance, saying it was reasonable to take out a policy, but adding: "You will probably already know that Captain John Boesman, President of the Netherlands Aeronautical Museum, always used to say: 'Ballooning is the safest sport . . . after angling'."

The final exclamation, after a request for a signature on the understanding that the balloon trip was based on a gentlemen's agreement, urged the signatory to throw his daily ballast overboard, come and enjoy himself. I signed the moment I reached the place to do so and, although alarmed at the possibilities of a chocolate milk baptism, felt more enthusiastic than ever about the flight. I would put the tune "You are my sunshine" as hard as I could put it. I would tie every penknife, pen and every other

34

object with the strongest of cords. And I would undoubtedly have my head in the clouds for as long as the balloon could keep it there.

Came the dawn of the day, and we made great haste to Birmingham. Outside the Cannon Hill Park a placard advertised the fact that a "Giant Passenger Carrying Balloon" would take off before the day was out. Giant passenger that I was, I hurried over to the zone allocated for the inflation, and there met the Boesmans. Both Jan and Nini speak excellent English, and both are the sort of people that everyone is bound to like. They have ballooned, one way and another, for twenty-five years, and they even left for their honeymoon by balloon. The two of them provide the energy which keeps the Hague Balloon Club going, and they pursue their sport wherever and whenever they can. They have landed in the forests of Java, on the mountain slopes of Norway, and in the sea. Once, when flying over Switzerland, Nini suddenly heard a vital rope break, but landed safely with only three still attaching her basket to its ring. On another occasion Jan, determined not to disappoint a crowd, and being supplied with much less gas than he had called for, was faced with the prospect of taking off beneath a half-inflated balloon. This is a hazardous proceeding, for such a balloon will continue to rise until the expansion of its gas has entirely filled out the envelope. There is nothing to be done in the meantime, as we learnt later in Africa, except watch the altimeter, and hope you do not go too high. Jan watched his altimeter rise to 19,000 feet before the balloon filled out, and before the accelerating descent began. He landed heavily, sorely frightened, and the possessor of a quite unintentional high-altitude record.

At Birmingham, apart from meeting the Boesmans, I also encountered a balloon for the very first time. I felt its fabric, wondered at the diminutive quantity of basket, and was amazed by the slenderness of everything, of rope, of cord, and apparently of the safety margin for nothing seemed particularly strong. Experience had trimmed the essentials to the bare minimum, but some of the ropes appeared almost naked of strength. I was also impressed with the weight of everything, once I started trying to move it around. This is not a contradiction. Most parts did look thin, and were thin, but the huge size of the balloon meant there was a great quantity of the basic items, such as netting and fabric, however thin they might be. It was the quantity that made the weight.

It is important to assimilate the size of a balloon, for much of what follows in ballooning hinges upon it. The reason a balloon goes up is because its own light gas has displaced the necessary amount of air. As air does not weigh much, a great deal of it has to be displaced before the weight of one man can be placed hopefully in the basket. In fact, if the man weighs 13 stone, and as air weighs 1·2 ounces per cubic foot, some 2,426 cubic feet of it have to be displaced to lift him. The easy way of displacing this air, without becoming involved in vacuums, is to replace it with something lighter, such as hydrogen. This gas is the lightest substance known, possessing only one proton and one electron per atom, and it weighs only one-fourteenth of normal air. Its weight, therefore, is small, but it does weigh something, and this means that a balloon can only lift an object thirteen-fourteenths as heavy as the weight of the air which has been displaced. So, to lift a 13-stone man by transposing air with hydrogen, it is necessary to displace more than 2,426 cubic feet, and 2,613 cubic feet would be nearer the mark. This, of course, assumes no balloon weight, and its weight must also be displaced by hydrogen.

A conventional man-carrying balloon, which stipulates three men plus a certain amount of equipment, is normally 20,000 cubic feet in capacity. This is big. Take the normal 10 feet by 10 feet by 10 feet room for comparison. It contains only 1,000 cubic feet, and so the average balloon must be twenty times bigger. The balloon we eventually transported to Africa was 55 feet from top to toe, by the time the basket was attached, and some 30 feet across. In other words, we took to the air with something about the size of a five-storey house. The balloon at Birmingham, by name Oxygenium, was slightly smaller. As I fingered it, and pulled it around under the direction of the Boesmans to make it ready for inflation, I learnt once again that it is all very well to read of a measurement. It is quite different to see it. It is even more impressive to lift it. The surface area of a sphere is $4\pi r^2$, and therefore a diameter of 30 feet or so means there are some 312 square yards of material to be cajoled into their correct position. Birmingham was the first occasion I realized quite how heavy much of the work could be that was associated with lighter-than-air flying.

Jan was there supervising things, and informing me that pupils of ballooning had to perform all tasks. Not only was it necessary, he said, that they should learn the job in every one of its aspects, but they could look eagerly forward to the day when they were balloon commanders, and could watch their pupils exerting themselves for the cause.

A further heaviness concerned the hydrogen cylinders. The gas was undoubtedly light, but to fit 20,000 cubic feet on to the back of a lorry means compression, and compression means cylinders of steel. In fact, the hydrogen had been forced into those cylinders to a pressure of 3,600 lb./sq. in., or 300 times atmospheric pressure. This procedure of fitting many pints into a half-pint pot meant that each cylinder consisted of a ton of steel, and there were ten cylinders, each with 2,000 cubic feet of gas inside them. In Africa the problem of gas was to be colossal. In Birmingham it was, by comparison, minimal. A man arrived with his lorry, and switched on the flow as soon as we at the balloon end of the pipe had need of it.

For the next three hours we all watched the balloon grow. As it did so, we steadily adjusted the sandbags around its rim. These were attached to the all-encircling net, and one mesh at a time we lowered them, while the fabric of the balloon within filled out with the gas from the pipe. I agree that the balloon could take no other shape than the one imposed upon it by its original maker, but its inflation did impart to us, or at least to me, a feeling that something was being created. It certainly looked increasingly beautiful, as its huge orange bulk protruded into the air, and later on it assumed a splendour of its own as the final cords of the net were gathered together, and attached to the basket.

Oxygenium, no longer a drab pile of canvas and rope, was a thing waiting to fly into the air. It swayed about exultantly, and plainly longed to be off.

Unfortunately, there were preliminaries. The tulip festivallers had to have their share of the balloon. Aldermanic individuals had to be given captive ascents on a long rope while they megaphoned their impressions to the gaping faces down below. After all, they had paid for the balloon, and the people had come to see it. Nevertheless, I overflowed with impatience. I scooped up the festival's tulip girls, and dumped them into the basket for their turn with the speed and diligence of a meat-packer. I retrieved them after their wind-blown flight with similar promptitude.

At last the balloon was due to be off. The wind had dropped almost to nothing, and the smells of an English evening were heavy in the air. I took my place in the basket, clutched the necessary maps, and watched Jan and Nini prepare Oxygenium for her flight to the unknown destination. This meant securing the instruments, making certain all ropes were disentangled, checking that toggles were safely through their respective eyes, and finally obtaining our equilibrium. A sack of sand placed outside, half another sack, a final handful and we were poised effortlessly a foot above the earth. The ground crew man-handled the balloon to the windward side of the park, with such wind as there was coming from the south-east, and there we shook hands with the festival's newly elected Tulip Queen. She smiled back, as three sandy hands took turns on her clean white glove, and all was set to go. Jan threw out another couple of handfuls, called "Hands off" to those still gripping our wicker rim, shouted farewells at people further afield, and jerked open the balloon's wide mouth with a happy grin on his own round face.

The magic of a balloon's departure then asserted itself. Without a judder, without the slightest tremble of motion, we began to move over the ground. As we did so, we rose gradually higher into the air. One foot, two feet, and then it was ten. Nothing was happening, and yet we were inexorably on our way. No one was doing a thing, and yet we were off. The Tulip Queen waved her long white arm once, then twice, and then merged into the others. The knot of people around our take-off spot became dissimilar to all the other knots, as we mounted higher and higher, and gasped at the fantasy of it all. The band was playing "Now is the hour when we must say 'Goodbye'", and even the bathos of that choice could not detract for an instant from the wonder of the world in which we were being transported.

It was the unreality that most frightened me. I understood why we were moving, and yet my senses failed to back up this understanding. To know that one will travel with the wind, to do so, and then not to feel a whisper of it is disquieting. I agree that we and the wind were as one, but the fact was hard to reconcile. It was also difficult comprehending the power of the hydrogen gas. I did appreciate how its properties could be put to lifting use in a balloon, and I knew it was absolutely colourless, and without smell; but somehow I was unprepared for looking into the gas-bag above us, for seeing right inside once the mouth had been opened, and for seeing nothing. It looked inside as air looks. It was invisible. It was not there.

Up we went, over the edge of that Cannon Hill Park, above the tips of the poplars, and out towards a reservoir while the music from the band died softly away. The three of us talked, and laughed, and pointed at people, and things, and marked our changing position on the map. The balloon was utterly silent, and from below came all the noises of a town. There were trains, and ships on the canals, and the unceasing growling of traffic, and the hum of people, and whistles, and shouts, and barks from the dogs, and strange sounds which belonged to nothing in particular. At ground-level all the noises tend to come from one plane, and therefore are confusing to our ears. Up in the air, and coming along a multitude of planes, the sounds are more distinct, certainly more audible and usually identifiable with their source. The yapping comes from that dog there, and not some indefinable canine half a block away. The screech comes from that car; the cat-call from that street, and probably that particular boy. Up in a balloon, noises were blatant and conspicuous, and far more so than ever down on earth. For one thing, we could hear them so much more loudly. Normally, when in the open air, our ears are slightly deafened by the wind moving past them. On the stillest of nights there is some kind of a breeze; but a balloon goes so perfectly with the wind that a whole new world of sound is set before the balloonist.

A whole new group of problems confronts him as well. These I left for the most part to the competent Boesman pair, and I listened to them reading the altimeter, checking our descents, and keeping in touch with the land before us. I watched a high-voltage transmission line passing slowly beneath, and saw another looming up. They have a sinister look about them. They are unnerving even when things are under control.

"There is a lot of tension here," said Nini, voicing both apprehension and her own observation of yet another file of pylons.

"Another handful," said Jan, and the sand splayed out on its way into the reservoir. While the two of them looked after the balloon, I drew our course on the map. We went over a railway line, and the train stopped while its crew got out to wave at us. We passed over a gasometer, and the three men sunning themselves on its convex roof sat up in alarm as our balloon floated by. We went over a cemetery, and a dog snapped back at us. It was then the turn of a lunatic asylum, and another railway, and a large park, as we travelled north-west in the general direction of Wolverhampton. Our speed was approximately 7 miles an hour. It was not a whit too fast, or too slow. It was superb.

Gradually I began to understand the procedure, and even interfered with suggestions.

"There's no need to throw sand now," I said. "We are not going down."

"No, but the land is coming up," they said, effectively quashing the remark.

The day wore on, and the sun sank lower in the sky. We veered away from Wolverhampton, and instead went towards Wednesbury. I agree these are industrial centres, with a dearth of garden parties nestling among castle grounds, but there is nothing aesthetically wrong in the sight of oily canals, slummish houses and the serrated roofs of a thousand factories when seen from a balloon. I know that most of the buildings were really hideous, with their ridiculous Florentine towers, and their acres of blackened brick; but I charge anyone to think that anything is ugly when he drifts over it on a warm spring evening, and the whole world is laid out entrancingly a thousand feet below. Unfortunately, although man-made objects of all sorts and even the sludge of the industrial revolution may look well from a balloon, there is nothing so like a field for landing on.

"It is time we came down," said Jan. "But I do not see anywhere."

I looked hopefully at the map. The English countryside was still a long way off, and the light was definitely getting worse very quickly. We all three peered ahead.

"Another tension," said Nini, and a 275 kV line passed slowly underneath. There was also another canal, and another four-track railway line, and then the three of us saw it at once. A recreation ground attached to a factory. The very thing.

Jan pulled for some 5 seconds on the valve line. Our floating serenity suddenly changed into abrupt descent. Down went the trail-rope, and down went we. Up came the ground, fantastically fast. Quite plainly, everything was out of control, I thought.

"Everything under control?" I asked.

"Oh yes, the landing is going nicely," said Jan. "It should not be disagreeable."

Disagreeable or not, the grassy football field was approaching with an unnerving speed. Surely, a basket was insufficient protection? Surely, somebody was going to do something? Surely . . . ? Jan interrupted.

"When we land, hold on to nothing."

It was while I was puzzling this one out that we hit. Once, and we bounced high. Twice, and less high. Thrice, and we stayed on the ground. The canopy of the balloon bucked about, and flapped like a sail when pointing into wind. I longed to get out of the basket to have a look at us, but remembered in time the words of the prospectus that such a premature move would be considered contemptible and infamous. "Just pull on this valve line as hard as you can," said Nini, and passed me the all-important rope. I pulled, and an old man came striding from the factory. He was plainly unmoved by our sudden and voluminous arrival.

"Who have you come to see?" he asked.

The Boesmans, completely competent in English, were utterly floored by any accent broader than the normal clipped manner they had been taught. As this man's delivery was as broad as they come, the Dutch pair looked blank, and I replied.

"Whose factory is this?"

"Smiths Castings," he said, pompously.

"Well, we have come to see Mr Smith."

"In that case, you've chosen a stupid day, being Saturday, for he never comes here on a Saturday, being his day off. Have you come from far?"

"No, only Birmingham."

"Oh well, that's not too bad then, but he's never here on a Saturday, not on his day off he isn't."

The Boesmans interrupted, and said it would be good if the balloon could be deflated on some car-park or other flat ground, for the grass was sodden, and it would not do to get the fabric wet.

"Where's your car-park?" I asked.

"Oh, you can't put that thing in our car-park. I'm afraid you can't do that. Where do you think the cars would go? I don't think Mr Smith would like that. In fact, I'm sure he wouldn't. In fact, he's given me express instructions about that car-park."

By this time quite a few people had assembled around the balloon, and the night watchman had real cars to worry about. As in all future landings, the assemblers soon became helpers, and they pushed us to a flat piece of tarmac on one side of the factory. There, with further long pulls at the valve line, the proud Oxygenium was slowly destroyed. The gas flowed out, and soon we removed the valve altogether

to make its passage easier. It was not long before the familiar
mass of fabric was lying empty, heavy, and waiting to be
rolled into its canvas sack. After a telephone call, the van
with its trailer turned up from Birmingham, and a small
posse of cars left for the nearest pub. The night watchman
was left to his deserted factory, his empty car-park, and the
three muddy patches on the recreation ground where a
free-flying balloon had chanced to return again to earth.
He was also left with a small spoon given him by the
Boesmans. Its handle had been fashioned into the shape of
a balloon, and it was proof, if he wished for proof, that two
men and a woman had come in a basket which had been
carried there beneath one of the most delightful creations
ever manufactured. However, I still doubt whether he even
bothered to show that spoon to anyone. He was one of the
most imperturbable of men, provided no one interfered
with the car-park reserved so diligently for Mr Smith and
company. Those who have seen a balloon landing, who
have been present at an unknown destination, must be
very rare; and he was most certainly a rarity.

CHAPTER FIVE

THE DUTCH LESSONS

THE Birmingham flight was followed by a curious ceremony in a Birmingham hotel. Each initiate has to be formally introduced into the fraternity of balloonists, and this involves a liberal pouring of champagne and sand over the victim's head. At the same time a certain chant is sung out, which has to be repeated by the one whose hair is changing from hair into a frothy muddy mixture the shaggiest of goats would disown. He reiterates the words he is told, and admits he is lower and less important than a sack of sand, that the balloon commander is all, that the passenger is nothing more than jettisonable ballast. It is an old tradition to introduce novices in this fashion, and the dull hotel was honoured by having much sandy champagne poured on to and trodden into its mud-coloured carpets.

The Birmingham flight was also followed by a change for the better in the expedition's fortunes. Quite suddenly, ways were seen of acquiring a balloon, some gas, and the cylinders to put it in. The Boesmans offered to arrange the balloon's manufacture. They said they knew a man in Belgium who would be prepared to make one in his own house, and in his spare time. It might take three months. It might take six. It would probably cost about £1,000. It might cost more. It might even cost less. At once, despite vagueness over such details, and despite the fact that I did not possess the money, I placed an order for one balloon, costing either more or less than £1,000, and deliverable by the autumn. It was a good moment, and it was arranged that I should meet the maker as soon as possible. The design would then be approved by the two of us.

The problem of gas dissipated immediately I learnt of East African Industries, a branch of Unilever, which was well entrenched in the margarine and cooking fat business out there. They made lots of hydrogen to stiffen these fats, because the bubbling of this gas through a fat makes it firmer the longer the bubbling—or hydrogenation—is continued. Their factory was in Nairobi, within striking distance of our proposed ballooning areas, and they had hydrogen to spare. Their compressor was small, but they had plans for ordering a larger and more powerful one, a machine exactly suited to our needs of packing hydrogen into cylinders to a pressure of at least 3,000 lb./sq. in. So there was a balloon, and gas—in theory.

There were also cylinders. We discovered, by a ramification I have never unravelled, that the Ministry of Aviation's supply depot at Elstow, Bedfordshire, possessed a large body of hydrogen cylinders. They had been used initially in the Christmas Island nuclear tests, for balloons of the conventional barrage kind had had to lift the explosive devices to a convenient height. When the detonations were over, and when the scientists had learnt how to pack nuclear assemblies within the confines of a bomb, there was no further need for the cylinders, and they had been shipped back to England. On a bitingly cold summer's day Douglas and I inspected them with a man from Aldermaston, and saw they were good and precisely what we wanted. They were all full, and we decided to take out enough cylinders for three inflations. Thereafter in East Africa we should shuttle them back and forth to Nairobi for re-filling. The first three flights would be with gas made in Britain, and afterwards we would rely on the local product. It seemed an excellent arrangement, and 180 cylinders were put on one side for us. They looked well, but they also weighed 23 tons. They were undoubtedly what we wanted, but the awkwardness of moving them around in the heat and bush of Africa was very evident even on that perishing day at Elstow.

At Birmingham, during the celebrations after the flight, the Boesmans had offered to give me the necessary instruction in balloon procedure, and arrange for me to take the exam for a Dutch balloon pilot's licence. It would be difficult travelling over to Holland for the remaining seven necessary flights, but it seemed the only thing to do. The flights would be expensive, but the experience of flying a balloon just had to be acquired. It is all very well thinking up schemes, dreaming of a voyage with the wind from Zanzibar to Africa, and curling your toes with anticipation before the glowing warmth of a cottage fire as your stomach settles down to digest a kilo or two of cockles; but you have to know something about the art. At least, that was how I felt. The technique of managing some 26,000 cubic feet of explosive gas, and of landing people by basket safely in jungle or desert or spine-studded bush, was plainly an art to be learnt like any other. Africa was certain to throw up aeronautical difficulties. It was obviously as well to know how to foresee at least a few of them.

Before agreeing to the Boesmans' offer I decided to make a final check on ballooning possibilities in England, for England was at least at hand. I went to see Gerry Long, the balloon flying adviser at Cardington who had for a considerable time been the only British possessor of a balloon pilot's licence. He is one of the nicest of men, and had been in the lighter-than-air business for almost fifty years. He told me tales from the old days, of being coxswain on the airships, and of the countless occasions when he had flown free balloons. Unfortunately, although his enthusiasm had not diminished one piece over the years, he possessed no balloon in which to take me up. He was the only man in the country qualified to instruct, but without a balloon it was no good. Mine was not to be ready until too late. The final blow came when Gerry Long's doctor thought it would be just as well not to renew his medical certificate. Over the years the doctor had learnt that ballooning is not always the plain sailing it should be. He thought it time his patient gave it up. And his patient did so, much to my regret.

Therefore it was up to Holland and the Haagsche Ballonclub. They were to be of most excellent worth, but before moving the scene over there I would like to linger a little longer at Cardington. It is a distinctive place, for the two gaunt sheds of the dismantled R.100 and the burnt-out R.101 are mammoth spectres dominating the station. Every battlefield is haunting to those who let it prey on them, and every grand failure casts its shadow long into the future. There is a bit of both at Cardington. Those two huge airships represented a tremendous struggle among men, and a hopeless end. Their sheds, still maintained and still as big, are the saddest constructions I have ever seen. It was such an effort; and such a failure.

Gerry Long introduced me to them. He showed me the place where the cigarette lighters and matches had had to be left in the old days. He showed me how the filling with hydrogen had been achieved. He tried to explain how large the airships had been, and what a thing containing 5 million cubic feet of gas had looked like. I had never seen those giants, and his stories seemed to come from another world. As he told me them, he was leaning on a dusty, flaking framework of aluminium. I asked him, casually, whether it had ever been part of anything.

"Good heavens, yes," he said. "This was a bit of one of the 'cars' of the R.33."

I immediately looked at the few remaining struts with reverence and touched their cold metallic shape.

"Oh, yes," he went on, "this was the R.33 all right. I remember once when we were at the Pulham mooring mast in Norfolk, and doing some maintenance, when the wind got up. One minute we were attached to the mast, and the next we were adrift with a lot of damage to the nose. Well, there were twenty of us on board, and plenty of fuel, so we started up the engines and got her under control. But we didn't make any headway against the wind. In fact, we did worse than that. We went backwards. Out we went over the North Sea, still trying to get back to Pulham. Things weren't so good, and by the time it got dark we were over Holland.

"By then we had been flying for ten hours, and we were round about Ymuiden. Well, all that night we didn't make much headway, but at dawn the wind began to relent. We still had plenty of fuel, but there was not the full complement of crew on board for we should have been twenty-eight. Also, no one slept. Anyway, at lunch time we crossed the English coast again, but this time going in the right direction. It was at three o'clock when we landed, having been up for thirty hours. It had been quite a trip, and must be about the longest unintentional flight on record. I had been duty coxswain when it had happened, and I got the AFM. Booth, the captain, got a bar to his AFC. He then became captain of the R.100, you know."

I touched the metal again. The world of airships was not only a thing of the past, but a world quite of its own. Screwed on to the outside of those gigantic hangars could well be a placard identical with that by the tea clipper *Cutty Sark*.

> "They mark our passage as a race of men.
> Earth will not see such ships as these again."

The fact that there is no such placard on the hangars, and somehow never could be, is part of the atmosphere of the place. It has all the feeling of something quite forgotten. That crash on the French hillside produced a shock that has never been surmounted. This may seem like exaggeration, but I suggest to the sceptics that they go there, and then see how it feels to them. For us, the situation was well summed up by one of the employees on duty at the gate.

"Do you realize," he said, as if it were possible we had not been informed of the fact, "that the R.101 took off from here? I remember watching her, when I was new here, and standing not 25 yards from where I am now. She dipped a couple of times, and that was the last we saw of her. Do you realize that was twenty years ago?" The poignant part of this particular story is that the flight had occurred thirty years before, not twenty.

However, Cardington was exceptionally helpful to us. They offered a grapnel, and we selected one from a rusty heap beneath a table. They offered baskets, and we chose a couple. One was a two-man affair, which would be suitable for the higher altitudes. The other could take three men, and would obviously only be used when the balloon gave sufficient lift not only to carry all three but the heavier weight of the basket. The men at Cardington, blatantly longing to do more ballooning, helped us in every way. One felt we needed a rope ladder, and settled down to make it. Another showered us with rope. "Can't have too many lashings with a balloon," he said. "Particularly where you're going." A third made a waterproof sheet to fit round our basket. This was a precaution in case we were forced to come down on the first flight somewhere in the Indian Ocean. When we finally left the hangar our car bulged with balloon gear of all sorts, and two baskets were lashed to its roof. The gigantic doors, installed to let out the R.100, were opened just a chink, and we drove happily away.

The collecting of the first equipment happened at about the time when the first bills started coming in. The Belgian attic balloon-maker had to have something. The forthcoming Dutch flights had to be paid for. The cylinders, loaned to us for a token sum by the Ministry of Aviation, were another account, for even token sums have to come from somewhere. Any expedition, and ours was no exception, acquires an earnestness it has not possessed before as soon as money has to be spent on it. The signing of large cheques is naturally important, and worrying, but the actual collection of money is doubly so.

We did have one interesting precedent to our expedition, and we examined his financial method with care and interest. In 1837, a certain Mr J. W. Hoare had floated an aeronautical company. His purpose was to explore Africa by balloon. He reckoned that he needed £8,000 for the venture, and plotted the trip from his offices at 110 Fleet Street. We therefore felt an immediate sympathy with him, for we were planning our own venture from my office in the *Daily Telegraph* at 135 Fleet Street, a few doors up the road. Mr Hoare had acquired his money by offering 4,000 £2 shares and, being an early exponent of hire purchase, had announced that they could be bought in two instalments of £1 each. So far all was well, for he had his balloon built "under the personal superintendence of Mr Graham", and he sold his shares. There was an understanding that the subscribed capital would all be paid back in twelve months, and the first profits would be realized in less than six months. He considered that the profits, even before he left for Africa, would pay dividends of 100 per cent.

49

Unfortunately, he then made a mistake, a colossal mistake. He took his "Great Mongolfier Balloon" down to the Surrey Zoological Gardens, and announced an ascent on Queen Victoria's birthday in 1838. He charged, foolishly, an admission fee from all who came. (After all, the profits had to come from somewhere.) Thousands came, and thousands paid; but the calculations made at No. 110 had plainly been at fault. In vain Mr Graham struggled to get the balloon off the ground, but the huge object failed to respond. It had room for 270,000 cubic feet of hot air, but the lift was inadequate, and the failure was absolute. As soon as the crowd realized this frustration it became a mob, and destroyed the balloon. Africa had to be left unexplored for the time being, and 4,000 shareholders licked their £2 wounds.

That was one way of raising money. It was also one method of failing. We decided on the more conventional habits of our own times, and set about extracting advances from various organizations. With infinite largesse, with great descriptions of the events to be encountered, we offered words and photographs for all we, and they, were worth. We spoke of those elephants sliding down Kilimanjaro, and the joys of a balloon, and the pressing need for publicising wild-life's plight. We talked of the superb vantage point suspended beneath the ropes. We described its possible uses, and the need for someone to make such a trip. We talked, excessively, at length, frantically, determinedly, and in any manner we felt would serve our purpose. One way and another the *Sunday Telegraph*, BBC Television, Allen & Unwin, and various foreign publishing houses became beneficent. Money, of a sort, began to come in. Like Mr Hoare, we started to have the necessary quantity of liquid assets to float both our enterprise and the balloon.

They enabled me, among other things, to go to Holland for those lessons. Sometimes I went over by night-boat, and sometimes with a friend, Geoffrey Hancock, in one of the planes from the Tiger Club. And sometimes I looked in on Holland when on the way back from somewhere else. At all events, the lessons were quite the most attractive that have ever been devised.

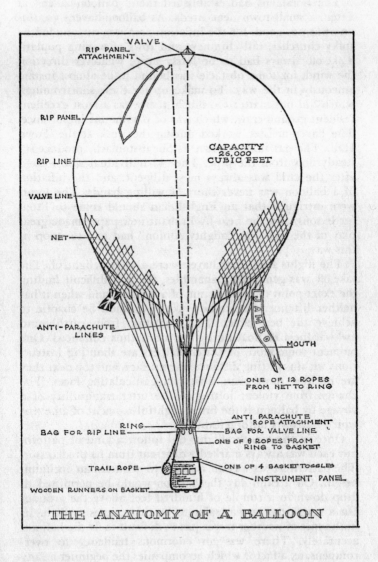

THE ANATOMY OF A BALLOON

VALVE

RIP PANEL
ATTACHMENT

RIP PANEL

RIP LINE

VALVE LINE

NET

CAPACITY
26,000
CUBIC FEET

ANTI-PARACHUTE
LINES

MOUTH

ONE OF 12 ROPES
FROM NET TO RING

ANTI PARACHUTE
ROPE ATTACHMENT

BAG FOR RIP LINE

RING

BAG FOR VALVE LINE

ONE OF 8 ROPES FROM
RING TO BASKET

TRAIL ROPE

ONE OF 4 BASKET TOGGLES

INSTRUMENT PANEL

WOODEN RUNNERS ON BASKET

JAMBO

The Boesmans had established their "balloon-haven" at Etten, a small town near Breda. As balloon-havens go, this one was not good, for the inflation area was surrounded by spiky churches, tall chimneys and rows of waving poplars. Take-off always had to be fairly steep, whatever direction the wind, for some obstacle was bound to be almost instantaneously in the way. To make up for these shortcomings, which did not matter too much, there was a most excellent resident ground-crew, which was of paramount importance. The haven-meister worked during the week at the Town Hall. The gas man, known as Sugar-stomach, produced a steady flow from the pipe. The old individual who looked after the sand was always most diligent, and the inflation of a balloon was never short of willing hands. The locals were intrigued that an Englishman should come to Etten for lessons, and the near-by Brabant newspaper made great play of the fact that "mighty Albion" had had to stoop in this way.

The flights from that haven were always delightful. The take-off was generally a shambles, for it is difficult finding the exact point of equilibrium of a balloon, and when it has neither lift nor weight; but take-offs should be chaotic to achieve the best effect. The transition from earthbound awkwardness to floating in the air is thus enhanced. One moment some score of Dutch helpers are shouting instructions within spitting distance of your face, and the next they are nothing more than a ring of gesticulating faces. The change from violent jolting to the utter tranquillity of a voyage by balloon is the first delightful moment of an event which is always unforgettable.

Once in the air, the flights did follow a kind of pattern, but each was always markedly different from its predecessor. The pattern we set was the attempt to maintain an optimum height. On a calm day the balloon would be permitted to drop down to a couple of hundred feet above the ground. On a rough day it was safer to be three times as high. In both types of weather it was just as difficult to fly the balloon accurately. There was an enormous tendency to overcompensate, a factor which accompanies the beginner at any art, and ballooning was no exception. For one thing, the handfuls of sand seemed much too inadequate. To be descending earthwards at 200 feet a minute, and to be told that two handfuls jettisoned over the edge will suffice seems a ridiculous contradiction. So the good instructor lets you contradict him, and ten minutes later not only are you not going downwards but you are going upwards at a similar rate of knots.

There was much to be learnt. It was necessary to get the feel of the balloon. It was vital to understand that the whole object, net plus fabric plus people, weighed at least three-quarters of a ton, and all of this weight was moving through nothing denser than air. Those few handfuls of sand were quite sufficient alteration in the balance of things, but they took time to have their effect. Perhaps only five minutes later did the balloon fully realize it was 1 lb. lighter. Its response was inevitable, but always slow. Therefore any idea the balloonist has of his needs in five minutes' time should be acted upon without delay.

He must realize that a lake passing beneath him will tend to lower his height in the daytime, for the lake will have colder air above it. A wood will have the same effect, and so will marshland, and sea. On the other hand, a town will send him up, just as a hot cornfield will, or a stretch of tarmac. If the sun emerges from behind cloud it will cook up his balloon, and send him up higher. When it disappears he will most assuredly come down. In theory, the sun never comes out from clouds, for both clouds and balloon are moving with the mass of air, but in fact it frequently does so for the airstream is not constant at all heights. It is possible to go faster than the clouds above you. It is more often likely that the cloud will win.

So the balloonist flies along, trying to foresee everything, estimating what is likely to send him up or down in five minutes' time, deciding what weight he wants to be then, looking out for electricity pylons, calculating whether the winds below or above his balloon are moving faster than he is, and keeping constant stock of a constantly changing situation. It is not easy. If you start going up, for instance,

53

you have to decide whether this move is being caused by the two handfuls you threw out four minutes before, or the sun becoming slightly brighter, or the farmyard you have just passed over, or if it were none of these three and instead a thermal has taken hold of you. Normally speaking, the balloonist should be able to detect whether he is about to encounter a rising air current. He can see hot patches likely to cause one, and he can watch the lie of the land. It may all sound easy and gentle; but, as I have said, it is not.

Once your three-quarters of a ton of balloon has built up its own brand of momentum, say downwards, it is difficult to stop it without excessive compensation. In theory, provided the balloonist has enough sand, he can arrest it. He can, perhaps, throw out a whole sack, a whole 30 lb. This is satisfactory if he wishes to avert some disaster, like an approaching pylon; but quite the reverse if he only wishes to stop the descent. The loss of 30 lb. will send him a few hundred feet higher, and may be the cause of his deliverance into the clouds. This is no great tragedy if they are of the gentle stratus sort, or if they are cumulus of not too great a size; but it is catastrophic if they are the nimbus thunder-clouds. In any case, not only is the balloonist forbidden to go into clouds, but he tends to lose his way when inside them. Floating within this absence of form may be aesthetic-ally pleasing, but such misty travel undoubtedly removes photographic merits of the ballooning vantage point. Besides, the object of the Dutch lessons was to learn all possible measures of control over the balloon, and not to rocket up into the clouds, however novel such a sensation might be.

So we floated over the dikes, the trim country, the steeply roofed towns, the windmills, the canals, of Holland. We muttered instructions at each other. "Now going down 1 metre a second. I think one hand here. Better make it two. Height now 210 metres. This is good. But Eindhoven is coming up. I think another hand. Perhaps yet another. Look at that girl. She's going to fall off her bike. Now we are going up. Yes, definitely. Coming up to 2 metres a second. Ah, she has fallen off."

54

It was also necessary to shout at the people down below, for they were always shouting up at us. The lack of wind around the basket made it fantastically easy to hear people, particularly when they were still in front of us. Once behind, it became harder to understand them. For me, of course, it was always fairly hard, but on those flights I learnt not only about ballooning but how to make the necessary retorts in Dutch. "Are you cold up there?" they shouted. "Why don't you come down for a cup of coffee?" "Are you going to land?" "Who are you?" "Where have you come from?" "Where are you going to?" Can I come with you. I am pretty." We used to shout back suitable remarks, suggesting they brought their coffee up to us, suggesting we met later on, inviting them to keep us warm. We also asked them where we were. This was partly because we were frequently uncertain, and also because the question regularly produced quaint answers. We would point at towns perhaps three miles off and ask their names. On the flatness of Holland the people on the ground could never tell which towns we were pointing to; but they were always ready to hazard a guess, or two guesses, or a score or more. The shouting went on frenziedly, until we had passed them by, and were still none the wiser for the passing.

Eventually came the landing. There has never been a balloon landing yet when I have known afterwards precisely what happened. Events are planned, but they occur far too swiftly for anyone to know if they acted according to the original idea. You valve a little. You start coming down. You choose your field, and unfasten the trail rope. You shout at people, if people there be, to catch hold of it. You throw out sand to lessen the fall, if it grows too severe. You start over-running the field. So you valve again to get down faster. You go too fast. More sand. The man catches hold of the rope. It pulls him off his feet. You shout at him. You see a barbed wire fence coming. You shout harder. His friend catches hold. You valve. You look for more sand. The ground comes up fast. You hit it, and fall into the bottom of the basket. You shout. You pick yourself up, and look for the valve line. You hit again. The basket hits the fence. There is a rushing sound of wind. More people are shouting, and they are not you. The basket is dragging over the field. You can't find anything. But you must rip. You must get rid of the gas. The poplars are coming close. You look for the red rope. You pull it. You take up its slack. You lose the rope. Then you pull it again, and this time you can feel it jerking open the rip panel. The balloon above you flaps wildly once or twice, and then lies down, softly, gracefully, on the bit of field in front of you. The basket is on its side. And all of you are lying there. And laughing. And asking each other if they are all right. And another balloon landing has been fantastically, miraculously accomplished.

On the original Birmingham flight most of the few people who had seen the landing, apart from the unimpressionable night watchman, had stayed respectfully at a distance, and had watched from there. This was never so in Holland. Hundreds would be around in no time. "Who are you?" "Where have you come from?" "How long did it take you?" These crowds were not only exceptionally inquisitive. In time, they became extremely useful. However clever the balloonist may have been in his attempts to land near a road, he has never been clever enough, and there is always the problem of moving the balloon, its basket, its net, its trail rope, and everything else back to the car. The car may or may not have seen the balloon during its final descent, but it is never hard finding the spot because all Holland is prepared to stop and watch for an hour or so. The car can always find the place without too great a difficulty. Into its trailer, and into its boot, goes the balloon. The crowd is thanked. Little balloon spoons are distributed to the most helpful of the helpers. The car drives off, and the crowd disperses to the clunking of clogs and the squeaks of the tall, aristocratic bicycles that are so much a part of the Netherlands.

These ballooning lessons were fabulous. By November 1961 I had completed six. There were two more to go, and there was the all-important examination. There was also a fantastic amount still to be done in England. The final month loomed before we were due to be off. It was quite a month. Douglas was now working full time on the expedition's affairs. Alan Root, the photographer, had been lined up in East Africa to accompany us. Our freshly appointed men on the spot, John Bridgman in Nairobi, John Newbould at Ngorongoro, Don Hutchins at Dar es Salaam, and Geoffrey Bell and Roger Bailey at Zanzibar, were all excelling themselves. In London, firms were helping us to get the expedition off the ground. Friends were being bludgeoned with determination and little sympathy. In short, the expedition was behaving in a thoroughly standard manner. Yet there were many occasions during that last month when I thought we would never make it.

CHAPTER SIX

THE DEPARTURE

DR SAMUEL FERGUSSON, the intrepid individual who had been Jules Verne's initial hero, and who had been our direct forerunner in the business of flying balloons over Africa, had also found that the purchase of a balloon was by no means the end of the preparatory story. By the time he had completed the English side of his adventure, he needed a whole ship to take him, his passengers, his gutta percha, and the rest of his chattels to Zanzibar. Fortunately, for he lived in the world of fiction, the Royal Navy provided him with one. We, existing in the world of fact a hundred years later, could not be so lucky; and our equipment became a major problem.

Douglas, a great man for lists, drew them up. We both examined them, at length, and tried to shorten them. This was difficult. From the vantage point of London it was hard judging the vital from the immaterial. To what extent would it be necessary to have a really long rope ladder? It would obviously be of inestimable importance in climbing down, say, a pillar tree whose branches start, or end if you are looking at things that way, a hundred feet from the ground. At all other times it would be an encumbrance.

To a large degree the tricky decisions of relating possible use to inevitable hindrance were taken for us by the cash available at the time. Douglas was also a great man for dreaming up resplendent ideas, and most of them foundered for the basic reason that money was involved. It was fine to see a man cleaning the lamps of Fleet Street from some aerial and hydraulic platform, and equally so to see in a flash that such a device in the wilderness of Africa would enable a peering camera to examine the world beneath it as if from a balloon; but hard cash crushed such a scheme to dust. Douglas's soul was somehow linked to the helicopter.

For him, its ability to go anywhere from anywhere in a straight line had a perfection he found admirable. He also found the machines were extremely costly, £38 an hour for the type he most cherished, but I am certain that one day he will hover from location to location while brilliant ideas are fulfilled before happy eyes and the inquisitive lenses of scores and scores of cameras.

The balloon expedition had money to achieve its aims, but not an excess of it. Therefore we tapped every likely source, and borrowed equipment wherever possible. To avoid repetition in letters, and to give somewhat more dignity to the enterprise, we printed a single page outlining the intentions. It detailed our purpose, our plans, our names, our procedure, and our support. It was extremely successful, and equipment began to accumulate. So we printed a four-page circular, and then an eight-page synopsis. They stated, among much else, that we intended to travel to Africa equipped with a balloon, and to make a number of captive and free flights from Zanzibar in the east to the Serengeti plains of Tanganyika in the west throughout January to March 1962.

The important thing about this brochure, which was most certainly pompous but which did at least have the merit of stating the facts, was that it enabled us to accumulate all the really vital equipment. Austins gave us a Gipsy, Negretti and Zambra produced instruments, Quadrant gave life-jackets, William Kenyons gave rope, McMurdo Instruments gave lights, Pye gave loud-hailers, Smiths gave a rise-and-fall indicator, the shipping lines knocked down the price, Johnsons of Hendon gave two cameras, Shell gave petrol, East African Oxygen offered technical aid when need be, British United Airways offered to fly us out on their freight planes, East African Railways and Harbours gave us a 50 per cent discount, the East African High Commission permitted our venture to take place, the necessary governments gave us their blessing, the Director of Civil Aviation expressed interest in the scheme, and the various game park officials and game wardens (the division of their authorities is initially bewildering) welcomed us to their domains. It was, in short, a useful brochure. People like seeing objectives stated definitely, and formally, on paper. It gives them something to get their various teeth into.

The expedition took a most positive step forward the day our 180 cylinders, each weighing 300 lb., and each compressed full with hydrogen, left the Royal Albert dock on the M/V *Trevose*. A third of them were bound for Zanzibar. The remainder were due for Mombasa, and then for Arusha, the Tanganyikan town that was to be our base. The despatch of these cylinders finally hammered home the notion that we were to rise or fall by hydrogen, and their going put paid to the idea of hot air.

For a long time this rival scheme had been debated. The obvious merits of lift by hot air, using the Montgolfier principles, were that air was universal, and we only needed to heat it to achieve our flights. The demerits were also considerable (see the calculations in Appendix 2 (c)). To achieve the same lift as a 26,000 cubic foot balloon of hydrogen, it is necessary to have a 125,000 cubic foot balloon filled with air at 100 degrees C. above the outside air temperature. This is quite a heat, and most of the fabrics we tried out tended to perish as soon as they were subjected to it for long. The R.F.D. Co. at Godalming, well known for dinghies and life-jackets, did the work for us. They found out that the fabric coatings tended to break down first at the high temperatures. In their molecular disintegration they released other substances, such as chlorine, and these quickly put paid to the fabric fibres on which they had been laid.

At the same time as these experiments were going on, the Nu-way Heating Co. at Droitwich were having thoughts about suitable burners for the hot-air balloon. In the old days, using such wisdom as they possessed, the aeronauts achieved hot air by the crudest of bonfires suspended beneath the paper canopy of the balloon's envelope. A hydrogen balloon of today is practically the same as its direct antecedents in the eighteenth century, but we felt a hot air balloon should be able to profit in the twentieth century by the modern fuels, the advanced techniques for burning them and the uninflammable and artificial fibres created by the plastics industry. At Droitwich they showed that a converted corn dryer, capable of delivering hot air both cheaply and fast, would be excellent for the ground-based unit. During the actual flight the topping up of the hot air would come from a simple supplementary burner, fuelled by tanks of butane or propane. To go up the balloonist would increase the flow of this liquid gas to his burners. To come down he would reduce it. There seemed no problem, at least on the heating side.

Eventually we had to scrap the idea due to the fabrics. That temperature of 100 degrees C. above ambient proved excessive. Admittedly it had been chosen arbitrarily; but, if there were to be less heat inside the balloon, the balloon would have to be larger. The idea of floating over Africa beneath at least 100,000 cubic feet of hot air presented too many other problems. Even our hydrogen balloon, only a modest 26,000 cubic feet, was 55 feet high from basket bottom to valve top when inflated. It was as much as a team of twenty men could carry when empty. Consequently, hot air was dropped out of the programme. Like the original balloonists of the 1780s, we forsook the Montgolfière in favour of the Charlière. We ordered our hydrogen cylinders, and they left by the morning tide for Africa.

Douglas's own particular concern was the photographic equipment. It was difficult to know what to take, and there is a full list of the final decision in Appendix 1. Photography, to the outsider, is one of those self-replicating processes whereby any advance is countered by the necessity to make two more advances. Acquire a good camera, and it demands first-class lenses to accompany it. Acquire a set of lenses, and the set cries out to be completed, with zooms and 500 mm. focal lengths, and really wide angles. Once there is good equipment it needs sound cases to cushion it against the harshness of life. In brief, if the reins are loosened for a moment, the photographer stands a good chance not merely of causing bankruptcy but of confounding himself, like the White Knight, in the midst of his gear. Douglas, managing to bite back such delectables as a signal generator, a constant

61

speed motor and an Enna 85-250 mm. variable focus tele lens, confined his final selection to a fairly modest array, the precise weight of which we were all to learn intimately as we carried it from place to place during the expedition's fulfilment. With regard to stock, we were fortunate in acquiring the still film at a cheap rate, and the 60,000 feet of cine was presented by the BBC.

The planning of an expedition by balloon cuts across many walks of life. I kept on hearing of balloonists, and meeting them. Sir Julian Huxley described a hazardous flight in which he and another zoologist happened to descend fast from the clouds, appear briefly before an astonished and unknown audience of earth-bound churchgoers, bounce roughly at their feet, and disappear abruptly into the clouds once more. That other zoologist, Sir Alister Hardy, my former professor, confirmed the story, and recounted others. Armand Denis, a globe trotter of the television screen, had ballooned in his time. So had Dr Arpad Eskreiss, now with British Oxygen, and formerly a weekend balloonist in Poland. Before the war he had taken part in the long distance races. Once, after setting off from Brussels, he had sailed high for days and nights before descending, so he said, to get his bearings. Recognizing a certain type of cattle, he realized Roumania was beneath him. Comforted, he rose again. A day and a night later he again descended. This time, when conditions were murkier, he saw only water. The very size of it confirmed his opinion that he had reached the Black Sea, and only by jettisoning everything but himself and his companion did the two of them reach the Odessa shore. Kings and princes fêted them, and three weeks later they arrived back at Warsaw. The remarkable part about this most remarkable tale is that their balloon did not win the race. Some fiend had managed to place himself in front of a storm. Without being destroyed in the process, he had been blown along at 100 m.p.h. over Eastern Europe. When his ballast had been exhausted he had landed in Siberia, and well to the east of the Odessa mark.

One day a small paragraph in a newspaper struck a chill into our systems. It stated that Twentieth Century-Fox were planning to film Jules Verne's *Five Weeks in a Balloon*, and would be on location in a matter of weeks. Douglas, never one to play down melodrama, and being steeped through reading in Scott's last expedition at the time, likened it to that fateful telegram AM GOING SOUTH that Scott had received from Amundsen. We debated what to do about it, and came to the easiest of conclusions. Nothing could be done. Then Douglas, still steeped, and still down on the south polar ice, went to the office door, made a blizzard-like noise, turned up his coat collar, muttered "I may be a little time," opened the door, and disappeared into the night.

In fact, unlike the unfortunate Oates, he had gone merely to look up cronies in the film business, and set them to work on discovering more about our rivals. The news they unearthed was comforting. The American company had no intention of flying a balloon over Africa, and the field was ours.

Those last weeks of preparation were fantastically full. There are two phases to every problem. In the first the general difficulty is overcome. Cylinders are put on board ship. A balloon is ordered. A Gipsy is obtained. Cine film is acquired. Then come the secondary worries. Where are those cylinders going to be stored? Who is to carry them there? Will they not be stolen, or the taps turned, or the caps lost? Will that Gipsy be at Dar es Salaam by December 31st, and painted like the balloon, and with a trailer, and a lock-up back, and is the insurance in order? Does the cine film need any documentation, and will the Zanzibar authorities really charge heavy duty on all unexposed film, and will the heat affect it, and how much will we need in Zanzibar, and then at Dar? Letters become more agitated, and reminders go off more hastily. Then cables make their well-meaning but expensive entry. And finally telephone calls become the only means of communication.

Enmeshed in all this flurry were the strident facts that I had as yet not passed my examination, and the balloon still had to be finished. The examination needed two more flights, as well as the passing of an interview laced with questions on the theory and practice of ballooning. The

Royal Dutch Aero Club would be in charge. Looking after the balloon itself was Albert van den Bemden, its maker. Bludgeoned by letters from me he replied in haste that everything was going ahead as fast as could be managed; but the ropes had been slow in coming from the factory. Also, his own job as a Pirelli salesman had been eating into his spare time, and his fingers were raw from work on the balloon.

We had to leave England before Christmas. The plan was to take off from Zanzibar on January 1st. The haste was necessary, and the dates had to be respected, because there was so much to be done before the long rains began on March 15th. Admittedly, that is an arbitrary date, and the seasons do not stick to the calendar; but around that time the heavens open in their own African fashion to turn the murram roads into sloshy causeways. Reports from Nairobi were none too good even during that frantic December, for the so-called short rains of the October period had lengthened out of all proportion, and the downpours measured many more inches than had ever been recorded in the century. If there was to be a dry period between the two wet ones it was certainly going to be short. It was up to us to make the fullest use of it. It was Zanzibar for Christmas, without doubt. It just had to be.

Way back in the calm of summer, one of us had suggested that there should be a pre-expedition party. Inexorably, the idea refused to die. In careless moments, we even mentioned the plan to others. They in their turn then mentioned it back. The party, so it seemed, also had to be. A day was fixed. Invitations were despatched to everyone who had helped. It was to start at 4 p.m. in my office at the *Daily Telegraph*. It had already been quite a day. The compressor had not been delivered to the ship on time. A lorry from Ipswich had therefore been chartered. King's Cross were wondering who The British Balloon Executive were. The arrival of a purity meter (for the hydrogen) caused curiosity, and therefore delay, in the letters department. A taxi had to be sent to fetch three life-jackets from near the Oval. A hide-faced hammer had to be bought. Some flasher units, for

The author

Take-off. Douglas takes this wide-angle picture with the camera on a pole. Alan works the cine-camera

A citizen of Zanzibar who had to stay behind

automatic lighting in water, had to be signed for. And then all of a sudden a guest arrived. In fact, three guests.

Fortunately London, or rather El Vino's, can deal with sudden requests for eighty glasses, and the right sort of stuff to put in them. The first arrivals only had to wait thirty minutes before they were suitably refreshed. Drink began to flow, but that did not stop the steady ringing of the phones. Yes, I must get to Holland tomorrow. It must be the first thing. No, I don't want to go to Nairobi tomorrow, too. That's for Mr Botting. Yes, B for Botting, O for . . . Yes, like blotting but you take the L out of it. Down went the phone on its gavel again. Occasion for a quick drink, a quick introduction of the former Captain of the R.100 to whoever was next to him, be it an expert on plastic foam, or the Serengeti, or the Straits of Zanzibar. Good heavens! Zanzibar! What about visas? Mary, ring them up. Who? Well, anybody who can say. Oh, you have. Well, have another drink. And answer that phone.

It was a good party, and was also the last I saw of Douglas for a while. He went off the next day to Africa, a week earlier than I was scheduled to go, to do some preliminary arranging. I remember reading a glass-stained note signed Du Bo, Du Bot, Du Bottin, which said that everything on his side was in hand. Judging by the facts that the note had many words missing, and had apparently been written by someone running at the time, I felt he was stretching his case; but the intentions were doubtless worthy, and aimed at placating one who knew all too plainly there was quite a lot considerably out of hand. There was, for instance, the balloonist's licence. There was also the balloon.

The Boesmans, Jan and Nini, met me at Rotterdam airport on a freezing Saturday. We drove down to Etten, the village possessing the balloon-haven, and arranged for the flight on the following morning. The small Hotel Victoria was full, and I spent the night with the haven-meister. In between food, which was more than generous, and gin of one sort or another, which was most welcome, I read the ballooning textbooks, and tried to infuse balloon-lore into my brain. The books were mainly in German, but the drink helped as I peered at them with heavy eyes through the lazy vapours extracted by my host from the cigar well wedged into his mouth. One sack of ballast an extra lift of 80 metres equals. In the northern hemisphere, if you your back to the wind have the low pressure on your left-side is. The winds at 1,000 metres twice as strong are as those at ground-level, and 30 degrees in direction different.

The next day we blew up the balloon Utrecht for my 7th, and penultimate flight. I had no idea when I would be able to make the 8th and final one. However, that problem would have to wait. Others were doing so. Many others. Besides, it is fun blowing up a balloon, even if a bitter December day is turning your hands into stumps, and knots are impossible to tie. A loyal group of Etten citizens, well muffled, well gloved, watched us go, and shouted greetings mistily as their words condensed in the chilly air around them. We waved back, pulled our scarves more tightly round us, and settled down to the business of flight.

As always, it was beautiful. In addition, it was warmer up there, because there was a haze over the ground. The sun, at 1,000 feet, could seek us out, and heat us up, a little. The sand was frozen hard, and I broke off lumps when need be before watching each fistful slowly drop to earth. Nothing else was stirring in the air that day. No birds were flying. At least, none that we saw. It was just us, and the huge mass of atmosphere moving us along. Poised up there, and realizing that all the air above us, below us and on every side was travelling at an identical speed, I suddenly felt as if in the centre of some mighty cohort. It was like being a cavalry-man, in the middle of a galloping line. It made me understand, for the first time, what massive forces must be involved when a 20-knot wind moves steadily from one side of a continent to the other. A balloon, unlike any other craft, enables you to feel part of the elements. A ship is an intrusion, bouncing about on top of the waves. An aircraft, and even a glider, crashes through everything; but a balloon is a cloud, a shape on its own, and going with the wind as part of it.

The sun sank early on that winter's day, and it was soon

66

time to end the flight. Just beyond a road lined with tall poplars was a huge, well-ploughed field. It was just the thing. Once over the road we dropped the trail rope, and pulled on the valve. Down we went. The rope touched the ground, and slithered along its frozen surface. Moments later we were throwing out some lumpy hunks of sand to break the fall, and suddenly we hit that field. It was like landing on iron. The basket shot off at once, and bounced uncomfortably high. The extent of this ricochet had taken us all by surprise, and more frozen sand was quickly thrown overboard. It was nothing like enough, for we came down much too fast, and hit the far wall of a frozen ditch with savage abruptness. Instead of the basket trundling along in its normal fashion, reducing speed all the while, our momentum was stopped upon the instant, and all three of us were thrown at that solid earthy wall. The rip had been pulled, and the gas left the balloon; but it took us a time to leave the poor distorted basket. Nini was clutching her shoulder. Jan had pain in his leg. And I was just tied up, in rope, and sandbags, and limbs of the other two. When we did get out of the ditch it was plain they were both badly hurt; while I, the novice, the cause of the flight, was utterly unscathed. Flight number 7 had not gone according to plan.

Two hours later, and over a most warming cup of coffee, the other two admitted they were in bad shape. The balloon and its trainee-pilot were still in working order, but the instructors were definitely not. Flight number 8 looked impossible. On the next day, with Nini painfully in bed, and Jan making one-legged plunges between the various furnishings of his sitting-room, it seemed even more remote. The prospect of a licence waned. As for flying from Zanzibar, that seemed pathetically remote.

As Holland formed an impasse for the time being, and no other instructors were available—for there are none too many of them at the best of times—I decided to catch a train for Belgium. I wanted to see how that particular problem was progressing, and whether the expedition would really be equipped with its own balloon by the end of the week. From Brussels station I took a taxi out to Ganshoren, and restrained my feelings briefly while the driver meandered round in circles looking for the right street. Eventually, after buying a map, we settled down on a more positive course, and it was about eight o'clock when I knocked on van den Bemden's door.

I was carrying a grapnel with me at the time, for I had found two in England, and knew he wanted one badly. It was with this most suitable object in my right hand that I was ushered into the main room, for the place was bedecked with balloon objects from top to bottom. Every picture was of a balloon. Every photograph was the same. Every silver cup was for ballooning, and every mug had some historic lighter-than-air scene beneath its glaze.

Albert was ecstatic over the grapnel, fingered it lovingly, and showed his wife where some earth was still lodged among the prongs. Actually that particular bit of dried mud had been collected from London Airport when I had inadvertently dropped the grapnel, but he and she regarded it as the nostalgic fragment of truth from some harrowing epic of the past. In a trice Albert was on the table and measuring the grapnel for size. Apparently, it was intended to act as the basic framework for some rather complex light fitting he had in mind. I say "apparently" most deliberately, for there were a great many people in that room, the conversation was in Flemish and French, and a piece of suburban comedy from America was booming thunderously out of the television set. There was, however, no sign of a real balloon, or indeed of anyone making one. I stirred some coffee in a balloon-emblazoned cup with a balloon-handled spoon after taking conventional sugar from a balloon-shaped bowl, and felt there was no time to be lost.

"Où se trouve mon ballon?" I asked.

Albert leapt off the table, and moments later we were driving round in his Mercedes diesel to the house, he explained, of the Schauts. Mrs Schaut let us in, and once again I was standing in a small room girt with ballooniana of every sort. She offered coffee, indicating a coffee set as she did so. I looked momentarily at the balloon-shaped knob on the coffee-pot's top, and declined.

68

"Où se trouve mon ballon?"

She led the way upstairs, and there was Mr Schaut in a sea of orange and silver fabric. His slippered feet strode over to greet the three of us at the door, and he introduced me to himself and the balloon. It was a great moment. I shook hands with him, and fingered it. It felt smooth, and very thin, and slightly chalky. It appeared quite the brightest orange and the most strident silver I had ever seen. It looked tremendous, but it also appeared only half-finished, for there were bits and pieces of unstitched fabric all over the place. I expressed dismay.

"Deux jours encore," said Mr Schaut, as he waded back into the middle of it all to make good the promise.

Mrs Schaut then showed me the net. That, too, had a lot of loose ends to it. It roamed all over the other room, and plainly there was more work to be done. I expressed alarm. "Encore deux jours," said Mrs Schaut, and Albert patted her affectionately on her arm. Everything was certainly being cut very fine. It was Monday. My aircraft was leaving England on Friday; and, as the East African freighter flew only once a week, I had to catch it. The balloon just had to arrive in England by Thursday to be put on that plane. This meant it had to leave Brussels on Thursday morning at the latest. There was certainly no time to spare. Both the Schauts and Albert had undoubtedly been working their fingers to the bone, and I shook their gnarled hands before being driven back to the station. By inches I caught the late-night train to Holland, and looked out into the night as it sped me back to the other problem. I wondered if Douglas was getting on any better than I was. There was much for him to do. At least he must have been warm when doing it. In Europe it was still bitterly cold.

The next morning I caught a tram from my hotel round to Statenlaan, and met Jan. They had regrettably been forced to a decision, he said. Their two injuries were so severe that a further flight for at least two months was impossible. Consequently, the advice of the Dutch Aero Club had been sought, and it had been decided that a licence could be granted without an eighth flight provided I proved myself fully competent in theory.

It is wrong to express delight because two people have injured themselves in a frozen corner of a foreign field; but, when the circumstances were as mine were, it is impossible not to show it. I expressed my deep regret, bubbling with happiness as I did so. I leapt around, shook all hands in sight, and then remembered with dread the examination. "The examining committee will be assembling at 2.30," said Jan.

I retired with my books, *Ballonführer Leitfaden* and the rest, to a near-by café with small carpets on its tables, and there drank coffee-cup after coffee-cup as I steadily absorbed the facts. I can assure all sceptics that a balloon exam is not just a matter of knowing which is the balloon and which is the basket. It is a matter, and so it should be, of attempting to appreciate the fantastic vagaries of our atmosphere, and their effects upon a freely moving object floating in the midst of them. Suppose the sun warms up 22,000 cubic feet of coal gas in a balloon by 1 degree C. By how much will the lift increase? Suppose the outside temperature then drops by 1 degree C. What will happen then? Does a big balloon travel faster than a small balloon? Which will go higher, a balloon filled with hydrogen or an equally sized balloon with an equal lift at the start that is filled with a heavier gas? How much gas, and how long a pull on the valve line, equal the jettisoning of two hands of sand (using two handfuls to a kilo)? As I said, I drank much coffee, and hoped the facts would also percolate into my system.

Exactly twenty-four hours later I was back again in my London office, sipping Mary's brand of coffee, and fingering the brand new balloonist's licence. It had a broad mauve strip diagonally across it, and was entitled: Bewijs van Bevoegdheid als Ballonvoerder. It entitled me to go where I wished by balloon. It was a most exciting document. A telephone call to Brussels then managed to allay my fears about the balloon. Albert and the Schauts were being as good as their word, for space had been booked on a Sabena plane leaving on the Thursday. In short, there was nothing

70

more for me to do; except answer the phone, and remember forgotten things, and fetch objects from Kings Cross, and collect money, and answer the phone, and chase people up who should be ringing, and wonder whether I would make that Friday plane, and whether everything would make it with me, and then wonder where on earth the time had gone that I thought I would have in those last three days.

The British United Airways freighter nosed its way round the complex pathways of London Airport, found the runway, took off, and headed for its first stop—Malta. I settled down to sleep with my feet resting on some machinery and my head comfortably lodged on the soft canvas form of Personal Baggage Item 5. It weighed 204 kilos, according to the other side of the label. A considerable weight; but it was, after all, a balloon.

CHAPTER SEVEN

THE ZANZIBAR WEEK

ZANZIBAR is a delightful island. I felt so initially as the local plane from Nairobi dipped low over its coral reefs, its acres of palms, its narrow, twisting streets. I felt so even more when, with Douglas and Geoffrey Bell, our man in Zanzibar, the taxi from the airport took us to Salim Barwani's guest house. That was our hotel in the town, and from it we rode forth each day on an excellent selection of bicycles not only to get things done, but also to improve our liking for Zanzibar in the process. Six days after I arrived, and two days after Alan Root had flown over from Tanganyika to join the expedition, we were all sitting in the Sir Tayabali Karimjee Club, drinking to the end of 1961, and more enthusiastic than ever over the attractions of the island. The two girls sitting at our table were both dressed in the twentieth-century type of sari, which combines the best from west and east, and the two of them were exceptionally beautiful. They had huge, clear eyes, skin the colour of warm, wet sand, and a way of moving their limbs which had all the grace and simplicity of a grass field waving in the wind. We drank deep, and thought that things looked well for 1962.

That New Year's eve was the first occasion for real relaxation. The previous days had been fraught with a displeasing variety of mishaps. A part of the balloon had mistakenly been carried on to Salisbury. Another part had remained rooted, uncomfortably long, in Mombasa. Telegrams had gone back and forth. The Customs authorities had delved into their files, and had then introduced the inevitable snags, all of which could have been banished the moment we signed the necessary cheques. They demanded, for instance, that we should pay large sums on all unexposed film brought into the protectorate. We explained that much of it would still be unexposed by the time we left. They asked us to estimate how much would be exposed. We countered by saying it depended on the speed of the wind, for presumably we were still in the jurisdiction of Zanzibar even if above it. They said yes, because Zanzibar extended to the three-mile limit, both for the sea and for the air. So we wrote out a sort of estimate of film, both still and movie, both colour and black and white, both 35 mm., 16 mm., and $2\frac{1}{4} \times 2\frac{1}{4}$, that would be consumed during our time in, above, and to one side of Zanzibar up to an infinite distance vertically and three miles horizontally. It was a pompous document. After receiving it the authorities relaxed, let everything in free, and the head of the department offered us a supply of toy balloons with which to test the wind direction.

As we sat at the Karimjee Club, holding tall glasses moist from the cold beer inside them, and talking with those fantastic gazelle-like creatures sitting by our side, the palm trees leant overhead as if trying to disguise the fact that the clouds above them were scudding along in quite the wrong direction. Throughout January, so the books had said, the winds always blow from the north-east. This was the season when the dhows set out from Arabia, and they have used the trade wind since time began. Despite the efforts of the overhanging trees, softly clicking their leaves together as the breeze pushed them this way and that, it was all too plain that the clouds were moving most positively from the northwest. If we were to take off in such conditions we would be having all the Indian Ocean to choose from in the way of a landing spot. If our luck was in we might hit Madagascar, but there is quite enough luck needed in ballooning without attempting to stretch it, and to hope for a landfall on a solitary island. The wind would have to veer more in the direction of the African continent before it was time to go. After all, the African land mass is a sizeable chunk, and to miss it completely would be a fatuous act. Even bad darts players can hit the wall at the far end of the room.

The season was an exceptional one in other ways, as we were told repeatedly. Rain, they said, was unknown at the end of the year. They even said it after our first choice for

73

a take-off site, a pleasant field of grass near both town and Barwani's guest house, had been transformed during one single ear-splitting shower into a lake. They continued to say it as our toy balloons, having been filled with hydrogen, sailed away briskly on bearings of 160 or so degrees, thus ensuring for themselves watery graves a few latitudes to the south of us and well within the immensity of the Indian Ocean.

Apart from the severe defect of the weather, and I agree that this matter tended to swamp the importance of all other issues, most of those other issues had gone well. The cylinders of hydrogen, sixty of them, were all intact, and the gas inside them was still at the original pressure. The aviation authorities had given permission for the flight, and every pilot flying in to Zanzibar brought with him his own predictions about future winds. The police, under Superintendent Suleiman, had promised eighty constables to check any crowd. The Coldstream Guards, recently posted to the island because of political disturbances, had offered a platoon of men to help with the ropes. The Acting-Resident had welcomed not only the idea but the three of us for drinks at his tall-pillared home. The Chief Minister had given the necessary permission, via his office in that most fantastic of all Zanzibar buildings, the House of Wonders, Beit el Ajaib, and the only place in town with a lift.

The town itself had also given its blessing, and help came from everywhere. Balloon safaris are far and few between these days, particularly in East Africa. No balloon had ever flown from the island before, but long memories pointed out that one visiting cruiser in the Great War had been equipped with a barrage balloon. Regular progress reports concerning our plans were transmitted by the ZBC, and before the first day was out we had no need to introduce ourselves. Zanzibar knew it had a balloon on its hands, and Zanzibar was kind enough to smile upon its fate.

In a sense it was fitting that we should start our expedition from the island. A hundred years ago, and we were celebrating a centenary, everyone wishing to visit the eastern quarter of Africa set off from Zanzibar. It was a vital terminal for men like Burton, Speke, Grant, Stanley and Livingstone. They arrived on the island, having rounded the Cape, and there took stock for their expeditions. They also hired porters, and many of the old lists are in the museum. For five shillings a man was hired, and few of them came back. The house that Livingstone stayed in before his final voyage is still on the edge of the tidal backwater just to the north of the so-called Shark Market. Stanley's room has an excellent view over the bay at the other end of town, and we even dined there when trying to borrow a launch from the house's present owner, Eric Stivens. The launch, we felt, could pick us up just in case we landed on the sea.

At the Karimjee Club, the arrival of 1962 was welcomed in the traditional manner. The gazelles got to their feet with the rest of us, sipped their fruit juices, blinked once or twice, and then smiled. 1962 began most excellently. It was still excellent some four hours later when the three of us, having mislaid the rest of the group at the club, wandered and sang and laughed through the capillary network of Zanzibar town. There were puddles, and it was hot-house warm. There were apparent blind alleys which then led, most surprisingly, most excitingly, on to superbly framed glimpses of the island's shoreline, with the moonlit surf breaking silently on the edge of a moonlit sea. There was, of course, the predominant snag. Every time we realized it there followed a miniature muscular contraction somewhere slightly below one's stomach. The wispy puffs of cloud were still there, still moving in the wrong direction, still threatening the fortunes of the expedition before it had even begun.

On the following day I woke up to a banging shutter and a fluttering mosquito net. A gale was blowing through the room, and indeed across the whole island. A cyclone over Mauritius was having this backlash even as far north as Zanzibar. In no time at all we were being told that such events were entirely contrary to the season's normal weather conditions. The new wind certainly put ballooning out of the question for a further period, but it also blew us Charl Pauw, who became a fourth member of the expedition. He was from Capetown, he had the thickest of South African accents, and was hitch-hiking around Africa. The gale had made it impossible for him to go swimming around the coral reefs—"Christ, man, those colours are fantastic, I tell you" —so he started helping us with our work—"Man, you're crazy if you think these blerry ropes are thick enough" instead of just wandering around the town—"But the place is lekker, I tell you, its lekker." He had with him a small bushbaby, and this used to hop around in his vicinity. When it felt tired the animal crawled into his pocket, and went to sleep. When it was hungry it ate grasshoppers apparently without any feeling of saturation ever invading its system. The end of a meal came when Charl could find no more.

Even though the wind put ballooning out of court on that first January day, the time we should have been departing according to the original London schedule, there was plenty of work. If you are going to leave abruptly, as a balloonist does because the point of no return is reached the moment he is lifted from the ground, everything to be done after the flight has to be done before it. Arrangements for transporting the rest of our equipment to Africa had to be made. The right people had to be thanked. The clearing up had to be done, so to speak, while we were still making the mess. The mess involved collecting sand from the beach, fixing the balloon—for I found the ropes between the ring and the basket were missing—checking with the airport tower, seeing about the constables and the guardsmen, and fixing up for a new take-off site. This last procedure was successful, but its manner of achievement had not been tactically perfect.

The local radio had announced the fact that we would be leaving from the playing ground of the King George VI School. The broadcasters had been told of our intentions before we had managed to pay a visit to the headmaster. He was reasonably disturbed at the outset, and more so when the Police Superintendent—whom I had taken as support— guessed the crowd might be 5,000 strong. As the conversation was by then sliding downhill, I threw in the facts that 10 tons of cylinders containing highly inflammable gas would arrive, that there was no guarantee of the hour or even day of departure once the balloon was inflated, that the fire brigade would have to be there, and there was always the chance of the balloon gaining the upper hand to cavort destructively downwind. Like a man who is prepared to fight one other, but who gives up at the sight of five, the headmaster forecast so many disadvantages to the idea that he relented graciously, and I and the superintendent shook his hand most warmly.

A trouble with Zanzibar is its sense of hospitality. Invitations are rife. We even had to make speeches—"Man," said Charl, "what is this Rotary Club effort? I'll prove to you they don't throw me out." We also learnt, with irritating ease, about balloon jokes. Perhaps it was ungracious of us to scoff at them, but a large number of people did make precisely the same remarks about balloons. This was reasonable, but each remarker felt his wit was his own, and was thereafter convulsed by his own brilliance. After a while, we began classifying these jokes, and pride of place was accorded to: "When does the balloon go up?" It is sad to relate that excessive numbers of people used not only to dredge up this remark but to hold their sides afterwards, to squirm this way and that, to find breathing almost impossible as their bodies were racked by the delightful pains of helpless laughter. Joke 2 said, and I repeat the remark in its entirety: "If you're filling it with hot air, there's enough of that around here." Once again there were the epileptic convulsions of a man at our feet. We watched the writhings with a dry and detached antipathy, like Massachusetts puritans who had been cannoned into by a drunk in the street. Jokes 3a and 3b, of equal dosage and demerit, were: "I suppose you call yourself balloonatics" and "Who do you throw out first?" More writhings in the dust. More puritanical aloofness and disdain. There were others about having a puncture, and the difficulties of personal relief in flight; but these and many more we would not even deign to number. After a time our own brilliance at being quite unmoved by these fatuities, when not one tremor of an impulse passed down our facial nerves, would strike us as being even

77

funnier than they, the perpetrators, had thought their remarks. When they had finished, and had brought their rib cages under control once more, it was our turn to grovel around with all the side-holding, breath-clutching, and muscular grimacing antics that they, in their minor way, had just been through.

Apart from people who were unwelcome for their jokes, although it was only the exact repetition that worried us, and they were not to know that, there were the straight-forwardly inane questioners. Once again, I suppose it was wrong of us to mock at their weaknesses, but large numbers of people did ask questions straight off the cuff. I think here a distinction should be made between lawful ignorance and outright idiocy. Plenty of questions were fair game, and to be treated with respect, even if they had been asked before. These included the material of the balloon, the type of gas being used, its size, the name of the maker, the method of attachment of rope to basket and net, the procedure for landing.

Forbidden questions were those which demonstrated that the asker had given rein to his questioning drive without, so to speak, putting his mind in gear. These included "How do you make certain of coming back to the same place?" with its subsidiary "How do you steer?" Questions that assumed either oxygen or nitrogen or any gas under pressure was used in the balloon always merited, or so we thought, no politeness from us. As the air around us is composed almost entirely of a mixture of oxygen and nitrogen, and as compressed gas of any sort weighs more than gas un-compressed, we asked these people in return how on earth they thought the balloon ever got off the ground. I admit we were frequently abrupt in our ripostes, but we con-sidered our counter-question a fair one, and sometimes followed it up by demanding how they thought a piece of wood floated on the water. Even to ask this question implies a measure of rudeness, but we felt sufficient justification if no sort of answer could be given.

On January 2nd the wind died down. That Mauritius cyclone had worked itself out. More important, the wind now blew from the north, a great improvement on north-west, and an indication that it was moving over to a point north-east of the island. Therefore we decided to go ahead, and start inflation on the following day. I was to look after the balloon. Douglas was to take the still photographs on the ground, and then join me in the basket. Alan was to look after the boat, for a fast launch had been promised, and then travel across with it filming the balloon until he had seen us safely over dry land. The boat would drop him off at Dar es Salaam. Charl, having spent two days splicing ropes and doing innumerable other tasks, had earned a place in the basket. His trade, as far as the Government was concerned, for we had to fill up the forms before leaving the island, was written down as coxswain. Geoffrey Bell, our first man in Zanzibar, was to film the departure. Roger Bailey, a second and most willing servant of the expedition, was to look after events on the ground while we were busy with the balloon, and then to clear everything up afterwards. (The schoolmaster had been rightly adamant about this.) Roger was also to settle outstanding bills, and pass the composite account over to us on the other side.

On that final evening we looked at the map again. Where were we likely to land on that other side? If the wind continued to veer at the same rate as it had been doing we would assuredly head for Kenya. If it stayed where it was we might just graze the continent a few miles to the east of Dar. On the other hand, provided it did not send us into the Indian Ocean, and provided it moved around to blow as it should be blowing in January, we would land somewhere between Dar and Bagamoyo. This was the contingency that should happen. Therefore it was the contingency we planned for. Alan's wife Joan was over in Dar with his Land-Rover. An Army friend of Douglas's named Don Hutchins worked there, and he had offered to look for us with our orange and silver Austin Gipsy. To both of them we announced by telephone, with the simplicity of direct assurance, that we would be landing as near as possible to the road linking Bagamoyo to Tanganyika's capital. On all our maps that road had been drawn with a bold, red stroke of the pen. It would be just a matter of looking for this highway, and then landing when we saw it. Either Joan or Don would be certain to see us. At least, that was the plan.

Flying control rang us up late that Tuesday night with the final wind readings, giving height, direction and speed.

500 feet	020/12 knots
1,000 feet	020/15 knots
1,500–2,000 feet	020/20 knots
2,500 feet	010/25 knots
3,000 feet	010/25 knots
3,500–4,000 feet	360/25 knots

Things looked well. At about 2 a.m. we all went to bed, having completed the packing. There was a large shipment for Nairobi, another for Arusha, and another that would have to follow after the flight had been made. The three piles entirely filled up the hall of Salim Barwani's house. He was the most forgiving, and the kindest of men. Having made the three heaps, having apologized again for them, and having nothing more to do, we then went to bed.

It was easy enough climbing under the mosquito net, and settling down into the foetal posture of sleep. It was much less easy to close one's eyes and actually go to sleep. I had never been in charge of a balloon before. My particular balloon had never been flown before. No one had ever flown a balloon before from Zanzibar. No helper there knew anything about a balloon. There were 35 miles of sea between the island and the mainland even if we went in the right direction. Five thousand people, so the police had estimated, would be watching the departure. Two people would be looking for us in Africa. What would the country be like where we chanced to arrive? There had been talk of sisal plantations, and sisal is razor sharp. If it wasn't sisal it would be jungle of a sort. There was clearly a difference between jungle and trim Dutch fields. Would the balloon get off the ground? Was there enough gas in those cylinders? Would the wind get up when we were half-way through the inflation, or even half-way across the Straits? Would the whole thing be a ludicrous flop, with a few shrunken figures trying to disguise the fact that they were catching a plane for the anonymity of somewhere else?

The following day had much to bring. Yet it was already that day. I had to get some sleep. I had to. There was so little time. Was that cloud moving as it should? It seemed bright. It could not be dawn already. I had to sleep. I had to.

CHAPTER EIGHT

THE POINT OF NO RETURN

THE next morning began with the suddenness of a pistol shot. Sleep vanished with an immediate realization that the day had arrived, and there was much to be done. It was drizzling slightly outside, but I rang up the control tower to receive the latest wind reports. They could have been better, but the flight was definitely on. Salim ordered the breakfast earlier than normal, and the four of us sat there with pencils in our hands jotting down the things to be done by each one of us as we remembered them. Flags, someone said. Yes, they should be ready. What about beer for the soldiers? And the final cable to the *Telegraph*. And a final word across to Dar.

I and the others left for the launch site, together with the balloon, in a hired truck. The drizzle continued, and I squinted through the compass as we took our own wind check of the day. The little balloon floated jerkily upwards, maintaining a steady course of 180 degrees. With luck, and if the weather reacted as it should, the day ought to bring that wind around to 200 degrees or thereabouts. The heating up of the African continent generally slewed the wind around by midday, or shortly afterwards. That was a chance it was necessary to take.

The guardsmen helped us drag the balloon into place. They then helped the net into its encircling position around the balloon, and I attached the valve, the gas hose, and the various other bits and pieces. It was an hour and a half later, and still drizzling, when we turned on the hydrogen. A schoolmaster, Ken Pascoe, had offered to act as gas man, and he was to empty the cylinders, one by one, as the day progressed. There is always a danger of fire with hydrogen, but there is no real likelihood of an explosion in the open air. Back at Cardington an expert had described the vivid

jet of flame, perhaps 30 feet long, that shoots out from a full
cylinder should the escaping gas ever catch alight. He
explained, with that irritating nonchalance of experts, that
such jets always go the way the nozzle is pointing. Therefore,
to turn off the gas, it was only necessary to approach the
cylinder from the other side, apply the key, and prevent
the flow. What made the whole thing easier, he added, was
that the actual flame did not manage to get a hold of the
gas until some feet from the cylinder. It was initially moving
too fast for the oxygen of the air to mix with it, and for
the combustion to begin. I repeated the gist of these remarks
to Ken Pascoe, but with one tenth of the expert's conviction.

The gas left the cylinders with a reverberating drone, lost
its 300 atmospheres of pressure, and travelled along the
100-foot hose to the balloon. There I, and the guardsmen,
and various other people dragooned to help, looked after the
steadily inflating shape. The procedure of filling up, and
then preparing a balloon for flight, is capable of making
use of almost any number of helpers. People never seen
before would drift up, out of curiosity, and would immediately be given a rope to hold, or something to pull, because
of their obvious suitability at that time and that place to
do whatever it was that had to be done.

Like so many tasks which should be simple, like putting
wallpaper on walls, or sloshing mortar between bricks,
everything can go extremely wrong if care is not taken all
the time. Any error that creeps in never creeps out. It either
stays or causes an exaggeration of its effect all along the
line. If the balloon is not symmetrical to begin with, it
never will be. The net must be made to take an equal share
of the weight on every side. The fabric must never be
stretched disproportionately. In short, there is nothing
intrinsically difficult about the inflation, just as laying one
brick on top of another involves nothing spectacular; but
one's attention to the problem must be complete.

By 11.30 the balloon was three-quarters full. The wind
was still 180, but at least it had not backed away from its
original direction. The crowd surrounding that precious
grass of the King George VI playing field was being well

controlled by the police, and Suleiman thought it already numbered 4,000. Someone even said that, barring meetings assembled by religion or politics, this was the largest gathering Zanzibar had ever known, and it was certainly increasing all the time. The drizzle was slackening off, and this meant the balloon ropes became steadily easier to handle.

I, personally, welcomed the drier weather for a reason quite apart from those associated with the misery of a rainy day. The textbooks had referred to "Shrinkage and Expansion of Net". Griffith Brewer had made the point in his customarily terse phraseology. "During an inflation in the rain the net naturally shrinks. As the net dries it recovers its original size, and in expanding it slips over the envelope, moving downwards in little jerks. The first time one experiences the dropping of the car (basket) a feeling of alarm naturally arises, so it is well to be prepared for this unpleasant phenomenon." I agreed wholeheartedly, but doubted whether preparations would ever be complete. The approaching departure from the island had quite enough risk involved, without the unnerving addition of little jerks downwards of the car.

At 12.30 I shouted to Ken to switch off the gas, for the balloon had had enough. It was larger by 750 cubic metres, or 26,000 cubic feet. It also, to my mind, looked most beautiful. Its main bulk was orange, but it had twelve silver stripes or petals coming up from the mouth which were topped by a silver band slightly below the equator. The design had been forced upon us by the quantities of silver and orange fabric which the Belgian Albert could lay his hands on, but it looked very well whatever the cause.

The headmaster approached, and asked when we would be leaving. I said as soon as possible, but at that moment Alan appeared to say that the promised launch's owner, not Eric Stivens but another, had let us down. He considered the sea too rough for his boat. Alan then hurried off to try and find another, but he was pessimistic. We had already combed the town for boats. It looked as if the trip would have to be unaccompanied. We did have three life-jackets, kindly given to us in London, but sharks live in the sea, and a following boat would have been a comforting sight. Anyway, that was apparently that.

The guardsmen brought up the basket, and with one man to each of the twelve ropes leading down from the enormous net I set about the final stage: the attachment of the slender wicker thing in which we were to make the journey. The method is first to fix a wooden ring to the twelve ropes leading from the net, and then to attach that same ring to the four other ropes leading up from the toggles of the basket. When this has been done, and the whole arrangement is still weighed down with 60 or so sandbags, the ground-crew have to remove the sacks and gradually take upon themselves the task of holding down the balloon. There is nothing difficult about this, for the basket is only going to lift three people into the air, and so twelve men should find no problem in restraining it. On occasion in the past the helpers have panicked. If one man lets go, the remaining eleven wonder if it's still safe to hang on. So there may soon be ten, and that increases the chances of there being only nine. Before the commander knows what is happening the others are letting go, and the final man is likely to be whisked into the air. Provided he lets go soon enough, only a balloon is lost. If he loses his nerve, and hangs on, he is as good as dead.

So, in Zanzibar, I stood in the middle, and told everyone what to do. The crowd was by this time fantastically large. The headmaster was still asking when I was leaving, and the balloons were still going on a course of 180. The day was clearing up, and things looked well for the time being. But I was full of apprehension all the same. "Make it three sandbags on the bottom metal eye. That's right. Don't worry about the swaying. Just let it sway. Now make it two sandbags. Everyone take one off, and just put it on the ground. Now let the two bags slide down each rope. Down towards the middle, so they're all next to the ring."

At this point the ring was lifted into the air, as it should have been. The basket was still firmly attached to the ring by its four ropes. The soldiers were doing well. The balloon was swaying more, but that was also to be expected for it

85

had grown taller with the removal of those bags. I set about removing the rest, and climbed on to the basket. "Now lift each bag in turn, and I'll take its hook off the rope. Right, this one. Just put it on the ground. Now this one. And hang on to the basket instead. Now this sack, and this one."

Suddenly to my horror I saw that one of the soldiers was examining the frayed end of a rope. It had just snapped. As I stood there the balloon and basket lurched again, and this time I heard a rope go. It was the other one at the same basket end. There were only two left. Another moment and those other two would go. And that would mean the balloon itself would go. Possibly with a couple of people hanging on to it until too late. Possibly. . . .

I know I should remember precisely what happened, but I do not. I remember a kind of liquefying of my brain, and shouting a lot, and pulling at things that wouldn't budge, and shouting some more, and then finally standing on the ground again with a feeling of utter despair. At least the balloon had been saved, for the ring was once again encompassed with sandbags. I looked at it, still wondering what had happened, and counted the bags to see there were enough. The ring was creaking, but half a ton of sand was keeping it at bay. "Has something gone wrong?" said a lace-gloved woman who had appeared from nowhere.

I walked to the soldiers by the basket, now detached from the ring, and had a look at those broken ends. The cotton rope, bought in Zanzibar, and spliced by us a couple of days before, had snapped as if cut by a razor. "That's the way old rope goes," said someone. "You don't get new rope going like that, however big a strain you put on it. It must have been donkeys' years old."

Alan, Douglas and Charl wandered up, and the four of us talked together. We must have made a depressing-looking bunch. Even though the situation had saved itself miraculously, there was certainly going to be no flight that day. More, and proper, ropes would have to be acquired, and spliced. Everything else would have to be checked. If a wind didn't get up in the night, causing us to deflate the balloon, we should be able to leave at the same time next day. There would obviously be hydrogen leakage during the night, and we would top up the balloon in the morning. That is, if there was enough gas left in the cylinders. We certainly didn't have enough for another inflation if the wind did get up.

The lace-gloved woman loomed up with another question dickering on her lips, and we dispersed. I went to Suleiman, and asked him to inform the crowd through his loudspeakers that the flight was most regrettably postponed for a day. I then went back to button-hole that man who seemed to know about ropes and listened to him as the people wandered away leaving the field to sixty red cylinders, to a length of hose, to those of us who remained, and to one vast orange and silver balloon heaving gently in the wind, and creaking just a little as it did so.

Twelve hours later I settled down to sleep under that same balloon. The day had been a long one, and much of it had been passed in the house of the Rasmussens. It had been one of that family who had talked about rope, and as his family house was the nearest to the balloon it became a headquarters building. None of us could eat lunch, and one of the Rasmussen brothers took us into town to find some stronger, better and newer cotton rope.

"Feel it," he said, over and over again, after we had found some. "Just you feel it. That's real Indian cotton. That's good and new. Just look at all those strands, and feel them."

The precious rope was taken to the power station, where the other brother worked, and there we tested it. Its breaking strain proved to be over a ton, which was more than enough in any circumstances. We then set about the business of splicing it. Unfortunately, although manilla is good to splice, and sisal is easy but rough on the hands, the splicing of tight cotton rope is frequently impossible. If you don't look out, it forms kinks and lumps which utterly destroy the strength and value of the splice. For the rest of that day we struggled with those ropes, because I had been told that Indian cotton was the best to have; but we achieved little. Of the sixteen splices needed for the eight new ropes, only five could be considered satisfactory by the time midnight had arrived. We decided that it would have to be manilla, and it would also have to wait until the next day. Rasmussen suggested African Wharfage Co. down at the docks. They would have it, he said, and splicers too.

At the balloon a small group of policemen posted by Suleiman sat about keeping guard over their curious charge. The gas inside it had cooled considerably when the sun had left the sky, and the fabric flapped in consequence—but not unduly. All the sandbags had been used to bed the balloon down, and everything seemed under control. The night was not too good, for there was lightning playing over on the African shore; but the wind was gentle, and that was the most important thing. We all looked at the broken ropes again, and realized once more how close we had been to losing everything. The local papers, in reporting the incident, announced that "a defect in the rigging" had been found, and this had delayed the departure. They later mentioned, with infinite tact and grace, that Mr Smith had detected a flaw during the inflation which had had to be adjusted. We looked at those frayed and useless ends, those flaws, those defects, and marvelled at our fortune.

Douglas, Alan and Charl then went back to Barwani's while I stayed with the balloon. I cannot pretend it was a good night. I had a sleeping-bag, but a slight rain began. This splattered gently, but exasperatingly, for the sleeping-bag was an inadequately long cocoon. I moved under the balloon, watched the lightning in the sky, wondered whether 26,000 cubic feet of burning hydrogen would scald a semi-encased individual lying beneath, and listened to the canvas jibbing at the wind. The police patrolled relentlessly, and changed shifts at seemingly five-minute intervals. The Coldstream Guards were having some kind of a night exercise, and files of men would pad breathlessly from one corner of the field to another. The relief when dawn came was considerable. I dropped the pretence of sleep most readily, and stood up with an alacrity rare on normal mornings.

The trouble with rising early, like arriving by night train at Kings Cross, is that everything else takes a long time to start. The Rasmussens had told me they did not rise before seven, but at that very hour I was knocking them up. Within a reasonable space of time I was scalding my lips on an excellent cup of coffee, and then badgering them to take me into town to see about that rope. We arrived, of course, even before the docks had started work; but the moment they did so we were hurrying to the rope department, and in virtually no time a group of Africans was splicing some manilla with a skill that I marvelled to watch. Their fingers were like iron rods, as compared with my own raw stumps after the previous evening's efforts; but I stretched them forward eagerly to receive the ropes when, some thirty minutes after starting, the Africans had finished them.

Back at the balloon was Alan with news that a boat had been acquired. It was the pilot launch and, although only capable of 8 knots, was most emphatically a boat, and very welcome. Due to this slight speed, which was probably less than half of what the balloon would achieve, the plan was that Alan and the harbour-master would leave one hour before the balloon. In theory I was to give them the word.

The wind was still persistent in its liking for 180, and it still made just as good sense as the day before for us to try and leave some time after midday. Therefore, even though that unnerving crowd began to assemble once again, and the soldiers were there, and everybody else, we did not begin the topping-up procedure until 10.45. In the meantime I went back to the Rasmussens, chewed my way through half a slice of cake, and lay back on a kind of couch. Fear of a sort was beginning to get the upper hand. Why, I wondered, was I in this ridiculous position? Why try and fly a balloon, and from Zanzibar of all places? Where will I be in three hours' time, or six hours, or nine? Where on earth will we go to, and what will we find there? Supposing it is the ocean. Or solid jungle. Will the ropes hold? Will we get off the ground? Will there be enough gas? Will there be some other fiasco like yesterday? The half piece of cake I had eaten was pushed resentfully from one side to the other by a stomach that wanted no part of it.

Such distaste for the immediate future vanishes the

moment you become incorporated in it. Back at the balloon there was much to be done, when 10.45 arrived, and we all did it. There was more than enough gas. The balloon assumed her proper, proud shape once again, and this time there was no difficulty in attaching either the ring to the net or the basket to the ring. The eight new ropes took the strain without even looking tight. There remained only the matter of equipping the basket with our requirements for the flight. So into it went one grapnel, one trail rope, one rope ladder, a bottle of champagne, some food, a lot of water, the camera equipment, a two-way radio, my instruments, two knives, spare rope and string, a stick of bananas, the bushbaby, and maps of the areas towards which we were likely to go. Above it, neatly tucked up, were the valve line (for a gentle release of gas) and the rip line (for a total release of gas). Around the basket we put initially a rubber cover, just in case we were forced down to the sea. Over this we placed one very large Zanzibar flag (bright red), one very large Tanganyikan flag (black, green and gold), and one extremely diminutive Union Jack, the largest to be had in town.

The three who were making the trip then climbed in, while Alan rushed off down to the boat, as it was plain our departure was near. First to get in was Charl (74 kilos), then Douglas (81), and finally me (91). I do not know why, but we were going through our paces like automatons. We did things as they had to be done. No one made any jokes about them, or any extra remarks of any sort. The previous twenty-four hours had taken all spare wind out of our sails, and we put on the life-jackets with the weary familiarity of men getting into their coats at the end of another day's work. Even the hauling aboard of the sandbags occasioned nothing superfluous. We lifted them in, and stowed them away at our feet until it seemed as if equilibrium was near. We were poised, or so I felt, with the right degree of buoyancy, and only the soldiers' hands kept us firmly on the ground.

At this point I should have made all the correct remarks to all those helpers standing near by. I should have shouted some greeting to everyone through Suleiman's loudspeaker.

In fact, I only continued with the take-off procedure. For twenty-four hours we had been wanting to go. The fact that the actual hour was near merely sharpened our impatience.

"Hands off!" I said to the soldiers.

They did so, and we stayed, toppling slightly, on the ground.

"Hands on again, and take this sack."

They all clutched at the wicker rim, and one man dumped the sack heavily at his feet.

"Hands off!" I shouted again, and this time we moved a couple of yards before sliding along on the ground.

"Hands on!" and they all came running up. I gave a soldier another sack, and asked him to empty half of it on the ground. The remaining half-sackful I clutched with one arm while I repeated the balloonist's immemorial phrase.

"Hands off again!" I shouted, ridiculously loudly, and at the same time pulling a rope to let the balloon's mouth open, thereby changing it from a sealed container into one where the gas could expand.

Instantly, the miracle of a flight started once again. Without a bounce, without any apparent movement, we were flying into the air. We said nothing to harm those first few moments when the incredible repeats itself and a balloon takes leave of the Earth with a grace that is unforgettable. Up we went, and smaller grew the people. The crowd broke through the police, and darted on to the field. How minute they were! How remote already! And how inaccessible! Our point of no return had already been reached. As if by a signal we three turned round in the basket, and looked ahead to see what chance and fate had in store for us.

CHAPTER NINE

THE TRIP TO AFRICA

VERY quickly I realized that it was not a good take-off. It is true that I had missed the trees on the edge of the field, but in making certain of doing so I had miscalculated the quantity of ballast left on board. Instead of cruising perhaps 500 feet above the town, we steadily climbed well in excess of that height, and were above 2,000 feet when crossing the coast of Zanzibar five minutes after the departure. However, that was a detail. The major facts, that the flight had been achieved, the ropes had not broken, the balloon had left the ground; these were unquestionable. There remained one important discovery to make. For a certain time I put off making it, and then slowly lifted the prismatic compass to take a back-bearing on that green field now speckled with the crowd. I let the needle settle down before daring to change the focus of my eyes and read the figures. It was fantastic. It was unbelievable. It read 020. The wind was precisely in the right quarter.

Suddenly, everything was immensely beautiful. There were little wisps of cloud around us, but there was no difficulty in seeing that the shades of blue and brown and green around the coral islands and their jutting reefs were perfect. Right from the start of the ocean trip we could see the coastline of Africa, only as a smudge on the horizon, but most comfortingly there. The town of Zanzibar had passed too quickly underneath, with dark streets, white roofs, invisible people. There had been surf all around its edge, and from the harbour there was a dot at the apex of a long, sweeping wake.

"That must be Alan, poor cow," said Charl.

And indeed it was, for I had forgotten to give him that planned one hour's warning. He had left when it was obvious we were soon leaving, and he had only reached the boat as we had sailed over the harbour. Already it was obvious we had more than twice his speed, but that wake looked consoling all the same.

"Christ!" said Charl. "Count me in on this ballooning effort."

"Well, we made it!" said Douglas.

Different words, perhaps, but the two of them had identical looks on their faces, and the sentiments were the same.

"It's still 020!" I said, entranced, and not being able to look enough through that compass. I kept on lowering it, and then letting the needle settle down again. This was not because I believed it might be faulty, and held back by the oil, but solely because it was such a wonderful thing to do. Time and time again the compass was made to give the good news. It was 020, still 020, and we were travelling on the reciprocal as straight as any die. Our course of 200 was slightly south of south-west, and we would most certainly cut across that Dar to Bagamoyo road.

"Christ!" said Charl, and left it at that.

Douglas just pushed the peak of his cap up, a fairly hideous cap, incidentally; but the gesture meant the same as Charl's expression of bewonderment. It was a supreme moment. Life cannot hold many such minutes in store for any one of us.

By then the balloon had stabilized at 2,300 feet. Nothing had been thrown out since our departure, and there was no need even then to lose a little weight. It takes time for a balloon to find its height, but when it does so it is quite content to stay there for a while. If the day is at all cloudy, and that day was, the higher you float means the greater the chance of being warmed by the sun. And this counteracts, for a time, the tendency to sink.

So we, well content with our lot, gently warmed by the sun, and with eleven untouched sacks of ballast at our feet, watched Zanzibar depart while the coast of Africa approached us in the other direction. The Straits were beneath us, the world was on every side of us, and no time could have been riper for christening the balloon. A treasured

93

bottle of champagne, bought by the expedition's secretary —Mary—back in London, was still both unscathed and unpopped. It was prepared with fitting solemnity.

"Hell, man!" said Charl, and his eyes bubbled over.

"Hell, man!" said Douglas, for Charl's accent just demanded imitation.

At this moment the cork flew up, and the froth spilt everywhere. I had failed to get the cork into the balloon's open mouth, the hole some 15 feet above us, and traditionally the aiming point in such ceremonies; but that did not diminish our appetite for the foaming stuff that fizzled everywhere. It plainly wanted to leave that bottle, and get drunk. We did not discourage it, and lapped it up greedily.

In between gulps, and while passing the bottle round, we named the balloon. Jambo is the first word that anyone hears and learns in East Africa. It is the Swahili for hallo, for greetings, for "how are you?" all rolled into one cocky sound. Back in England it had been decided that this word, with its pleasing undertones of something rotund and large, would be a most excellent name for the balloon. So in turn we christened her "Jambo", and looked up with admiration at the huge orange and silver form happily poised above us.

It was then the turn of the bushbaby. Much of the unintentional libation exuded by that enthusiastic bottle had run into his pocket in the canvas, and he was wet when we lifted him out. Being a nocturnal animal, and the sun being fairly bright, and the whole world around him being frighteningly different from the shady trees in which he normally lived, I cannot pretend that he welcomed our idea with any other emotion than disgust. He sipped at no champagne. He refused banana. He would not even uncurl. He behaved for all the world like a nocturnal animal suddenly woken up to blink at bright clouds and three happy faces beaming equally brightly down on his moist and furry form. We replaced him in his pocket, and pulled down the flap.

Charl and I worked out our position on the map. We took

94

cross bearings, drew them in, and then put a mark and a time inside the small cocked hat these lines produced. The track was still exactly 020 from our starting place, now invisible, and we were travelling at slightly over 20 knots. The poor launch, capable of 8 knots even in the best of weathers, was not even making that speed in the choppiness down below. Our map was only a paper one, and a large thing when unfolded, but it was perfectly manageable in the balloon. On the ground, even during the gentlest of days, such maps contort themselves into unfoldable shapes whenever confronted by a breath of wind. We were sailing along in a force 4 breeze, and yet nothing ruffled that map. I repeat that flying with the wind means that you feel no wind. It is not like sailing. It is not like gliding. It is an experience entirely of its own. The wind takes you, as fast as it pleases, and yet causes not a single hair to ruffle in the process. This complete lack of draught of any sort is extremely hard to comprehend for the novice balloonist. He looks down, as we did, upon a buffeted world, and yet he coasts along above it all, unblown, untouched by the wind, and yet in the very midst of it.

After some forty-five minutes we slowly started to descend. I saw no harm in flying slightly nearer the sea, and so let the movement build up. Winds are stronger the higher you go, twice as strong at 3,000 feet as at sea-level, and I thought we could afford to travel a little more slowly. If we found it too slow down there, or radically different in direction, we could always come up again. So we went down. Every so often I threw out a hand of sand, enough to stop acceleration but not sufficient to halt us completely. At 500 feet we levelled out, and took stock of a different world.

High up, the sea had appeared flat and remote. Low down, it became a thing of noise and fury. Never before had I heard the sea. When in a boat the water had always lapped against the sides making a dominant noise. I could never then be certain what noise was the sea, and what was being caused by the boat's intrusion. A swimmer cannot listen either, for his ears are slapped by the water, and the waves run into him. If he stands instead on dry land the predominant sound is the surf. Whether it is the big rollers breaking on the shore, or those diminutive ripples that flap about at his feet, the real sea noise is beyond him, away from coastal disturbances. So we all heard something we had never heard before as we sailed along at that lower height. It was an incredibly angry sound. Waves suddenly formed, and hurled themselves at each other. Other waves skidded along the surface, trying to disconnect themselves from the main mass of the sea. And all the time the roaring, and crashing, and breaking went on. It was another world down there, unfriendly, harsh, and violent.

At this moment a Dakota came to look at us. The Zanzibar flying control had been repeatedly asking all pilots within its radio range for wind information, and so it was only reasonable that the pilot flying the regular run between Dar and Zanzibar should turn aside to look at us. In a tight bank the aircraft circled round. From the frailty of our basket, it looked a monstrous thing that could destroy us without even being aware of doing so. We waved back, determinedly, and shouted at each other above the roar. It naturally eclipsed anything the sea could do. In a sense we felt infinitely superior to that metallic and heavier-than-air machine. Balloons had taken to the air exactly 120 years before its kind had succeeded in doing so. We were there first. Admittedly, it could steer, and travel at faster speeds, but we had been flying for nearly two centuries. It was entirely right for the rule of the air to stipulate that engined machines should give way to gliders, and that gliders should steer clear of balloons. The DC3 thundered around its predecessor, waggled its wings in salute, and then rumbled off in its own noisesome fashion.

Immediately afterwards we realized the balloon was going down fast. The trouble with waving vigorously, and feeling superior, is that this takes your mind off the matter in hand. The altimeter read 200 feet, and we were descending rapidly. The sea was increasingly boisterous.

"Quick, Charl, throw out two hands."

Down they went to land inaudibly in the sea.

"Now, two more," and Charl burrowed again in the

The Manyara inflation, with Alan Root at the cylinder end

The coastline of Zanzibar beneath us

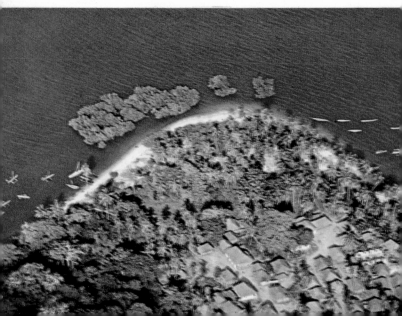

bottom of the basket. I watched the altimeter, saw it slow down, and then almost stop. It is as well not to throw out too much even in a tricky situation, for in escaping the deep blue sea the devil of going far too high may be upon you. Charl was poised with another handful, while I watched the needle. The sea was precisely 55 feet beneath us, none too far, when the needle gave another tremor downwards. Charl threw out the handful as if it were something red hot. This time we heard it, but the needle flickered upwards in response. Soon afterwards the balloon rose steadily away, and the five modest handfuls had turned a watery disaster into the tranquillity of flying further on. At 700 feet we were stable once again.

It was still at that height of 700 feet that we reached Africa. It was a landfall in the most grandiose sense of the word. Without an effort, with only exclamations of enthusiasm from the three of us, we passed over the surf and then dry land was beneath us. With equal abruptness the sound of the sea changed into the eternal insect chatter of a tropical world. It was as if someone had pressed a button. One moment the waves were crashing into each other; the next they had been left behind. The waters had been parted, and there was land. The 30-mile flight from Zanzibar had been satisfactorily accomplished.

Douglas had been busy throughout the flight trying to record it on film. The holding of an Arriflex with a 400-foot magazine clamped to the top of it, the burrowing down into the basket to change the reels, or the lenses, in fact the whole complex business of photography, had given him more than enough to do. It was he who first realized that the need no longer existed for those life-jackets, now soaked with our sweat. In turn we took them off, for one pair of waving arms soon uses up the available basket space. In turn, we dropped them among the sandbags, and then pulled off the rubber covering which encased our wicker platform. That, too, was no longer necessary, but there was no point in having it ripped to pieces during the landing. Having registered our landfall in this manner, all three of us then leant over to have a look.

I do not know what I had expected, for the maps had been vague, and I had never been in the area; but I was amazed at finding such a virginal piece of land. There were trees everywhere, and in the few gaps between them were bushes filling all the space. There were no paths, no tracks. There were certainly no houses, and there were definitely no people. Apart from the insect noises, there were occasional croaky sounds as a bird or two took to the air well below. I could see no stream, and hear no water. Yet there was great warmth to be felt, and a hothouse smell to be savoured. It was all ripe for people, like a Garden of Eden; it was all ready, and fruitful, but no one had yet arrived. We shouted down in case there was anyone hiding beneath the trees. We called out "Jambo" with a new significance, but no one called back at us. A few more birds flew off, and settled again a little farther on: It was eerie; and yet most beautiful. Also, for I swear that no one can make such an arrival from the sea without a feeling of relief, we were glad to see the land for its own sake. Had it been most foul, we would have welcomed it. Instead, it was breathtaking, and the three of us were mainly silent as we leant over the edge not wanting to miss a thing.

Moreover, we had no intention of missing that road, but it seemed initially no place for a road of any sort. Charl and I looked at the map again, extended the line from the take-off place to our last known point, and made it cross the African shore. There was nothing to show whether it corresponded with our actual course. The map only indicated "Bush", and left it at that. Occasionally it mentioned "Farm", but without any real confidence, for not even a line had been drawn between the edge of the farm and the start of the bush. The road was the only thing to look for, and that lay not less than 5 miles and not more than 10 from the shore, according to our position. Suddenly, I saw a scar between the trees.

"There's a track down there!" I said.

We all scanned it eagerly, looking for people along its brown and muddy surface; but it weaved its way silently and emptily. We looked at the map again to see if a track

98

had been marked. It had not, and the realization came almost audibly.

"That was no bloody track," said Charl. "That was the bloody road!"

He was bloody right; and something had to be done about it right away. Even at that lower height we were still travelling at some 20 m.p.h., and therefore moving away from the road very fast. Every extra minute in the air meant another 600 yards walk back to the road. It was easy enough drifting over the trees, but hacking our way through them on the ground was certainly going to be a different matter. I pulled for two seconds on the valve line, and our descent began. At the same time we cut loose the trail rope, and its 200 feet were fully extended shortly before the tip touched the trees. It did its work, and at some 100 feet above the fast-moving tangle of branches we flattened out.

So far, so good; but where on earth to land? I saw nothing approaching. No open space. No marshy area. Certainly nothing resembling a farm, and fortunately nothing looking like sisal. It was cooler just above the trees and, despite the rope, we had a tendency to sink. I was at the front of the basket, and Charl—if such terms can be applied to something only 3 feet long—was at the back. Each time we sank I asked for another handful to go, and it was in this leap-frogging manner that we penetrated farther and farther into the heart of Africa.

"Another?" said Charl.

"Not yet. No. Yes, now!" and up and over we went. "It's going to be a long walk," said Douglas.

"Christ!" said Charl.

"Another hand."

"Hand gone," said Charl, and a tree passed by a few yards beneath.

The rope and the lower height must have slackened our speed to 10 m.p.h., but the trees flashed by alarmingly.

"Another."

"Another gone," said Charl.

"A very long walk," said Douglas.

And then a dead tree suddenly appeared, straight ahead.

It looked craggy, and its limbs were mossy white.

"Another hand, Charl. No, stop! Don't throw it, let's hit this. We'll crash into it."

That was all there was time to say before our basket hit it, so to speak, in the chest. The three of us ducked, and saw flashes of branch. The noise was tremendous. The basket juddered, and got caught up, and then released itself, and then was free. I stood up, and pulled for all I was worth on the rip cord. We were temporarily motionless, still not caught up by the wind again, and there seemed to be a space between the trees. I pulled and pulled at the rope, and down it came between my hands. Then we were going down, fast. I remember one bounce, then I pulled some more, and at the next bounce the basket fell on its side. The three of us, and much else besides, were thrown face downwards into the grass of Africa.

"Christ!" said Charl, though his voice was muffled.

We all scrambled out, and stood firmly on the ground. No one was hurt. The balloon, with still a little gas inside, looked well. It had draped itself over a young and bushy tree. Forty yards back was a very dead and shattered tree, the means of our landing, and over it stretched the trail rope now at rest after its cavorting, twisting, snaking journey. We had arrived. It was just two hours after take-off. Where we were, we had little idea. But we were safe. We had arrived. Even the bushbaby looked relieved.

The singing in our ears changed into the steady noise of insects. This was Africa. For a time we did nothing but congratulate each other, and tell each other the facts we all of us knew about the trip. We laughed. We waved our hats in the air. We laughed again. Only slowly did it dawn upon us that no one would ever find us in that spot. It was up to us to find them.

CHAPTER TEN

THE RECOVERY

ONE of the epics of ballooning history concerns the flight of Andrée and his two fellow Swedes. In an attempt to cross the North Pole by balloon, a foolhardy effort it would seem in the light of present-day knowledge, the crew were forced to land on the ice at 83°N. So much snow had collected around the valve and the fabric that the extra weight was more than the lifting capacity could bear. A landing was made, and the aerial plan came to nought after sixty-five hours. The men took photographs of themselves, and their half-deflated balloon. Then, having sledged for many miles, yet still with a stock of food, they died three months later. The world rightly assumed they had come to some sort of grief, but where or when was a mystery. It was not until thirty-three years later that their remains were discovered by the side of the last shreds of their equipment. The camera was found, and its exposed film, preserved in the extreme cold, was carefully developed. The pictures were clear, and showed much of what had occurred. There is great poignancy to them, for the men knew exactly what had happened, and what was likely to happen. They were fit— for the time being. They were safe, and yet had little hope. They carefully arranged the camera, and pressed the button. The bedraggled balloon lying on the ice was behind them.

I cannot pretend that we were in the same boat, although we took similar photographs of our own place of return to earth. Douglas, always one for putting himself in other situations, talked of snow and ice-floes and the bitter cold as we set about packing up the balloon in the lush, vege-tative heat of Africa's coastal belt. The situation was not nasty, for I considered we were no more than 2 miles from the road; but it could so easily have been very much worse. Without that dead tree, now a little deader, I do not know how we could have slowed down sufficiently to land. Had we continued at that speed, and held our horses looking for an open patch, I think we would have gone well into Africa, well off our maps, and far away from any road. Had we just taken our chances of landing in the bushy forest as if it were an open Dutch field, and had just descended like some aircraft exhausted of fuel, we might have made a satisfactory landing. On the other hand—and there were a good few other hands to choose from—we might not. The sudden arrival of our basket in a tall tree might have enmeshed it sufficiently to trap us there. The balloon itself would then have been above us, still gusted by the wind, and a menace. There is nothing quite so graceful as a balloon flying through the air; but, according to reports of tree-landings, there is nothing quite so unmanageable as one which mistakes the so-called forest platform for a piece of open ground. Often the balloon has to be sacrificed, and cut away. In short, Jambo on her virgin flight had done well, and was quite unharmed. That dead tree had made the sacrifice on her behalf.

To jump ahead momentarily in the story, the tree was pleasantly misrepresented by a local newspaper. In answering questions about the landing, I had said it was standard ballooning practice to look for some means of slowing down the horizontal speed. I did not add that the normal means were getting someone to hold the trail rope, or attaching a few sandbags to its end or, if the wind was sufficiently gentle, throwing out the grapnel. Such methods are impossible when a stiff breeze is blowing over a fair-sized forest, and I reported that we took advantage of the fragile-looking tree. In the paper it was then written that "Mr Smith adopted the normal ballooning procedure of looking for a dead tree, hitting it, crashing through it, and landing on the other side".

To jump back again, we packed up Jambo into its basket within two hours. The rubber sheet inverted its rôle and was fitted over the top in case of rain. This diminutive package, no bigger than the basket of 3 feet by 4 feet, was all our proud craft became. It had been the size of a five-storey house at Zanzibar, but it looked most humble when folded up. Beside it was a little pile of sand, a small contribution of nine sacksworth brought over by air.

"If anybody wants sand delivered here from Zanzibar," said Douglas, gazing at it wistfully, "we're in business."

Picking up the compass, we set about finding our way out of that bush in such a manner that we would be able to retrace our steps. This meant the traditional blazing of the trail, walking on exact compass bearings from dominant tree to dominant tree, and writing down a general description of the route. Charl had the bushbaby tucked away in his top pocket, Douglas carried as much camera gear as he felt made a load, and I drew a sort of map of the way we were taking. It was less than two hours before we stumbled, abruptly, on the road. From the point of view of any onlooker, which there was not, three men appeared suddenly from nowhere, took stock of a situation that was little more than a muddy track, thought about walking, dismissed the thought, and settled down on the edge of the road to wait for something to happen, like a lift.

From a long way down that road an African appeared, walking our way. He carried coconuts. The very thing. We all, at once, felt in need of a coconut, or two. Douglas completed the transaction.

"Unaweza ku-pa nazi kwetu?" he asked, and there was instant response.

With swift ease the man lopped the tops off three of his bunch, and we were soon drinking the cloudy water. He then fashioned those tops into spoons, and we gouged out the soft insides. The events of the previous forty-eight hours had given us all a backlog of food and drink. Stomachs had been like shrivelled forms, frightened of the future, and had shrunk their shapes like sea-anemones when danger is near. With the satisfactory crash into the jungle they had re-emerged, empty of food, and full of desire to fill themselves out again. Of course, due to our complete lack of interest in the subject before take-off, the food placed on board had been microscopic in quantity, and had been engulfed in no time. Hence, the appeal of those coconuts, and the desire for more.

"Leti nazi nyngine tafadhali," said Douglas, and more were prepared.

Those who have not eaten coconuts fresh from the tree, apart from not knowing their excellence, cannot know quite how much residue they create. The whole green husk is hacked off in slivers, and the central nutty core is tossed to one side in all its fragments. The enthusiastic coconut consumer almost buries himself in the results of his work, and it was from behind such a rampart that the three of us stepped out at the approach of the very first car.

Ten minutes afterwards, when we had explained ourselves, an Indian merchant was taking us to Bagamoyo in his truck. It had been full of people and things before we joined it. It then just became fuller, and it sloshed towards the town along the 20 miles of mud and open waterway which formed the road. Admittedly, this was quite the wrong direction, as Dar was our destination, but the route had not been excessively lumbered with traffic, and we were grateful—after a while—for anything using it. The actual business of getting from Bagamoyo to Dar could be sorted out later. Where the ground teams were, we did not know, but we could guess. The more we sloshed towards Bagamoyo, and the more mud we slithered through, it became steadily obvious that they must be bogged down somewhere. They had winches, but were plainly having difficulty, and we saw no reason why we should not be in Bagamoyo while they were having it. The Indian driver said the southerly portion of the road was worse, and we were on the northerly section.

"This," he added, as his windscreen-wipers pushed the cascades of liquid mud to one side, as the four wheels drove a path through lake and rut and temporary river-bed, "this is nothing. Here it's drying out fast."

There was no sign of our friends at Bagamoyo, and we waited for them a little while as we sipped through straws at a gassy drink in an Indian store. We also bought postcards, but there were only views of the Post Office or group-shots of Papuan natives. Bagamoyo had been important in the slaving days, as it was then the main port for Zanzibar; but, when you look at it now on a wet night, drinking an unlabelled fizz from a crooked straw, having just completed a deal for every Papuan card in town, it seemed a desolate spot.

As Douglas had an acquaintance at Bagamoyo, a man who owned a salt-farm, as well as a fast boat at Dar (hence the original interest in him), we decided to look him up. The Indian driver offered to take us to the home of Alister Stanley. The thought of a comfortable house on the soggy night it had become brought back our spirits.

"What's the name of this river?" I asked facetiously as the Land-Rover breasted its way through some deep water. "This is no river," said the pedantic Indian. "This is a road."

At the end of it appeared a huge and dripping veranda. Beyond the drips there sat a man, and for many more hours that evening there sat the three of us as well, watching the rain, drinking beer to make up for that eternal backlog, telling the story of the flight over and over again, and trying to keep awake. When we did go to bed, still talking, it was still raining, and we still felt dry inside. Yet, when we doused the lamps, sleep came instantly. I have the feeling that not a muscle moved throughout the night.

During the next three days we prepared for our departure from the coast to the game areas of Tanganyika, some 500 miles inland. Joan Root and Don Hutchins had turned up at breakfast-time on the day after the flight, having seen us arrive over Africa some four miles to the north of their vantage point, and being incapable of following because their truck had become engulfed in the mud. They had arrived in Bagamoyo extremely late, too late to find out where we were, and had slept elsewhere.

After an extremely lengthy breakfast, with the same old thirst being drowned this time in coffee, we set about retrieving the balloon. At a sisal farm fairly near to our point of arrival we collected labour. Some of them had seen the balloon, while the others knew all about it and wanted to see its landing place. We drove the truck into the bush as far as was possible, and then set off on foot to find the lonely basket. The Africans were disinterested in my notes about our exit route, and just plunged ahead along our tracks. They picked up the path without trouble. It might have been made by an army on the march for all the difficulty they had in finding where we had come from. A sudden whoop of shouting ahead of us indicated the end of the line.

Carrying the balloon was another matter. The men of the Bagamoyo area have a tradition of being good porters that stretches back through the centuries, but they had not met a balloon before. One man took the 90 lb. of net away on his head. Another took the valve and ring, while the rest bundled the 450 lb. of balloon into the 94 lb. of basket, and then lashed the lot together with long poles. Thus it was in the traditional manner, behind a file of chanting Africans, with the loads swaying this way and that, and with a man at the front hacking a path for the column, that we returned to the road, and the Gipsy. Afterwards Joan and Don pointed out the various places, as we made detours in the forest around them, where the truck had become stuck the day before; but 7 miles north of Dar there was an obstruction which took even them by surprise. It said "Bridge closed".

Sure enough it was. The flood water surged by beneath it, while the bright lights of Dar twinkled ahead. Like everyone else we just left the truck, and caught a lift on the other side. This time the thirst-slaking went on at the Hotel Etienne. The beer was just as good, and the rain came down as before, but there was a foreboding about the next stage. That bridge had been a warning. Other bridges were down. The main road to Arusha and the northern province had been closed. The floods were sweeping everywhere. Even the Serengeti, the main game park, had closed its gates at the peak time of the year for visitors. The papers printed the only weather report received from the area. It just said "Fantastic". Each new arrival at the Etienne had a hazardous tale to tell of immobile lorries and liquid roads.

The arrival by balloon, the floating over all these Earth-bound difficulties, had been ideal. Our predecessor, Dr Fergusson, had had a balloon that could stay up for ever, but then he was a most remarkable man. We were subject to natural laws, unfortunately, and had to make do with them. Our balloon had to come down, unlike his, and we had to make a series of hops instead of his one, huge, all-embracing stride. We had to contend with impassable roads, and the effects of some unprecedented and untimely rains. We envied him, enormously. Yet we had one great point over his flight. The mind of Jules Verne had never imagined the sights we were going to see. He had never thought of plains filled from horizon to horizon with galloping forms. He had never dreamed that such vast herds could exist. Dr Fergusson occasionally had seen an animal, and had then shot it. We intended to see thousands upon thousands. In this one aspect we intended to excel.

Unfortunately, there was the tricky problem of actually arriving at the next take-off zone. Our planned destination was Manyara in the Rift Valley, but it was said to be wetter even than the Serengeti. We sipped our beers, thoughtfully; and watched the rain with awe.

CHAPTER ELEVEN

THE JOURNEY INLAND

BEFORE leaving Dar es Salaam, Tanganyika's capital, the manner of our arrival had to be settled with the authorities. The relevant form was spread before us, and we did our best with it. Port of Departure: King George VI playing field. Port of Arrival: Near dead tree 2 miles west of Mile 25 on Bagamoyo road. Type: Balloon. Name: Jambo. Number of aircraft/ship/car: OO-BDO (Jambo did have this number, but on paper only, for there had been no time to paint it on). Crew members: Anthony Smith, captain; Douglas Botting, camera operator; Charl Pauw, sandthrower, general hand. Equipped with radio?: No (but loudhailers). Radar: No (but telescope). And so forth about berthing facilities, and hangarage, and tugs, and more besides. We did justice to the form in a meaningless sort of way. A big stamp of entry was put in the brand-new logbook, which had been sent with the balloon from Brussels.

The Customs authorities had tried to reach us on the day of our landing. Two men, obviously happy with the idea of a spell out of town, had set off for our probable point of arrival. They had seen us cross the road, when we were still having illusions about it being a track, and they then set off into the jungle to find us. Unwittingly, we eluded them. This was a shame, for it robbed them of a rare moment in any Custom officer's life. They had visualized themselves appearing, stamp and chalk and documents in hand, at our point of arrival. With deadpan faces they had intended to greet us with the supercilious welcome so much a feature of their trade, and to go through the patter of asking for goods to be declared, for reasons of voyage, etc. It would have been a great moment, had these two emerged solemnly from the jungle around us. Unfortunately, the very thickness of the jungle, which should have heightened the effect so dramatically, also prevented it from occurring.

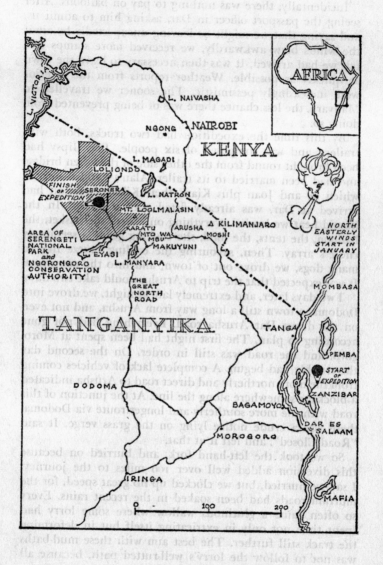

Incidentally, there was nothing to pay on balloons. After seeing the passport officer in Dar, asking him to admit us, and saying that we might be leaving unexpectedly by air if the winds blew awkwardly, we received more stamps and felt we had arrived. It was then necessary to leave the town as quickly as possible. Weather reports from the interior were increasingly pessimistic. The sooner we travelled to Manyara, the less chance there was of being prevented from doing so.

By this time the expedition had two trucks, both with trailers, and was composed of six people. The Gipsy had been brought round from the other side of the fallen bridge, and had been married to its trailer. Alan's Land-Rover, in which he and Joan plus Kiari, their Kikuyu servant, had arrived at Dar, was already fitted with a trailer. In the humid heat we loaded everything on board, the basket, the balloon, the tents, the food, the cooking gear—a seemingly endless array. Then, savouring the cooling breeze like so many dogs, we drove out of town, and into the continent. It was expected that the trip to Arusha would take two days.

Two days later, and extremely late at night, we drove into Dodoma, a town still a long way from Arusha, and not even on the direct Dar–Arusha road. Everything had not gone according to plan. The first night had been spent at Morogoro, and the road was still in order. On the second day the trouble had begun. A complete lack of vehicles coming from the more northerly and direct road to Arusha indicated a blockage somewhere along the line. At the junction of this road with the more southerly and longer route via Dodoma, there was a crude notice lying on the grass verge. It said "Road Closed", and left it at that.

So we took the left-hand fork, and hurried on because this diversion added well over 100 miles to the journey. I say we hurried, but we clocked up no great speed, for the murram roads had been soaked in the recent rains. Every so often came a glutinous wallow where some lorry had spent time not only in extricating itself but in deforming the track still further. The best aim with these mud-baths was not to follow the lorry's well-rutted path, because all smaller wheels would surely succumb, but to engage low gear, all four wheels and then drive fast at anything resembling road rather than canyon. This particular manoeuvre, chancy at the best of times, became additionally tricky when both ridges and ruts were submerged. On one 50-yard stretch, already dotted with a few marooned lorries, Alan plunged into the water in the traditional manner. He may have thought he was driving to begin with, but the ruts and the front wheels took over very quickly. They combined to hurtle him sideways at a lorry piled solidly with coconuts. He missed the lorry, but a fresh set of ruts pitched him over and he ended up with one side three feet deeper than the other.

This sort of thing may be all in the day's work for the average driver along dirt roads in tropical areas, but it means that any attempt at unruly haste is reciprocated in full. Every hazard has to be encountered, surveyed, respected adamantly, and then overcome. Any attempt at pretending that the river is not deep, or that a little skill will be more than enough, is careless. Four hours later you appreciate fully its depth, and you know everything there is to know about winding, first rope, then wire, around a revolving capstan. The road has plenty up its sleeve for the disrespectful. It was after Douglas had taken what he called a trick at the wheel that we behind him saw his truck skid through 180 degrees, following a sizeable lurch here and there, and then run backwards into a ditch. Truck and trailer turned over with infinite grace while we behind slipped to a halt in the mud. A door was on top, and Alan and I jerked it open.

"For my next trick . . ." said Douglas's voice from somewhere down in the cab, a voice impeded by Charl's frame lying on top of it.

It took three hours to put that truck on its wheels again. When we did drive away the damaged machine had to be towed. It was then only 40 miles to Dodoma, but it was dark, and raining, and it was cold because the windscreen had gone, and the towing truck flung dust and grit into the face and eyes of the man keeping the second truck on its course. It was not a good journey, but when there has been an accident and no one has been hurt, there is always a tremendous feeling of relief. This particular state, of having an accident or some form of disaster, and getting away with it, was to be a feature of the next few weeks. I sat there, not knowing this at the time, with someone's vest over my head, with a partly torn polythene bag helping it to keep the grit away, squinting at those two reflector lamps, feeling frozen stiff, wet through, holding a deformed steering wheel, and yet enormously happy that things were as they were. "For my next trick . . ." he had said, and I laughed in the remembrance that no one had even been hurt.

On the following day at Dodoma the truck was given to a garage, and the garage was asked to make it work. By this I do not mean that everything to be done had to be done. I mean only that the truck was to be made fit to drive once again under its own power. For a new windscreen, a new roof, and various other refinements, it would have to wait until Arusha. The rain had been continuous during the night, and the journey to Arusha was obviously becoming harder every minute. That town was important because it was the jumping off place for Manyara and all the areas over which we hoped to fly. We knew we could get from Arusha to those more westerly points, but it was becoming increasingly doubtful that we could get to Arusha.

Every hour or so one or other of us would walk from our sleepy hotel down to the garage to inspect progress. A Cypriot named George was taking it all very much in his stride. Situated as he is in the centre of Tanganyika's road system, or web, he receives the wrecks of cars much as a spider ensnares the carcasses of flies. It is not a good road system, and his business is prospering. He was treating our Gipsy confidently and quickly, much as he had treated a motor-bicycle of mine seven years before. On that occasion, when I was midway between Capetown and the Mediterranean, I had presented him with a machine apparently cracking apart. It had suffered, that bike; but he had welded the whole thing together again, and had seen me on my way. I had had further difficulties on the trip, but never again did the structural portion of the bike give any trouble. Therefore I had confidence in the man as he also brought the Gipsy back to life.

Shortly after lunch it was ready. We reloaded the equipment, and were all set to go when the manageress of our sleepy hotel rushed out to say a bridge was down at Mile 80.

"Many thanks," we shouted, putting the trucks in gear.

"But it's down I tell you!" she squawked. "You won't be able to get through to Arusha."

"Goodbye," we called out into the dust of our wake.

Somehow, she urged even greater haste in her efforts to warn us, and the threat of one broken bridge was insufficient to stop us leaving. Besides, with one bridge already down, with the promise of more rain building up blackly on the horizon, there was no occasion for dalliance.

At Mile 80 we met the bridge. The woman's story had been partly true. The river had been over its surface, but as it was of concrete, and as the water had since subsided a few feet, we were able to drive over it without incident. On the way we learnt that a couple had been struck dead by lightning on that section the day before. The man had been looking for something in the boot. His wife had been in the car, and a dog had been beside her. Quite a few cars went by before the occupant of one thought their postures looked a little odd, and he stopped to check. We also heard that it was still raining heavily further along the road. Therefore, once again, we continued on.

When we met the rain the lack of a windscreen became as important as before. My clothes took up their compliment of wetness, and then dripped. The night and I grew rapidly colder. The lurchings, the slooshings, became worse and worse. For mile after mile we drove on, feeling that bridges behind us were falling like flies, and wondering why the torrents surging beneath those we crossed had not already carried them away. Then sleep started taking over. It became harder and harder to see what was what, what was road, what was treacherous bog, what was narrow bridge parapet. Eventually the inevitable happened, and the trailer slewed round to overtake. I allowed for the skid. I over-allowed, and skidded the other way. The trailer came up on the other side. The steering wheel spun back, and then with nothing more than a soft jolt both trailer and truck slid into a bank. "I think," I said, as Alan came rushing up, with an anxious look on his face, "that we'll stop here for the night. After all she's well parked."

No damage had been done, and five minutes later six shapes had scattered themselves among the various corners of our equipment. In five minutes five of those shapes were soundly asleep. Joan, Alan and Kiari were in the Land-Rover. They looked supremely comfortable. Charl had even made the Gipsy's sodden, windowless and roofless front seat appear appealing. But what was worst of all to one who suddenly felt disastrously ill, and who had been allotted the softest spot of all—on the balloon inside the Gipsy—was that each time he got out to make another foray down the road, the snores from inside the basket were sounding loud and clear. How Douglas slept in it I still do not know. That basket was 3 feet 11 inches by 2 feet 11 inches and Douglas, when he takes his hands out of his pockets, stands over 6 feet tall. Yet the snores were there all right, resonant, tremulous, and determinedly persistent. They never stopped, so far as I was concerned, throughout the remaining four hours of that disenchanting night.

At the very first hint of light I woke the others up, and a much bedraggled group continued on its way. It was still raining slightly, but on the other side of an extremely tortuous section we met the tarmac. After that we sped along the Great North Road into Arusha in fine fashion.

Coffee, as is well known, does wonders to the bloodstream. It turns haggard, droop-eyed, grey-faced individuals into reasonable humans once again. It also makes them think that a wash and a shave would be quite in order, and that a hot breakfast would not be resisted unduly. The New Arusha Hotel is used to this sort of thing. Filthy vagabonds arrive from all parts of the countryside, sign their muddy names in the book, disappear for an hour or so, and arrange a metamorphosis. As caterpillars become butterflies, so were we a markedly changed group as we strode out into the town to go about our business.

There was much to be done. The Gipsy was put in the hands of the Gailey and Roberts garage. Barclays Bank was visited. Immense amounts of food were bought from the Fatehali Dhala store. Photographic arrangements were made with Malde's Camera Shop. Peter Champney, the local information officer, was visited, for he was to be of considerable value in liaising with the outside world. Permission was sought from John Owen, director of the Tanganyika National Parks, to camp in them. Permission was also sought from Henry Fosbrooke, chairman of the Ngorongoro Conservation Authority, to camp in his area. (The wild life may not know it, but they are the responsibility of a complex assortment of independent organizations.)

At the end of the day we drove out to Brian Mahon's farm on the M'Ringa Estate, for he had been acting as addressee on various sea-going consignments from Britain. Prominent among the goods received were the 120 cylinders for our inland flights. They were to be lifted back and forth to Nairobi for refilling as and when we emptied them. That little lot weighed 15 tons, and the problems involved in the shuttle-service were to prove a major millstone for our organization. Once again we had reason to envy Dr Samuel Fergusson. His original filling of hydrogen, made with iron and acid at Zanzibar, had lasted him throughout his five-week journey. The world of fact is very different. No free-flying balloon on record has ever kept a single consignment of hydrogen for one-eighth of that time. Yet we had cylinders, the strength of which Dr Fergusson could never have dreamed of. I tested the pressure of a few to check them. All was well, and in the heat of Africa the inside pressure had risen to 4,000 lb. a square inch. We should get three flights out of those 120 cylinders, if everything went as planned.

We made arrangements for one-third of them to follow us out to Manyara, and then we ourselves set off. The world's first balloon expedition in central Africa was under way. It looked precisely what it was. The basket had been attached

115

to the Gipsy's roof. The grapnel was hanging on one side. Rope bulged from everywhere. And the six of us inside the trucks waved back vigorously at every passer-by whose curiosity in our shape made him stop and stare and hold up a wary hand.

Manyara was a mere 70 miles away. The first leg of the route down to Makayuni was along the Great North Road once again. It was tarmac now, or rather that section was; but, when I had ridden along it seven years before, the section south of Arusha had been one of the cruellest of the whole 7,000-mile journey. Perhaps it was at this very spot, as the motor-bike lurched uncontrollably, and I listened to the banging of its suspension system, that thoughts of a balloon had first come to mind. It was noisy, that machine, and very dusty, and it did pass on a good few of the road's unevenness to a well-battered spine. I had caught glimpses of animals as they had hurtled away, with staring eyes, with fast-moving hooves. It had been thwarting not to see more of them. In any case, noise and dust or not, battered vertebrae or not, I had to stick to the road. Its destiny had been mine.

I can well imagine how it was that I then thought of silence, of floating peacefully, of a calm and dustless air, and of a journey that led nowhere in particular, but over everything in general. A balloon is a logical next step after a motor-bicycle. It has everything that the bike does not possess. It takes you, purposively, on a journey of its own. It does not demand 100 per cent attention to keep it even in an upright position. It does not induce myopia in its rider as he gazes inexorably at the converging road in front of him. It gives him instead a complete view, an unhindered survey of the entire world this side of the circular horizon. Almost certainly the idea had been born during one particular bounce on that well bruised saddle. Then it had festered inside me. Now, at last, it was coming to pass. The Zanzibar trip had been an introduction. The real journeys, those over the wide open plains and the huge herds, still lay ahead. Manyara was to be the first.

At Mile 48 we turned off the tarmac, and on to a dirt road

116

once again. The great western wall of the Rift Valley lay ahead, and beyond it were the Crater Highlands of the Ngorongoro district. The whole area was rich in game, and was fabulous country. It would surely be even more fantastic when seen from a point suspended silently beneath the huge gaseous canopy of a free-flying balloon.

CHAPTER TWELVE

THE STORM

FOR those who come reasonably fresh from London, a safari camp is a remarkable change of life. For the initial night, and for many subsequent nights, I found it hard to reconcile that only a few tent-pegs and guy-ropes stood between us and any creature that chose to inspect the camp. On the first evening, having walked a short distance away from the others, I stood there looking up at the near-perfect Southern Cross, and felt exceptionally edible. There were hippos not so far away, booming their low-pitched chuckle into the night air. Admittedly, they are herbivores, but they are big, all the same. Every now and then the sawing sound of a leopard, the regular kerr-krr kerr-krr, joined in with the hippo background. And, of course, there were lions as well. A male lion does not roar, at least not in my understanding of the word. Instead he produces a series of groanish grunts, a whole arpeggio of them, which rise steadily to a climax, and then take an age to die away. The whole song of power can be heard for miles. It always seems to sound close, and then sounds closer. When near by, and we were once privileged to hear the call a mere 5 yards away, it is frighteningly loud. The tape-recorder was quite incapable of recording it, because the whole device tremored with unreasonable vibration.

For those straight from the London jungle, such African days and nights are most awesome. Our camp was on the edge of a delightful wood of yellow thorn trees, tall and smooth with a greeny-yellow bark, and we looked out over the open plains of the Rift Valley floor. Every morning a group of giraffes strolled past our camp, elegant and aloof. Every evening they strolled back again, for they had to escape the daytime bites of the tsetse, and tsetses will never leave the shade if they can help it. Every morning too, perhaps an hour or so after dawn, pelicans and flamingos would fly over the camp. On the ground both types of bird could be improved upon, for the pelican is flabbily fleshy about its neck, and the flamingo is a spindly thing of feather and gawky limb; but the air transforms them. Thousands and thousands of the most graceful shapes, spearhead after spearhead of well-ordered lines would sail by. If they were high, then we could see more of them. If they were low, and hurtled suddenly over the tree tops, a great torrent of noise would then hit us. There are several millions of these birds in East Africa, and they constantly change their minds about the lake of their choice. Whole populations then get up and go, and provide an unforgettable spectacle for anyone beneath who may be shaving or just passing the time of day.

In fact, we had more than enough to do, pelicans or no pelicans. It was just superb being able to do it in such amazing surroundings. Wake up to see a monkey having a look at you, and the task of the day—whatever it is—cannot begin to be a drudgery. The first jobs were all connected with our own maintenance. There is a saying that any fool can be uncomfortable in a camp, and we saw no virtue in proving this. So we fixed up a liberal supply of water, a shower of sorts, plenty of firewood, a lavatory with a most delightful view, and generally made certain that we were comfortable.

The first consignment of hydrogen cylinders then arrived. These had to be unloaded and, despite the fact that each one weighed nearly 3 cwt., this was a paltry labour as compared with the unscrewing of their caps. Each cap was a thing of iron threaded on to the valve end of the cylinder to protect the relatively delicate valve mechanism during the inevitable rough and tumble of travel. It is an iron cap, and the cylinder threads are made of brass. The reason these receiving threads are not also of iron is that no oil or grease is allowed. If it were used, and if there happened to be a slight leak of the hydrogen gas, there could be an explosion. In some way the hydrocarbons of the oil can combine disastrously with the hydrogen, and the rule against oil is rigidly applied.

In theory, as the caps are not screwed on tightly, and as only one thread is of iron while the other is of brass, the two should not rust together. In practice, after lying idle in the rain of Elstow, after a sea-voyage of many weeks, and after a certain amount of cooking up in the tropical climate, the caps were almost welded on. We had enough trouble with them at Zanzibar. In mid-Africa, with fewer facilities at our command, we were to remember each cap almost as an individual. According to the books, and it is good never to lose sight of what should be happening, a simple spanner gets them off. In fact, we needed every inch of two 6-foot monkey wrenches. One was clamped round the body of the cylinder. The other was wound round the cap. Even though this afforded leverage of a high order, it was insufficient. So one end of one monkey wrench had to be thwacked with a sledge-hammer, and under this sort of punishment the caps were persuaded to revolve.

Because hydrogen can explode in the presence of air it is normally recommended that any little tapping applied to the spanner, during those allegedly rare occasions when some friction is encountered, must come from leather hammers. These have heads of well compressed and hardened hide, and are therefore incapable of generating sparks. For a time we had worked according to the book, tapping softly here, placing the spanner there, and had achieved absolutely nothing. The book might as well have asked us to hammer in nails with a fly-swat for all the progress we made. Hitting the ends of giant monkey wrenches with a sledge-hammer was so far away from the written instructions, and sparks flew so frequently, that we made frantic haste just in case our luck would not hold for ever. Finally, after a large number of extremely exhausting hours, all the caps were off. We sat our sweaty bodies on the pile of cylinders, and felt gratitude for their unexploded state.

Another task was mending the balloon. The Zanzibar flight had left the fabric unscathed, but there was the rip panel to be sewn back in. It is the pulling open of this flap that allows the gas to escape extremely rapidly. Pulling it open during flight would naturally be fatal, but when landing in a strong wind the failure to pull it can also be disastrous. To prevent a full gas bag bounding along the ground, inevitably towards some spiteful obstacle, the rip has to be pulled at the right time. The correct moment has to be judged between regarding gas as a vital necessity and as a lethal handicap. The parachutist has to do the same, and he must be quick to spill the wind from his canopy or unbuckle his harness.

Anyway, the rip once used has to be mended. The panel is about 15 feet long, and both sides have to be glued and stitched together. The glue must not only stick panel to balloon, but must ensure no leakage of gas. The cotton stitches are to hold everything together reasonably well just in case the glue begins to melt, as has been known. (In ballooning, or so it seems to the freshly initiated, every possible disaster has happened once. The facts of each case have been duly chronicled, and the modern procedure of balloon preparation is just following one safety measure after another.) Neither the cotton nor the glue is strong enough to resist the pull from the basket once the balloonist takes that rip-line in his hands, and pulls as if he means it.

During those early days at Manyara we were very dependent upon the near-by village of Mto-wa-Mbu, pronounced mmtoewumbu, and meaning mosquito river. It had a shabby air, looking like a cross between Main Street in an early Western film and a forsaken village where the jungle is reclaiming its own. Representatives of seventy African tribes were said to live in it, fugitives from the various wars of the past who had somehow collected together in this particular area. While the others shopped at one Indian store, I wandered over to the other. In some cunning fashion, its proprietor was never without a week's growth of beard. Even cunninger, he made the same shirt and trousers last apparently for ever.

"Is this a nice place to live?" I asked.

"No," he replied, "and I should know, for I have lived here fifty years."

"What's wrong with it?"

"For one thing, the people are lazy. They are all lazy. All they do is drink, and have sexual intercourse. These things I like as a hobby, but not full-time."

Within a few days of our arrival at the Manyara camp we had accumulated a mixture of pets. The bushbaby still reigned supreme, and ate grasshoppers with contented abandon. When he was asleep he was the nicest pet in the world. When he woke up, at sunset every evening, it was not that his energy knew no bounds; it knew nothing else. From table to chair he leapt, then from chair to someone, and from that person to someone else. As the Indian shopkeeper would have said, such activity was all right on occasion but not when unceasing. It tended to prevent anything else. A plateful of food, or a tableful of dismembered camera parts, would suddenly receive one bushbaby in its midst. An adult bushbaby would have been an even longer but a more accurate leaper. As it was, our creature practised on us, and around us, and underneath us; but we liked him, all the same.

Pet No. 2 was a python. Alan was an expert on snakes, having in his childhood collected them, and he found a 7-foot specimen. As pets go it had shortcomings, for it refused to eat, presumably preferring to digest what was already there; but it was a magnificent creature to watch as it climbed, and moved, and slithered along the branches. Also with shortcomings was a colossal snail, but even it had grace as it shifted itself from one patch of grass to the next. An animal, to our minds, with no defects at all was the chameleon. He was not an expert at the customary colour-changing, but he was perfect with flies. Each breakfast he lay along a twig suspended above our communal table, and from there he picked off the flies beneath him. The 5-inch tongue took one-twenty-fifth of a second to reach its target, and slightly longer for the return journey. One day the stickiness of his tongue's bulbous end dried up, and flies were merely clubbed unsuccessfully. Yet he would not drink, and even if placed in a whole bowl of water would only swim about in undulating symmetrical fashion, with right fore-limb moving in conjunction with left hind-limb, and vice versa. This movement, combined with a flexing of the backbone, is the primaeval basis of progression for all tetrapods; but he survived the experience with a tongue as dry as before. It was only when we remembered his real existence, and the fact that chameleons rarely encounter streams, that we thought of dew. We sprayed water over a plant, placed him on it, and were entranced to see him lick the wet leaves with a parched and arid tongue. From that moment on, each fly was doomed the moment those round and independent eyes had decided it was within a chameleon's remarkable range.

Our praying mantis had attributes none the less fantastic. It was a female, some three inches long, and had a face that turned to watch its watcher. She, like the bushbaby, lived on grasshoppers, and ate them from one end right through to the other. She held them delicately, took bites when necessary, and then chewed until her mandibles had left room for more. A man does not eat celery with two hands, but if he did the effect would be similar to a mantis at mealtime. Every so often she laid a great frothy egg, which expanded and solidified the moment it left her. Nothing happened to this for several weeks, but then suddenly miniature mantises squiggled their way from the myriad compartments of which it was composed. They dangled on the thinnest of gossamer threads, found a resting place for their gesticulating feet, and then began their lives. Joan was their keeper, and flicked minute insects into their jar to keep them happy.

However, these creatures were incidental to the main purpose. A week after our arrival, when we had learnt all there was to learn about the local winds, we blew up the balloon. The wind was blowing regularly from the north-east, roughly 040, and tended to become violent at about 3 p.m. Therefore the intention was to take off at midday. The position of our camp site, and the wind's direction, indicated an almost ideal flight. First there would be the Manyara forest to cross, then the marshy and impenetrable area bordering the lake, then the lake itself, and finally the 2,000-foot cliffs of the Rift Valley's western wall. Either we would ascend over this wall or travel farther on down the valley. In either case the flight would have unparalleled scenery on all sides, and there would be plenty of opportunities for observing game because the forest and the lake's edge were well stocked.

The actual inflation was, of course, most markedly different from the one at Zanzibar. The crowd of 6,000 had been reduced to a motley three, a trio of non-Swahili-speaking Africans who had appeared mysteriously from the forest. The platoon of Coldstream Guards had been replaced in their sandbag and rope-holding duties by as many Mto-wa-Mbuians as the Gipsy could carry. With their help, Alan looked after the gas, Douglas the photography, and Joan and I the balloon. It all went most smoothly, and by 11.30 the basket had been satisfactorily attached. We placed the eighty sandbags inside it, and went off to have some food. The balloon looked perfect. The wind was calm, blowing precisely from 040. The auguries, so far as we could judge them, predicted an excellent flight. This goes to show just how wrong both we and some auguries can be.

The food break was to last half an hour. At the beginning of it a light plane appeared from the north, circled our camp, and then landed between us and the browsing giraffes. Hugh Lamprey and John Newbould stepped out, one a biologist, the other a botanist, and both acquaintances from the past. They had seen the balloon when some 25 miles away during a flight from Arusha to Ngorongoro. They said it was like an orange in a pygmy land, and they had come for a closer look. They accepted beer, and we all sat around gazing at that bright and globular thing. There had been no occasion for such peaceful admiration at Zanzibar.

While we looked at it, talking of last-minute jobs to be done, accumulating the bits and pieces to go in the basket, and munching bread, pickles and cheese, the balloon suddenly became even brighter. High up on the Rift Valley wall a cloud had appeared. This then grew, alarmingly, before our eyes. The air was calm, but more and more of that cloud came over the cliff. There was nothing to be done, beyond watch it. The cheese and pickles stuck unchewed around our teeth. The beer was left, half drunk.

The balloon started swaying slightly before we felt the wind on our faces. Every sandbag we had was already acting as ballast; so nothing could be done on that score. Besides, a balloon can withstand winds up to 30 miles an hour or so. The cloud gradually engulfed the air in its path, turning the blue sky dark and thundery. We stared at it, transfixed, while our stomachs contracted within us. The wind grew stronger, and the balloon swayed increasingly. The white puffy edge of the black cloud passed over our heads, and the dark shadow rushed along the ground.

I think we still had beer mugs in our hands, and half-consumed fragments of bread and cheese, when the first raindrops fell. Someone suggested a move inside the tent, and we then stood beneath the awning watching the weather get worse and worse. Quite suddenly, its character changed from mere turbulence to viciousness. A squall came from nowhere, and the rain flooded from the sky. A muffled sort of screech went by as the wind became a gale, and at the same moment the balloon began to move.

We rushed out, shouting at Joan and Douglas to bring up the trucks. It was deafeningly loud. The balloon bucked back and forth, almost hitting the ground with its bright orange sides. Alan and I splashed along, skidding in the mud, shouting things, and then throwing ourselves out of the way as the balloon heaved itself suddenly in our direction. We caught hold of the basket, now jerking along in huge strides. Water poured from the balloon as from some gigantic tap. This was coming from its surface as all the rain sluiced down those running sides. Holding on to that basket was like standing in a waterfall, except that it bounded along with only the wind in control.

The trucks came near. We thought they might hold it. Alan put a rope round the basket, and then rushed for a truck. But a big heave from the basket pulled him over, and he fell backwards in the mud. Up again, he flung the rope round the trailer hook. Another heave from the basket, and the rope left his hands. We on the basket seemed capable of nothing. Our combined strength and those three-quarters of a ton of sandbags were as nothing. Each heave, each bucking of the balloon, went on unhindered by anything we could do.

Then Alan got the rope attached, and someone put the truck in gear. All four wheels spun round. They showered mud everywhere, but nothing happened and the basket heaved and creaked its way over the ground as before. Through battered eyelids no one could see much, but the truck must have been pulled back, for the rope never broke. However, we could see that the clump of thorn trees was getting steadily nearer. Once the fabric met those trees, it would be shredded instantly. Even normal trees would have torn the thing to bits, but those ones had 2-inch spines on every available twig.

I climbed up on the sodden, water-logged basket to reach the rip line, and then held it as the balloon leapt back and forth. It had lost a lot of gas, and the wind blew shapes into its dripping surface. It flapped about, like any sail in any storm. It banged about, like any piece of canvas caught by any contrary wind. And all the time, in multi-yard strides, it picked itself up, and leapt towards those trees. I remember shouting to myself: "I can't pull it yet. But we can't hold it. I must pull it. Not yet. But I must. I must, I must. Those trees. I must pull it." And then I did.

The effect was most rapid. There were one or two slaps from the wind, and then the whole proud shape crumbled and died before our eyes. The heaving, cavorting, un-controllable thing became just a heap of shining canvas. It collapsed at the very foot of a yellow thorn tree's trunk, and we all stood around, panting, and amazed by its trans-formation. How could we have been powerless before this heap of fabric? How could it have pulled all of us, that sand, that truck, as if we were nothing? Yet it had, and now all that remained of our well-augured flight was the very wet hulk of a free-flying balloon. Even as we watched, two frogs leapt from the grass into the puddles lying among the folds. And as we stood there, still battered by the rain, we felt too confused to speak. The plans had most plainly been destroyed, and 26,000 cubic feet of precious hydrogen had been lost for ever. Yet, pathetic thing that it looked, we still had the balloon. The trees, the wind and the rain, had been thwarted; but only just.

CHAPTER THIRTEEN

THE TAKE-OFF FROM MANYARA

HAVING seen to the balloon, and having watched it collapse at our feet, we returned to the deserted camp. It was still raining hard, and I do not know who first noticed that the tents were under water. I remember rushing into the big one and finding four Masai standing there. Their long limbs were in water that was awash with film and notebooks and food and clothes and all the rest. Frantically, I started picking everything up, putting the sodden belongings on the camp beds, and telling the Masai to help me. They did absolutely nothing. I fished around among their feet and pulled out dripping objects. They still did nothing; except fill up the tent.

"Either you help, or get out," I said in English, knowing no other way of addressing them, but feeling they must understand when they see bread and cameras and books floating around in water.

As they neither helped, nor got out, nor even moved, I picked up their four spears, which were by the tent flap, and threw them in a cluster out into the rain. The Masai continued to stand around for a while, and then went to retrieve their weapons. Neither they nor their spears came back. In the meantime I and the others salvaged everything, and by the time the job was over the rain had stopped. My watch still ticked, and from the first appearance of the cloud to the completion of the storm, a mere thirty minutes had elapsed. Africa seemed as incapable as ever of doing things by halves.

One advantage of being sent back to Square 1 in any enterprise is that the whole job is easier to do a second time. We moved camp to a higher spot. We took our ground crew back to their village, and sent off a message to Arusha for the second consignment of cylinders to be brought up. We also inspected the balloon, when it was dry, and glued and sewed that rip panel once again. The storm even repeated itself, for at precisely the same hour on the very next day a large cloud poked its fluffy shape over the edge of the Rift Valley wall. After putting everything inside, and fastening every tent flap, we watched the approaching form with the fore-knowledge of what it would bring. Once more the sun was blacked out, as the air scudded around. We were fascinated at the power coming straight our way. Sure enough, the rain started like a thunder-clap, and the wind screeched out of the sky. We moved to the shade of a tent, and I stuck an arm out to measure the wind. The paddles of the anemometer flew round, and the needle danced jerkily at 35 miles an hour. If the wind was as fast as that, even in an area sheltered by bush and tree, small wonder that the towering bulk of the balloon had taken such a beating.

Shortly before this second storm arrived Hugh and John had taken off in their Piper plane. The grass where they had landed was waterlogged, but they found another spot and flew off from there. The rest of us, having brought everything in for the second storm, then took it all out again to complete the drying. In fact, this was to be the pattern of the next few days. For the peak of the dry season, it was being a most remarkable year. As we paddled around our camp, we reckoned that anyone not equipped with flippers and an aqualung would surely perish when the wet season came.

A further proof of Africa's ability to do what it liked with the elements came two days after the storm had hit the balloon. We were in the Manyara Forest, and had been filming all morning. We had initially been concentrating on a group of Sykes's monkeys, and then on some fresh-water crabs that had had a fierce desire for chicken bones. They had tugged for possession of these remnants of a picnic meal with satisfying vigour, and had provided good material for the cameras. We had then moved on to the dry bed of the Marera River. For two or three hours we took shots of the Gipsy making its way across the rocky river floor, and then up the steep bank on the further side. There had been a

Inspection at Manyara, with a thunder-cloud building
up behind

All balloon landings are little more than controlled accidents

sort of bridge, but this had been washed away, and the site was good for action stuff showing travel off the beaten track. It was genuine, too, for the boulders had to be levered to one side, the Gipsy had to make its jerky way across the stream, and then winch itself up the other side. Afterwards, for what reason I do not know, we drove the Gipsy back again. From it we took the picnic things, and made ourselves comfortable on the rocks of the empty stream.

The day was calm. The huge forest trees towered above us, and the insects maintained their perpetual fervour. There were plenty of elephants and baboons in that forest. We listened for them, but the insects drowned everything. Then a deep rumbling started to compete.

"Must be a lorry going up the escarpment road," I said, and everybody agreed for a while.

"But the escarpment road isn't up there," said Alan.

"Well, it sounds like a lorry."

"But it can't be," said Alan. "There's nowhere up there you could get a lorry."

Alan then stood up to hear better, but I think we all saw it at the same time.

"Look out! It's the river!"

Each of us suddenly caught sight of a few dancing movements behind the stones further up the hill.

"Look out! It's coming down!"

I remember grabbing a collection of gear, for we had all our stuff lying around, and running with it to the bank. At that moment both the water and the roar turned round the corner upstream of us. We each stared momentarily, and then rushed for another load. But the stream was coming down fast, in a big arc, and smooth at the front. Everybody dashed up the bank, just in time to watch the broad wave go by. Somewhere in that first second our food and knives and things must have been washed away, but we never saw them go. We stood there transfixed by the almost instantaneous change in the scene. In fifteen seconds the dry river bed was 6 feet deep, and sounded volcanic in its rumblings.

Huge boulders were being invisibly hurled downstream. We heard them bowling and bouncing and crashing beneath the waves, and watched the waters rise along the banks. A subsidiary stream rushed round our island vantage point, threatening to wash the Gipsy away even with this smaller watercourse. We drove the truck through those relatively minor torrents on to higher ground, and returned to watch a river gone mad. Had the Gipsy been in the main stream, it would surely have been washed down into the Manyara lake. Had someone been in it, he would have gone as well. Had anyone been caught by that flash flood, he would not have stood a chance. We all stood and looked at it, and shook our heads at each other. It was like regarding the havoc wrought by a time-bomb seconds after passing that way. It shrunk one down to size.

"I wonder what happens next?" said Douglas, and he gave a sort of laugh.

That evening, by way of a change, we drove up to the Lake Manyara Hotel. Our camp was undeniably in a raw piece of countryside, and wild life of all sorts did wander near by, but perched high up on the cliff above it was an extremely modern and well-built hotel. From every room up there was a fantastic view over the enormity of the Rift Valley, and from down below came the trumpeting of elephants. It was a remarkable spot. In its swimming-pool we swam and splashed around, and appreciated this adjunct to the simple life under canvas. To round off the evening we played darts, sat on bar stools and drank well of a brew called Tusker.

We told our tales of the sudden flood, which had all but taken us with it, and of the sudden storm which had almost put paid to the balloon. In return, we had been told another of the difficulties of film-making in Africa. A large company had come out to Tanganyika with a definite script, and some ideas about wild life. The first of these was that animals could be persuaded, provided sufficient financial resources were behind the enterprise, to do anything the script demanded. In the instance of this particular film the story called for an elephant charge. During a fierce stampede the creatures were to pour through an animal trapper's camp, wreck grass huts, kill people, and generally create a crisis. On the camp's other side was to stand the hero, who, or so the script said, would stop the charge with one or two well-placed shots, and thereby earn a lifelong place in the heart of some khaki-clad girl.

Well, or so the story said, a collection of elephants were assembled in a suitable neck of the woods. An African camp was built with the trimmings of cooking-pots roasting over fires and dummy people attending them. The elephants were duly maddened by thunder-flashes, and away they went towards the camp. Iron bars nailed to trees saw that they went in the right direction, and countless cameras recorded the fact. The elephants arrived at the camp right on schedule and were travelling along at the right sort of pace for an uncontrolled stampede. Unfortunately, for elephants have a finesse about them even under such conditions, they all hurtled through the camp correctly, but not a grain of damage did they do. No cooking-pot was overthrown. Not a single straw left its berth among the eaves. And, which was worst of all, not a single dummy was made to flinch, let alone receive a pachydermatous footprint in its midst. The camera had trapped nothing of the Africa which is alleged, by scripts, to exist. The movie men were made to think again.

A resourceful lot, they soon had another idea. If big elephants were no good, what about small ones? Great, someone must have said, just great, because a little time later on there was a group of infant elephants collected in that same neck of the woods. The theory was that children of all species tend to be more waggish than their elders. They are puppyish; they are kittenish; it was therefore to be hoped that elephants would run true to the general rule. As neither puppies look like dogs, nor kittens cats, so was it necessary to alter the infant elephants. Their woolly backs were shaved, and little wooden tusks were strapped round their necks in the appropriate position. In the meantime, the camp had been miniaturized. Micro-huts had been built, with midget cooking-pots smouldering over dwarf fires, all suitable material for the stuffed manikins who were dotted about. The great moment came. The elephants were sent careering down the chosen path, and arrived at the camp. With their trunks, and for the hell of it, they lashed this way and that, and then happily went their way. Pots had been upset, huts torn apart, dummies disrupted. Gratefully, the camera men turned away from their machines. Justice had been done to the script. A piece of Africa had been immortalized.

Coming down that night along the steep and twisty escarpment road from the Manyara hotel we met elephants, and lurched to a halt. They are huge; but so gentle, and controlled. Watch a human-being walk through a bush, and it is a messy business. Watch an elephant encounter a thicket of twig and thorn, and he seems to flow through it, amoeba-like, until he is standing just as peaceably on the other side. We stood on the road looking at the vast dark shapes until we realized that they had all—every one of them—disappeared.

The following day, not only did Charl have to go off back to South Africa, but the fresh consignment of gas arrived. Two four-wheel-drive Bedford 5-tonners came whining in a low gear over the giraffes' strolling ground, with all wheels skidding on the muddy grass. We rushed off to collect another body of Mto-wa-Mbu citizens, and found no difficulty in recruitment. Pay was two shillings a day plus a packet of Four Aces: no other cigarette would do. The tasks were lifting down the full cylinders, lifting up the empties (which were virtually identical in weight), and helping us to unscrew the fresh lot of caps. The job was done well, the money and cigarettes were handed round, and everybody was once again packed into the Gipsy's hold. There was a hole in its metallic roof, made for camera work. From it smoke poured forth as from a chimney. Off went the Gipsy, apparently under steam, as a score of men from Mosquito River consumed at least part of their payment.

That night we decided upon a flight for the following day. The wind had been correct, the gusts never above 20 m.p.h., and the storms had apparently relented. We had arranged to collect the now more experienced ground crew at eight, and noon seemed as good a time as any to take off. We ate well—it was basically a rice dish but much had been added —and then completed the plans. Afterwards, for no particular reason, we had what might as well be called a musical evening. At the time we thought it amazingly funny, and grovelled around in pain at our own antics. The procedure was to choose a tune or song, and then fill in with the correct instrumental noises. Whether bagpipes, or Greek barrel-organs, or merely harps, we thought our imitations were astonishingly funny, and laughed and laughed as the tape-recorder played them back to us. From this one tent in the middle of an open stretch of Tanganyika's vast domains, a torrent of noise poured out.

Suddenly, with one accord, it stopped. A drop of rain had hit the roof with an awesome loudness. It was followed by more and more, and then the wind came. We sat in the tent, crushed at once, not singing another note, not playing back any more, not having the slightest wish to do so. Would Africa never let up? Would the whole of our scheme collapse in a season of inclemency and rain and storm? We turned down and then blew out the lights. After all, it was time for sleep.

The next morning it was still blustery, and we postponed the flight for twenty-four hours. Joan went off to the village to inform the helpers, and also to get more food. Douglas, Alan and I initially let off pilot balloons, and watched them go this way and that. The night's storm had left everything about as settled as the whiskers on a mouse's nose, and the air quivered in every direction. It was most blatantly a day for sticking on the ground.

Anyhow, we decided to do everything by way of preparation that could be done to the balloon, without actually putting any gas in it. We laid it out, connected the valve, attached the various lines inside the balloon, joined up the gas tube, fixed that to the first batch of cylinders, and then arranged the sandbags round the net. So far as that side of things was concerned, it was only necessary to turn on the tap. We also fixed the basket more effectively. During the storm one top corner had snapped. There was a danger of the whole thing becoming diagonal rather than rectangular, and so we took the axe to look for a right-angular piece of green wood which would act as a splint. Having found a suitable elbow of the right length and size, we tied it into position, and felt happier on that score. Everything else needed for the flight we piled up punctiliously in little heaps.

That evening, having watched the meteorological signs more avidly than any Roman ever inspected the entrails of a sacrificial fowl, we felt a trace of confidence never experienced before. It did seem as if the weather was relenting. On no side was lightning playing. There was no ominous stillness to the air. There was no hint of torrential treachery as far as we could see. It did appear, and we would gladly have copied the Romans had we known the formula, as if it was a night bearing good tidings. We sang no songs, for the mood was different; and it rained no rain. Oddly enough, despite the calm and the fair prospects, it took us all an age to go to sleep.

On the following morning the sky was perfect, with not a cloud to spoil it. The breeze was gentle, and kind. The great day had undoubtedly arrived. Coffee was sipped standing up, and we then walked briskly to turn on the gas. The Gipsy lurched off to collect the men, and the inflation began. The gas poured from the cylinders with the characteristic tortured sound, and the balloon swelled up rapidly. Our confidence expanded with it.

When it was fully inflated there were some smallish thunderclouds peeping over the hills, but nothing of immediate concern. The balloon books say: "On sighting cumulonimbus formations, deflate at once." However, had we followed that particular instruction to the letter, we would have created the first balloon safari on record that never flew a balloon. Such clouds were as much a feature of that part of Africa as the flat-topped acacia trees. Anyway, Alan looked up at them, and quoted the instruction once again, for we were often talking of it.

"'On sighting thunder-clouds, deflate at once.' Are we ready to go?"

This was to be his first flight, for he had been launch-bound at Zanzibar. He was to take the stills, and generally act as animal observer. Douglas, who was to look after the cine-camera, answered him:

"On seeing thunder-clouds, look in the other direction. Let's go."

The three of us clambered in. I began the ritual of finding Jambo's equilibrium. Hands were raised. Hands were put back on the basket's rim. A sandbag was removed. Hands were lifted off again, and then replaced. Half a bag went overboard, and we were ready to go. I looked downwind at the thorn trees to judge what angle we should take off at, and felt our existing lift was more than enough to clear them. I counted the bags. There were six. That was five fewer than at Zanzibar, but now we were over 2,000 feet higher. Anyway, it was enough. We shook hands with the ground crew who were now grinning hugely, and said farewell to Joan. Where she would find us, and when, and how, was another matter. That was for the wind to decide.

So without more ado, I called "Hands off" for the last time and let the breeze take over. We rose quickly and gently, and the magic of another flight had begun. In no time at all we were in that other world.

CHAPTER FOURTEEN

THE THUNDER-CLOUD

THE main purpose of this first flight over part of the African continent was to assess the reaction of the animals in as wide a variety of habitats as possible. No one knew how they would behave below a balloon, but plainly their particular environment would influence them. The Manyara area was a complex of utterly different types of countryside. Our camp bordered, as we knew almost to our cost, on that large coppice of yellow thorn trees, and the Rift Valley wall was a few miles to the west of it. At the foot of this cliff, and running along in its shelter, was true forest. Identification of the plant species indicated that this belt of trees had formerly been connected to the huge tropical enclave of the Congo basin. It was now a fragment, but large enough to support a population of forest creatures. The balloon would surely drift over it for at least part of the journey. Then there was the lake. This was either bordered by reedy or dusty marsh, the haunt of buffalo and reed-buck and hippos, or flat and muddy shore-lines. Anything might be wandering about on those wide-open spaces, such as giraffes and gazelles, but the actual watery and weedy part of the mud is the home of an infinity of birds. Some 600 species have been spotted at Lake Manyara, and its mixed environment makes it an ideal place for observing such a representative collection of African bird life. It is also an amazing spot for flamingoes and pelicans. Sometimes there are a million of these two species living on that stretch of water, sometimes even more.

The lake was swollen from all the rain of the recent months, and was probably 30 miles long and 10 miles wide. No one knew exactly. The heavy rains had also drowned the traditional points of access, and even we from our camp site had been unable to get at it. Besides, if someone had been able to survey its dimensions, the next bout of rain would have added a mile here, half a mile there, and confounded the calculations. People agreed it was probably about 300 square miles in extent, and were content to leave it at that. However, its swollen size did mean it was inadvisable for us to come down either in it or on its shores. It was normally possible to drive, or at least to progress, through the forest and the stretches of mud-flat beneath the Rift Valley's western wall; but now that was out of the question. The track had been passable for a mere 7 miles when we arrived, but the sudden and amazing flooding of the Marera River had knocked another 2 miles off even that diminutive journey.

Therefore, for the balloon flight, it was necessary to get well away from the lake before coming down. On the high ground to the west of the cliff wall there was a road, a frequently blocked one—but a road none the less, that led from Karatu southwards to Mbulu. From Mbulu there was a cross-road of sorts that led to the Great North Road, the north-south highway of Africa. Therefore our flight plan, so far as it could be predicted, was at least bounded by a rectangle of roads. It would plainly be advantageous if we landed near one of them. How, or where, or when was not in our control. Therefore, as we took off from Manyara, these crucial issues of the future were well at the back of our minds as we sailed, effortlessly, wonderfully, into the vast blue expanse of sky above our launching site.

"Sign me on as a balloonist," said Alan, when the take-off had been achieved, and the thorn trees were gliding easily beneath us. I laughed, and watched the camp recede at some 10 miles an hour. Joan was there with the waving hands of the ground-crew team, and so were all the vehicle tracks. There were the big lorry marks. There was the path we took to look for hippos. And over there were the tracks leading up to, and then away from, that giant termite hummock of red-brown earth. Very quickly the camp was being swallowed up by Africa. The huge tree which had shaded the cylinders became as nothing. The tents disappeared; and last of all to go was the white tarpaulin on which Jambo had been inflated. Yet long before that had happened all three of us were looking ahead, rather than back. The world was just as exciting in every direction but, in a balloon, it is almost impossible not to look forwards. What has passed is only interesting in that it indicates the line of travel, and therefore predicts the course that is still to come.

The balloon stabilized itself at 1,000 feet, rather better than at Zanzibar. In no time we were at the lake's northern edge, drifting over the huge and impenetrable wilderness of reed. It was Alan who first pointed out that certain blobs were buffaloes, the first animals we ever saw. There were thirty of them, doing absolutely nothing, and flapping their ears in the itchy heat. And then came two warthogs, snuffling along busily, and making much noise about it. At last, I said to myself, at last I was in a balloon, and having Africa pass by beneath me. For no reason beyond that, but that was more than enough, I grinned hugely at the others, and then laughed with the joy of it all.

With the lake coming along, and with so much of it to cross, this was no occasion for letting out gas to test the animals' reaction to us. I had not touched the six sacks of sand, but the lake looked long. So we left those buffaloes behind and, still at the height of 1,000 feet, moved out over the water. In theory, and at midday, a lake should bring a balloon down towards it; but this lake was so shallow, and consequently so much hotter than any normal lake, that we rose a little on reaching it. In fact, it was at about 1,500 feet that the three of us coasted down the Rift Valley for the first part of the trip. We were comfortably in the shade from the balloon, and life was very pleasant.

It also had a razor edge to it. It must be possible to be blasé about standing in a basket a third of a mile or so above the earth, but such complacency is hard to visualize. The basket is strong, and even kicking a hole through it would be an exceptionally wearisome business; but when it is your whole support, this thing of twisted osier, its apparent fragility is considerable. From time to time it creaks. It certainly does so any time anyone changes position, but it also creaks on its own accord. After all, we three, our sand, and our equipment, were quite a burden for such a slender thing. However, far slenderer than the basket were the ropes. The eight hastily spliced lengths from Zanzibar between the ring and the basket's toggles were very taut during flight. They were undoubtedly strong enough so far as breaking-strains were concerned, but they looked uncommonly thin. Yet thinner still were the toggle connections to the basket. These were not of rope but of wire. Also, there were not eight of them but only four. Again, from the point of view of breaking-strength, they were more than sufficient, and they had been woven into the basket to join up with their opposite number from the other side. It was a perfect arrangement; in theory, but each wire looked pathetically feeble. The total of their twisted strands added up to a diameter not more than one-quarter of an inch. They were sufficient, those four metallic lengths; but the margin of safety did seem to have been cut most fine.

As for the balloon, the huge orange shape sitting so silently above, it was hard to know how to worry about that. Its fabric was extremely delicate, its net was of string rather than rope, but these considerations were quite outweighed by the ridiculous fantasy of being supported by an open container of gas. I could never quite comprehend this fact. Through that open hole was gas, invisible and without colour or smell. By its unaided efforts our whole device was hanging in the air. Adding every weight together, us, the basket, the net, and the casing of the balloon itself, that gas was contentedly holding over three-quarters of a ton 1,500 feet above a lake and slap bang in the middle of the sky. To be precise, our total lift that day was 1,693 lb. I do not think that anyone can be nonchalant when engaged in such a remarkable phenomenon as a balloon.

However, putting aside the feeling of awe engendered by such flight, there is still a strong residue of straightforward fear. We pretended it did not exist, but it was there all the same. After all, it had reason to be. Where were we going? Would the ropes and basket hold? Would we land well, or badly? What about clouds, and sudden storms, and downdraughts? We well knew what Africa could get up to on the ground. We were infinitely less capable of controlling our affairs once we had committed ourselves to—as it has been called—the bosom of the air. The bosom was capable of plenty of upheaval. It was all very well being a piece of gossamer, but this could plainly have its drawbacks.

For the first hour of that flight we floated over the lake, roughly parallel with the western cliff, and on a course of 200. This was precisely the wind at Zanzibar, and it still blew just as steadily. The cliff runs almost north and south, and so we gradually edged nearer to it, and nearer the shore at its feet. This was excellent. As we approached it, I was content to let the normal seepage of gas lower us gently towards the water, and I refrained from throwing out sand that would prevent this steady descent. At the water's edge, and extending in clusters from it, were the pink streaks of thousands of flamingoes. Occasionally, a streak flew into the air, and a long skein of birds moved along the shore to settle somewhere else. It was all so remote. They were busily engaged in finding food, and had no relation with the woods behind them, or the open plains, or anything beyond the mud which supported them. They certainly took no heed of us.

When we were still a mile from the shore, a group of shapes suddenly appeared as giraffes. They edged out of the wood, and wandered across to the water. One even walked into it and then, spreading himself with legs astride, contrived to drink in the only manner possible for his species. At 600 feet we passed over these splendid creatures, and knew that had we been in an aircraft they would have scattered in every direction. As it was, they did nothing. In fact, one sat down, and folded his legs tidily beneath him. His 7-foot neck still stuck up like a pole pushed over, and at some 60 degrees to the ground.

Our steady course then took us over that shore. At this point, known as Endabash, there was an enclave in the cliff through which a river ran. For millennia its waters had eaten into the wall, and now a triangle of land stretched back from the lake with cliff on two of its sides. Into this region we floated, still at 600 feet, but with 2,000-foot ridges of rock looming up before us. For the time being we continued to watch. An elephant was down there, flapping his giant African ears widely back and forth. Suddenly, there were three more. And then, down by the stream, were a herd of buffalo, perhaps sixty strong. Then there were more elephants, and more buffaloes. This was precisely what we had come to see.

Unfortunately, as soon as we were seeing it, the flight was being threatened by the cliffs. We were not fulmar petrels who could coast all day by such high walls, and never be in danger. We had to take the necessary steps to avert it. I decided to let down the trail rope and hope that this would help us lift over them. After all, the air mass was going over, and the rope would be an added safeguard to ensure we followed suit. Wherever it touched, provided there was a slight slope on the cliff, we would rise accordingly. So we cut the string holding the rope to the basket, and down it went.

From that moment on, the simplicity of the flight ended. The rope had not uncoiled correctly. There was a loop in it. This meant it would not slide easily over the trees or the ground or whatsoever it encountered; instead it would hook itself on to something, and we would be pinioned above it. If the wind was strong, this could be disastrous. There was only one thing to be done, and the three of us started hauling that 200-foot length of rope into the basket. It was extremely heavy, and unwieldy. For anyone who has had difficulty in unravelling a piece of string, think of sorting out such a mass of rope when confined to a basket. I threw out two handfuls of sand to give us some more height, and watched the approaching cliff. Douglas and Alan unthreaded the massive coils of rope, and prevented the camera equipment or anything else going overboard as each coil was pushed over the edge.

Eventually the rope was disentangled. The three of us held parts of its length over the side, and then all three threw our sections together in such a way that a fresh entanglement did not create itself on the way down. No new knot was caused, but as the rope's end was suddenly halted it cracked like a gigantic whip. The sound reverberated round the cliffs, and a small puff of smoky dust indicated where the crack had been made. The rope's end was all frayed, but nothing could be done about that, and the approaching cliff now formed the major consideration.

I felt we were safe, as we approached it, if we were about half its height. I did not wish to be too high, and to fight too shy of its rocky walls, for then we stood a better chance of being lifted up into the cumulo-nimbus which was sitting, as clouds tend to do, on its summit. That particular cloud had been growing throughout our journey, and was causing concern, but I felt there was room to be lifted over the cliff without actually entering the crown of a cloud. There were about 2,000 feet between the top of one, and the bottom of the other; not much but probably enough. Certainly, no one was making jokes about deflating in the presence of cu-nims any more. The situation was too real to be mocked.

Suddenly, a wind struck us all, and the basket swayed one way. The Jambo pennant was blown to one side, and we all took a firmer grip of the edge. The trail rope, instead of hanging straight and lifeless, was twisting about in long sinuous undulations. I looked at the instruments, the altimeter and the variometer—a device for indicating rise and fall, but we were going neither up nor down. A moment later the shadow showed us our movement. The wind had just reversed itself. We were heading most purposefully out of Endabash and towards the lake again.

"Ah, well," said Douglas, who could put a lot of meaning into that short sentence.

Alan and I agreed with him. A balloon is a balloon; you have to take what comes.

Sure enough, our shadow danced over the final trees of that enclave, crossed the patch of dried mud, and then tripped out over the wavelets of the lake. The time was two hours after the start, the height was 1,000 feet, and five sacks of sand remained. Having ventured a mile or so over the lake, we then turned southwards once more on our old course, and were again travelling parallel with the cliff wall. Yet all was not as it had been. For one thing that place where the contrary wind had hit us was now shrouded in the mist of rain. For another, we were now travelling at twice the speed, and the big cloud sitting on top of the cliff was beginning to grow alarmingly. We were safe enough at our height, but its expansion was blotting out the sun. For a little while longer our shadow continued to bounce along over the lake, but then it disappeared in the shade of something so infinitely bigger.

Almost at once, we started dropping towards the lake. A hot sun playing on a balloon heats up the gas within, thereby adding to its lift. With the removal of the sun, we started losing this extra buoyancy, and sank in consequence. I threw out sand fairly steadily, but the sun's heat had been considerable, and a whole sack had gone before the descent flattened out. By then we were 100 feet above the lake, and the trail rope was dragging along in the water leaving the sharp cleavage of a wake behind it. We continued along at an estimated 20 miles an hour, and straight for the southernmost shore of the lake. Behind it was farmland, and it looked a fair place for a landing. Some Africans were standing on the lake's edge, and there did seem to be a few open spots. We thought one or two looked particularly promising, and assumed the flight might end in one of them.

All assumptions are fatuous in a balloon. At the very moment of making up our minds which of the two spaces was preferable, the wind dropped to nothing. Also, the air became cooler. That cloud up there was building itself into an afternoon storm. I continued to throw out sand, used up the third sack, and was soon reaching for the fourth bag since the journey had begun. Handfuls from it splattered down into the water beneath us, noisily. They made ringlets in the lake, and these spread out to pass the trail rope hanging limply near by. It confirmed, by its complete absence of wake, that we were moving nowhere. The sand continued to pepper the area around it, as I prevented the cooling balloon from dropping below that height of 100 feet.

It should not be forgotten at this point that the waters beneath us were charged with soda. The lake had accumulated it over the centuries, as other lakes with no exit collect salt, and this was an additional hazard. To land in it would be to expose ourselves to its caustic properties. The heavy rains had at least reduced the concentration, but to have one's eyes even in diluted soda is looking for trouble. We knew it felt slightly soapy to touch, but had no idea how our skin would survive were we to swim for a long time through it. And how far could we swim? I am a bather who likes to imitate the actions of a raft, not a motor-boat, and I have never tried myself over lengthy distances. This lake was huge in every direction. A swim even to the nearest shore was likely to be a major operation.

For some twenty minutes we stayed there, quietly poised and motionless above the water. The cloud above grew darker and more ominous. The sand supply was running dangerously low with only a little over one bag to go. Should the supply be totally consumed the balloon would either sink downwards or could be constrained from doing so by the jettisoning of more valuable commodities than sand. There was the remainder of the drinking water, and what little existed of food. Afterwards, shoes and cameras and filmstock would have to go. I realized this was a time to do something drastic before it was too late.

"I think," I said, "that I'll throw out half a sack at once to see if there's some sort of air movement above us. We must get away from here."

The other two nodded, and watched a 15-lb. cascade of sand rain down into the water. Shortly afterwards we started to rise, and the end of the trail rope was quickly flicked out of the water. The cloud base was about 4,000 feet above the lake, and the intention had been to let the balloon stabilize itself roughly midway between the two dangers. Unfortunately, it continued to rise above that half-way mark. I watched the altimeter needle move on quite steadily past the point where I thought it should have stopped. No one was saying anything, least of all me. I had made the decision, and my hasty calculations were apparently awry. We continued upwards at the same unnerving speed.

There is no reasonable way of stopping such an ascent. The physics of ballooning ensures that, if some gas is then released, the balloon will rise just as determinedly. This paradox is caused by the fact that a rising balloon is invariably losing gas from its mouth as it ascends into a more rarefied zone, and the gas is escaping to even out the pressure. Therefore the release of gas merely means that it escapes from the valve rather than the mouth. The result is the same: the balloon continues upwards. Yet had I released so much gas that, by removing such massive quantities of its lifting power, the balloon was bound to descend, the ascent could certainly have been stopped. This action was in the last ditch category. The rise could have been turned into a fall, but nothing could have stopped the fall. The sand supply was by now hopelessly inadequate, and even boosted by cameras and shoes and everything else, we would surely have plummeted into the waters swifter than any gannet. Therefore it was necessary to let the ascent continue.

At 6,000 feet above sea-level, and 4,000 feet above the lake, the altimeter gave the first signs that the rise was slackening. Miraculously, the cloud was still above us, perhaps a thousand feet higher. We could still see the Endabash enclave, with the stream running through the middle, but we could now also look down on the top of the cliff walls surrounding it. I have never taken less comfort from such a remarkable view.

"There's Lake Eyasi," said Alan in a flat voice, squeezed dry of interest by the situation we were in.

"Uh-huh," said Douglas, registering that he had heard the remark, and leaving it at that.

Both of them looked down at the altimeter in my hand, and saw the needle was still rising. They must also have noticed that my hand was trembling wildly, but this they didn't point out. I saw that my other hand was still, and so transferred the altimeter. The act also transposed the quivering, and idly I switched the instrument back and forth to check the automatic reaction. It worked every time. The important hand fluttered like a poplar leaf. The other one stayed calm, and still the needle rose.

Seen from far away, the edges of a thunder-cloud appear sharp and bold. Seen from near and beneath they do not exist. As the needle crept up to 7,000 feet above sea-level, or a mile above the lake, we just became more enmeshed in the darkness of that cloud. The ground and cliffs were still visible to one side, but half the lake had disappeared in the mist. The time was very near for that drastic release of gas, for that plummeting earthwards, that gannet-like descent to the waters below. The air was certainly charged with static, and I did not know what would happen if a deluge of hydrogen suddenly emerged into it. There would be one of two results: either it would catch fire, and the balloon with it—or it would not. Ignition by static electricity of an inflammable gas is not something that works in half measures. It is either catastrophic, or ineffectual. To avoid it, the best course is not to be in a situation where it is likely. Releasing two or three thousand cubic feet of hydrogen at the base of an active thunder-cloud is an extremely probable situation. I had no intention of pulling that valve line until absolutely necessary.

The cloud above rumbled continuously. It did not produce a series of claps, but a regular noise like a piece of corrugated iron battered by the wind. It was a growl more than anything, a token of the forces at work within. Had we entered that cloud there would have been no hope for us. No counter-measure, however drastic, could have prevented us being hurtled up to 40,000 feet or more. We would have died from cold, from oxygen lack, from rapid decompression, and from the flames of our own buoyant gas. Such clouds have destroyed strong aircraft, chewed them up into little pieces, and then scattered the fragmentary remnants of man and machine over the countryside below. Our chances were even less, if there can be less than that. The great black shape murmured thunderously, and we just stood there not knowing what to do.

The altimeter was still at 7,000 feet. Gently I tapped it, just to see if the needle had stuck. It didn't move. I tapped harder. It stayed quite still. Could it be that we had stopped? Or was some complicated pressure system affecting it? I tapped again. If we were still rising, and it wasn't moving, that would mean the pressure was rising. But why should that be?

"I think we have stopped," I said, very quietly, fearful that it might be wrong.

"Uh-huh!" said Douglas.

And then, from nowhere, and beneath that dark world of cloud, came a breath of air. We all looked at each other. Yes, surely we were moving, and sideways? Surely? The altimeter stayed where it was, but we were definitely changing. Definitely. Going to the east, it seemed. Away from the cliffs, and the escarpment, and that enclave. Out into the lake. But what did that matter? We were going away, away from that treacherous thing. The air became lighter. Yes, lighter. The mist above, so far as we could see it, was becoming brighter. And then, magically, the sun broke through.

As soon as it did so, we could look back at the cloud. It was no longer black but white. It was brooding over us no more, but clearly and puffily to one side. The sun warmed us again, and the altimeter started working up from 7,000 feet. But this didn't matter now. The whole sky was above us. We could go any height we liked. The cloud was to the west. That could do what it liked. We were now independent objects once again. We were now a free-flying balloon, not a thing being sucked into the aerial equivalent of a whirlpool. The altimeter went to 8,000 feet, and then to 9,000 feet, and shortly afterwards it settled down. In fact, it was at 9,500 feet that the needle stopped altogether, and I sat down in the basket, full of incredible weariness.

It was at this particular point in time that I started to think about this book. Therefore, as the point is a valid one, this is where Chapter 1 begins. I have already described how the flight continued, how we stayed there above the lake, how an evening breeze took hold of our balloon, and sent us over the land to the east of that Manyara lake. The flight had ended with satisfaction, and we had coasted along over that area south of the Tanangire River at the most satisfactory height of 150 feet. Perhaps it was the hair-raising events we had gone through, perhaps it was the realization of remarkable fortune and a lucky escape, but I shall always prize those last thirty minutes of that day's flight. The air had lost its venom, and was stable and warm. The fierce heat had gone, leaving us to drift with perfect ease over the surface of the land. This was ballooning. This was perfection.

The final crash of the basket upon the rocky ground was an excellent landing. No one was hurt, and we all scrambled out to shake each other by the hand. Our cloud, that monstrous thing, was now shrinking away in the evening light, and we looked back at it almost with affection. The great lake we could see no longer, and even the cliffs were receding as the sun sank down behind them. A fantastic day was ending. In turn each of us leapt on top of the basket to get a better view, and then, laughing, and interrupting each other, and pointing out things all of us knew, we started packing up the balloon, and wondered only a little how to get back to camp.

CHAPTER FIFTEEN

THE NGORONGORO CRATER

ODDLY enough, we spent that night back at our old Manyara camp. Joan had watched the entire 60-mile flight from the lawn of the cliff-top hotel, and had then driven round to pick us up. By the time of her arrival, a couple of hours after she had seen our shape disappear into the brownness of the land, we were standing on the main road waiting for something like her to turn up. Our landing place had been within half a mile of the Great North Road, a notable piece of fortune. Moreover, it had also been one mile off a PWD road camp unit, and its members had seen us land. Nothing, in short, could have been easier. If only I had been a little more patient I think we could have landed on the road itself and, had we seen it, even nearer that camp. But there was only one quarter of a sandbag left when we did finally hit the ground, nothing like enough for any emergencies. If a tree had loomed up in our glide path during that final landing run we might have been able to soar over it had we jettisoned the lot, but then we would have had nothing to break the subsequent fall. In short, it was as well that we landed when we did. The day's remarkable run of luck could not have lasted for ever.

It is hard to realize immediately that something has not been 100 per cent successful, particularly when it has so nearly been fatal. Certainly we did not as we drove back to camp that night. Nor did we as we all laughed at Kiari's surprised face of wonder when we materialized once more, and out of the night. The next morning, as we packed up the trailers and trucks with all our goods, in a shimmering heat quite unlike the earlier days, we did have twinges of regret about the flight. On no occasions, except for the final descent, had we come nearer than 600 feet to the animals. It is true they had cared not a fig for us at that height, but it would be necessary to come lower to test out those ideas about a balloon's vantage point. It was also vital to be less preoccupied with our craft. We wished, somehow, to be a raft in the air, and to pay as little attention to our conveyance as raft-men do. However, during storms, even raft dwellers must become involved in the antics of their platform, and we had been similarly beset with the turbulence of the atmosphere.

So we decided to move off to Ngorongoro, the crater area so rich in game that flying over hundreds of animals would be inevitable—or so we reasoned—whatever course we took. We had to discover their reactions. I had plenty of doubts about the value of an unsteerable, free-flying, conventional, hydrogen-filled balloon, but the basic plan was to see whether animals resented its shape. Before the arrival of the motor-car no one had predicted that it would be such a valuable tool in game observation. I do not mean it was unforeseeable that the observers could cover great distances in it, but that the final length between them and the animal of their choice could be so short. For various reasons, some known, some only guessed at, the animal looks upon man in a truck as if he is a fellow creature safely in his lair. Yet if the car door is opened a fraction, if one foot is put towards the ground, the animal rapidly bounds away.

This reaction of animal to car was unpredictable, and has been most valuable. No one could say how they would react to a balloon, but someone had to find out before any further plans were made. If they disregarded it, then balloons could do valuable jobs. For instance, incredibly little is known about the behaviour of a lion, how often it eats, and how much it eats at a time. Also much more needs to be learnt about its method of attack. A balloon of the barrage type, aerodynamically shaped, able to withstand winds, and roped firmly to the ground, could give a superb view over an entire coppice. The lions living there could be studied in a manner impossible from down below. A drinking hole could be watched on a twenty-four-hour basis. An entire migration through some region could be observed, and counted. Yet none of these things was possible, none even worth considering, if animals had an innate distaste for a silent and inflated object poised in the air above them. Its effect upon them was the very first thing to find out.

Alan, Joan and Kiari travelled in the Land-Rover. Douglas and I followed in the Gipsy. We filled up at Mto-wa-Mbu, shook hands with the ground crew, talked with the two Indian storekeepers, and finally sped off up the escarpment road. We then drove over the Karatu plain, well stocked with Wambulu farmers, before accepting a lower gear, and driving up towards the crater area. Mosquito River was 2,000 feet above sea-level. The crater rim was nearer 7,000 and the two trucks pulled steeply up that twisty, well-surfaced road. At the so-called Wilkie's Point we had our first breathtaking view of the Ngorongoro Crater, and stopped at once.

First impressions are important. We were looking down the crater wall into the huge saucer-shaped dish before us, and Douglas voiced my own worry as well as his.

"But where are all the animals?"

Alan and Joan scoffed, and pointed them out. It was as if the focusing of our eyes had been at fault, and had then made the necessary correction. Quite suddenly, hundreds of dots became animals. The perspective of the crater had misled us. It was 12 miles across, capable of holding the bulk of London, and yet there was nothing in it to indicate this huge size. Admittedly, there were trees and a lake and steep walls at the edge, but nothing that immediately gave the dimensions away. I had encountered this difficulty in Africa before, of being presented with some vast view, and being given nothing with which to measure it, no road tapering into the distance, no house or village, no finite feature to make the rest comprehensible. At Ngorongoro this effect was most striking. Douglas and I floundered in our lack of judgment. Were those bushes, or trees, on that slope? Was that wall 200 feet high, 1,200 feet, or 2,200 feet, or even more? It was quite remarkable how many illusions could exist when there was nothing really concrete on which to base one's estimations.

Field-glasses are satisfactory when confronted by this kind

of spectacle, not just because they bring everything nearer, but because they destroy all misconceptions. Douglas and I could not see those wildebeest to begin with because we were not looking for ants, and our eyes glanced fleetingly over them. Through field-glasses one looks for shapes, and shapes are therefore recognized, irrespective of their size. Even so, that crater appeared a most remarkable phenomenon.

It is the largest crater in the world. Its walls are steep, between 2,000 and 3,000 feet high, and it encloses an area of some 130–140 square miles—according to where it is reckoned that the crater floor ends, and the walls begin. No one knows how it came to be, for normal craters do not approach this size. A strong theory is that it used to be a tall volcanic mountain, with the 12-mile diameter being the size of its base. Then, due to some collapse of the Earth beneath it, the whole top fell inwards to form the saucer-shaped structure of today. The surrounding area is still volcanic, and the many mountains near by such as Meru and Kilimanjaro are extinct volcanoes with their subsidiary blow holes dotted about them. There is also one active mountain, the conical Ol Doinyo L'Engai. This sprouts out of the Rift Valley to the north-east of Ngorongoro, and becomes active in a minor way once every seven years or so. All this volcanic activity was fairly recent, but Ngorongoro is as inactive as they come.

Certainly nothing eruptive has happened within it in the past few thousand years. Its steep walls grow trees, and permanent streams ensure fresh drinking water for all the animals. The crater bottom is porous, and therefore the water can drain away. Less than a hundred years ago it was discovered for Europe by a German explorer. Shortly afterwards, and at the turn of the century, a pair of German brothers moved in to farm the fertile spot. They built houses some 8 miles apart from each other on the crater floor, and began to grow the conventional crops. Naturally, both the animals and the local pastoral tribes were an encumbrance; and were dealt with summarily, whenever they interfered. After all, this is the nature of agricultural invaders. Everything else must be sacrificed to their cause.

The Siedentopf brothers fought the animals, fought the Masai, and also fought the many natural hazards. It cannot have been an easy existence, however barbarous their methods, and when the Great War came they had to give up altogether. Tanganyika was German-occupied territory, and Kenya was not very far to the north. A small contingent of Germans kept a large army of British and South Africans on the move throughout the war, but plainly it was no time for farming sisal and wheat in the Ngorongoro Crater. In fact, the German force did not surrender officially until news came through of the Wehrmacht's collapse in Europe, but for practical purposes it had been defeated a couple of years before.

With the arrival of peace, and with the British taking over Tanganyika's affairs, there was a fresh chance of the crater being allowed to revert to its former role—a paradise of nature. It very nearly did nothing of the sort. The Germans had begun farming it, and therefore arrangements were made for British farmers to carry on with the work. The two houses, the one at Lerai, and the other to the north, were still standing; but for the time being there were more convenient agricultural pickings nearer to the towns and the railways. By the time people were beginning to look elsewhere, the crater was being regarded as a protected area, even though no legislation had been made to this effect. When a conservation law was eventually passed, the 130 square miles of the crater formed part of a huge national park collectively known as the Serengeti. This covered 7,500 square miles.

Unfortunately, although most of the area was uninhabited by man, a part of it was a traditional grazing area of the Masai. As the ways of animals and man conflict, it was subsequently decided to remove this area from the park, and to give it a different status. It is now known as the Ngorongoro Conservation Authority, and the Masai are permitted to live and graze over its 2,400 square miles. This move, and the later repercussions, are the subject of fierce controversy. Many people feel it was wrong, particularly in an age when natural areas are being eaten into all over the globe, for any park to secede part of itself for any reason. Others felt the Masai had more than enough room, perhaps 90,000 square miles to graze over, and they should not be allowed to jeopardize the future of one of the world's wonders (which the crater undoubtedly is). The main trouble with the Masai, quite apart from their love of cattle, apart from their desire to keep many more than they need, and also apart from their cattle's ruthless grazing technique, is that they induce in many Europeans a certain complaint or blindness known affectionately as Masai-itis.

This must be explained, as it is the root of many remarkable decisions, not least the one to take the crater area out of the Serengeti park. Generally speaking, the Europeans in Africa have, since the beginning, encountered two types of African. There have been those who were oppressed before the white man arrived, and those who were the oppressors. These were the subject and the warrior races. Again, generally speaking, and I am aware that there have been exceptions, the oppressed groups dropped their tribal customs, and donned dark glasses, short trousers, and open-necked shirts. They became clerks, and very useful to the invaders. However, in the background, and often a pain in the neck to the invaders, were the old warrior tribes. They had more to lose, and resented losing it. They were the traditional Africa, with fierce customs, rigid ideas, and an implacable disregard for change. They caused headaches for the administrators, but earned respect. They were malleable to nothing, and changed those who were trying to alter them.

Such a group were, and are, the Masai. I understand that some individuals have been to school, but the majority live in huts of wattle and dung, and obey their laws but no one else's. The men do no work, and have virtually no interest in money. They are apparently content with the old days, and welcome nothing of the new—except for the fact that the vets keep their cattle free from rinderpest. This aloofness from the twentieth century is the cause of the split among those who know them. Some resent it, as being almost unnatural. Others welcome it, and feel at last they have met a proud, dignified, courteous race who merit admiration.

This second group, as like as not, become champions of the Masai. In their opinion, and protagonists of any movement tend to become too one-sided, the Masai can do no wrong. The blindness has infected them. Masai-itis has got a hold.

Both points of view are equally understandable. Unfortunately, the second one, the affection for the Masai, is often misinterpreted as being a desire for the past merely because the past is going. Many tourists are like this. They want Africa to remain a huge anthropological museum, full of leaping natives, circumcision rites, tribal dances, and skull-bedecked grass huts. They want it to be almost as it always was, still with the colour but without the old wars, still with the simplicity but without the disease. When they meet and see the Masai, they feel this is as it should be. In fact, one of the arguments for having the Masai in the crater is that the tourists like to see them there. The black natives are all intermingled with the savage beasts. The old Africa is still alive.

Logically, I suppose, it is wrong to be enmeshed in the problems of the crater before descending, physically, into it; but any visitor does become immediately involved. He sees the fantastic amphitheatre full of game. He also sees the wandering herds of Masai cattle. Inevitably, he asks if the two are compatible, if the old relationship of man to animal can continue when man is suddenly presented with vaccines for his cattle and antibiotics for himself. As soon as he does question someone, that someone is bound to be partisan to one idea. Then the visitor will take one of the two main sides, while wishing he could believe in the middle course. He will either consider that everyone must be kept out of the crater area, because it is such a fabulous remnant of the animal world, or that the immediate demands of the local human beings should take precedence over such fanciful notions. He would like there to be a compromise, that the Masai who are now there should continue to live there, that their present cattle population should not be allowed to increase, and that the existing status of man and beast should be preserved; but he doubts if such a compromise is possible for long. Man's demands will increase. The Masai will not be content for always with wattle and dung. Even if they are, their government in Dar es Salaam will not let them be. Schools will have to be built, and hospitals, and shops, and lines of communication, and the result of all this will be that the magic of Ngorongoro will have gone. At present the situation is almost all right, even though the drought of 1961 turned the crater into a dustbowl as hundreds of Masai from other drier areas brought their scrawny, starving, dying cattle into the crater. It survived even this onslaught, but nature is not indestructible for ever.

As Douglas and I looked down into that crater for the very first time, and peppered Alan and Joan with questions about its future, we instantly became partisan. Perhaps one does so because everyone has a built-in despair about what can go wrong. The hand of man has the brute delicacy of a club more often than not, and there is something fearful about looking down on the Ngorongoro Crater, and the 15,000 big game still living there. A small piece of mismanagement, a bad year, a certain amount of political pressure, and this wonder of the world could go. Its shape would remain, but would predominantly serve as a reminder of what had been. At present, Ngorongoro is still hovering, tremulously, on a brink. In the next few years it will either be saved for future generations to see; or, most emphatically, it will not.

From Wilkie's Point the road winds round on the crater rim. We followed it before getting permission to go down into the crater itself. Only four-wheel drive vehicles are allowed down that cliff road, and the good sense of the rule becomes more and more apparent with each rocky hair-pin bend. A tractor once fell off the road and although the driver fell sensibly off his seat at the outset, he was later able to recover no pieces that a child could not have carried in one hand. It is not a route for those with vertigo. It is also not particularly good for the trucks, and on occasion is more like driving down a flight of steps than a road. A similar track runs up the side of the Rock of Gibraltar. Both are brilliant bits of engineering, and with both there is relief for the novice when he reaches the other end.

We lurched down into the crater, with our balloon, our two trucks, and our two trailers, and then drove along to the camp site we had chosen from above. As we did so, groups of zebras leapt out of the way at the last minute, and the wildebeest either frisked about or stopped and stared. It was an enchanting world down there, and we pitched all our tents beneath the spreading limbs of one gigantic fig-tree. That night over supper, with the pressure lamp hanging from the grapnel, we discussed our plans for flying over the crater. The winds would have to be checked. So would the animal movements, and their present positions. Above all, there was the problem of the cylinders. We would have to test all roads with them very much in mind.

At that moment, when our ears were half cocked for the reverberating throb of a lion's roar, or the happy whoop of a hyena, or any sound from the open zoo around the camp, a fantastic noise filled the tree above us. I remember ducking from its loudness, and wincing as if hit. I had never heard a noise like it, and could only think for a description of someone tearing a directory apart where all the pages are of corrugated iron. It had a rending, painful, tortured note to it, and came in bursts. Dante would have relished its infernal agony. Douglas and I, in mid-chew of our cheese biscuits, paralysed with curiosity, looked helplessly at Alan. "A tree hyrax," he said. "You would think. . . ." But any thoughts by anyone were quashed by another sort of noise, blatantly from the same anguished animal, which then split the air. The previous exhalation was dove-like by comparison with the second string it had to its orchestral bow. I have never heard ten navvies being strangled simultaneously, but I now know what they would sound like. How that creature's tortured windpipe survived those laryngeal lacerations I do not know, but they continued for a full minute before the world assumed a silence it had never known before. Then, after a respectful pause, just in case a shred of vocal chord survived still capable of further vibration, another hyrax in another tree answered this love-call to shatter all others. Like bagpipes, the nature of those cries was really only audible when far away, and we listened in amazement as the sound

157

was taken up from tree to tree. Again and again that evening our own hyrax answered back, apparently exceeding all the others by a factor of four or so. Had we possessed wine glasses at the start of the evening, I am certain they would have lain shattered by the end of it.

Anyway, whatever the effects of his calling that night, whether it established territory or earned a mate, the animal put paid to further rational discussion. I imagine quarry workers feel the same when they have laid their charges, and are ready for the detonations. Perhaps, in mere decibels, larger animals can produce a greater volume of sound, but I do not think the tree hyrax can be bettered for sheer strangulation of effort. I never did get over its call, and the last thing I remember that night was Douglas chuckling beneath his mosquito net after another agonizing minute had been spent by the small and rabbit-like furry form somewhere in the huge tree above us.

CHAPTER SIXTEEN

THE FIG-TREE CAMP

I FIRST heard the drumming in that indecisive period between sleep and wakefulness. Vague suggestions meandered through my brain concerning the cause of the noise, and were then dismissed as other thoughts became more and more coherent. Then I knew it could be nothing else than the hooves of animals. It must be zebras, for wildebeest would never make a noise like that. They went by in droves, and the earth tremored beneath them. I lay there listening, not wishing to get up immediately, not wanting to disturb them, and soaking in those sounds. Perhaps waking up in the past on military expeditions had been like this, as cohort after cohort of cavalry prepared themselves, and moved into position. Certainly the zebras were being most orderly, and only occasionally yelping with their high-pitched dog-like barks. And all the time the hooves were thundering over the ground. Day was dawning in the Ngorongoro Crater.

I pulled back a tent flap, and saw it was arriving in a rather slovenly fashion, for a heavy mist hung about. I levered myself out of bed, and into clothes, to have a look at things. A group of zebras, fat rumped and stocky, bounded off from a spot just 15 yards away. Their own drumming merged with the sounds of the many other columns who were all making their way past our camp. They appeared out of the mist on one side, some walking, some galloping, and then disappeared in the soft white light on the other. A thousand or more moved into sight and out again before leaving the place to its own once more.

That striped cavalcade was to go past us every morning, for they and we both took water from the same stream. The zebras like to drink at least once a day, preferably twice, and the herd had grown accustomed to that particular water source. Every morning they drummed past, plumply, friskily.

It is difficult telling the males from the females, because external signs are hard to assess. The males tend to be stockier, and slightly stronger-looking, but the distinction is not easy to make out. However, it is remarkable how one's eye becomes more skilled just with time, and how the comparisons become easier. Each morning we watched the parade, or looked at it over our shaving mirrors, or over our breakfast cups, and became more skilled at telling age and sex and mood; but we never ceased to wonder at its beauty.

On that first morning we drove out in one truck to take stock of the crater. The heavy rains had saturated it, as everywhere else; and we wished to know what possibilities there were for take-off sites, and what chances existed of reaching them with the hydrogen cylinders. So we left the fig-tree and just drove where we wished and how we could.

I will come to the driving part later, but in the meantime I must try and do justice to the crater itself. It is, as I have said, part forest, part lake, part open plain, and part swamp. There are always at least two streams flowing into it, and usually many more. These streams act as spokes which have to be negotiated, and during wet periods they all run into a central lake which is nowhere more than a foot or two deep. The crater walls are steep, but trees still hang on to them on one side, and it is possible for animals to get in and out of the bowl even though many never make the effort.

When driving about in this crater, it is possible to meet a greater variety of habitats in a far shorter time than is normally the case in Africa. Generally, everything on that continent is of massive dimensions, but within the crater all has been changed. One moment you are driving through the Lerai forest, meeting white-tusked elephants, watching baboon families, and looking out for leopards. The next moment, and quite suddenly, the lake is before you. Thousands of flamingoes are picking their way through the mud. They are all, every one of them, busy with their heads in the water, filtering that mud through their beaks, and walking slowly along, one angular stride at a time.

At one side of this lake, over towards the Goitokitok spring, is marshland. Impossible to enter, it is the world of

Jambo within the Ngorongoro crater

The shifting sands, or barkan, just outside the Serengeti

Disillusion sets in after thunderstorm floods on the expedition's camp near Lake Manyara

the hippopotamus. His grunting chuckles show that he is content with the bog and water and reed and mud that make up this particular quarter of the crater floor. On its fringes, and in the lush grass, the rhinoceroses are happy to exist. They are a belligerent lot, and will charge a truck often enough for its occupants to plan a fast exit route whenever they see a rhino lurch into view. His method is to stand up from whatever wallow he has been lounging in and then face the intruder. At this time, with his tail held high, his nose curling at the air, one old primaeval notion is going through his cranium. Douglas summed it up well, as a rhino stared at us, by putting this thought into words: "Ter biff—or not ter biff," he said, in what he judged to be a rhinocerean accent. "Shall oi biff 'em—or shall oi not biff 'em?"

It is a Jurassic sentiment. But then a rhinoceros does not rightly belong to this quaternary age at all. He is worryingly devoid of cunning. He is disturbingly stupid, and will rarely leave a drying-up water hole until he is too weak through water lack to move on elsewhere. Consequently, he is not faring so well now that the pressure of man is being brought to bear increasingly upon the animals. The white, or square-nosed, rhino is in particular straits, but even the black rhinoceros is finding survival steadily more difficult. That biffing thought, such as it is, is about the limit of his mental exertions.

On the first day when Douglas coined this apt phrase, the rhino did decide in favour of giving us a knock. From 30 yards he moved rapidly into a gallop, and we moved most speedily through the gears. It was astounding to see something so heavy moving so fast—roughly 25 m.p.h.— and even more so, to hear for the first time, the snorting that goes with this turn of speed. His nostrils puff the air out with steam-engine explosiveness, and this is a terrifying aspect of his charge. It would also be fairly frightening to be hit, for a rhino weighs more than the truck he is pursuing (2 tons *versus* 1½); and Alan let the snorting animal come no nearer than 3 yards or so to a collision. Thereafter it trundled away, with its tail still held perpendicularly upright, and its reputation for having a primitive crack at things happily endorsed.

There were thirty-five rhinos in the crater when we were there, some living in that high grass, some spending more time on the open plain. This expanse was the home of the herds. The wildebeest, with their grey backs, their fly-whisk tails, their lolloping canter, their shaggy manes both above and below their necks, were the predominant species. Next were the zebras, and the groups intermingled at random with each other. The third contingent was of gazelles. There were Thomson's and Grant's; the first more numerous, slightly smaller, rather less horned, and with their eternally moving tails placed a little higher up relative to the white patch both species carry so conspicuously behind them. Like all animals in the crater, however many round worms they actually carry within them, and however many ticks they possess externally, they always looked in superb condition. Their shiny black hoofs leapt eagerly over the ground, and every animal was perfectly made. The babies could run well from the day they were born, but had a different style. Instead of a normal galloping rhythm, with each limb slightly out of phase all four legs jerked along together, and they ran over the tussocky ground as a coiled spring might run.

Naturally there were no fences in the crater, and predators and prey were all in the one huge arena; but it was often possible to tell where lions might be merely because the area seemed empty. A light brown shape was the first sign of a lion, and an extremely indolent animal it always turned out to be in the midday heat. They cared nothing for inquisitive trucks, and lolled around, and flopped about, and turned this way and that with a bored nonchalance. Their coats were thick with flies. Particularly so were their red wounds, possibly from the last mating, and the flies only bothered to move when the great black tuft on the tail clouted them, or the whole tawny shape rolled over on to its other side.

It was strange sitting so nakedly in a truck, with all windows removed, just a few yards from carnivores of such muscle and power; but they were full of contempt for trucks. However, open the door a chink, put one foot half-way to the ground, and adrenalin would instantly be coursing through everyone's systems. The lions would growl, and crouch, and lose all resemblance to their former dazed state. Reality would exist once more. The pecking order, if such a timid term can be applied to an animal like a lion, had been re-established. A cuff from one of those paws, and any human being would be most instantly dead.

Driving round the crater floor is a business of keeping your eyes open, and then being rewarded most handsomely. Perhaps a cheetah would slide away, more like a snake than a quadruped, and vanish into grass less than half its height. Or a leopard would look disdainfully down from a tree. Or a family of bat-eared foxes would start to play. They use their huge ears to listen for insects in the grass, and then pounce on them. It is wrong ever to imagine that creatures just grow up to be capable of fulfilling their particular role in the animal kingdom. They have to learn, generally speaking. Those fox cubs were only too plainly not hearing insects; but they listened, and they pounced, and more likely than not they rolled over uncontrollably at the end of their leap. A family of jackals near by was also trying to get the feel of its limbs, when suddenly the mother bayed into the air. The babies looked at her, hesitated, and then followed suit—as best they could. Anyone hearing their sounds unaccompanied would not have known what they were; but, coming after the mother's splendidly eerie and drawn-out howl, they were obviously pathetic imitations of the same thing. The only part they did effectively was to throw their heads back; the rest was a confused nonsense of whimsical whimpers being ardently wailed.

At all times of the day, and for much of the night, there is bird song in the crater. There are many kinds of cuckoo having variations on the standard cuckoo theme. There are bee-eaters, pleading plaintively for someone to follow them. There are plovers, wheeling and whooping as eternally as they do over European fields. Every now and then there are strange croaky sounds coming from the bustards, about as near the conventional idea of bird song as a motor-horn. Always, there are birds to be seen, such as Abdim's storks treading their way through the long grass looking for frogs, or the same storks soaring effortlessly in the hot thermals of an afternoon. Then there are crested cranes, and maribou storks, and stately secretary birds, and ducks, and larks, and finches, and hoopoes, and they all intermingle with all the other animals there. Those who live in cities inevitably think of animals as zoo keepers do, with each in their own compartment, each species separate from its neighbour. In the crater, due to the abundance of water and the ever-changing variety of ecological environments, the extent of the mingling is remarkable. This is an outstanding feature of a glorious place.

Driving back to camp that evening, having gorged our retinas on unforgettable spectacles, we felt more determined than ever to float by balloon over that breathtaking chunk of countryside. However, there were plenty of difficulties ahead before achieving this aim. The crater was wetter than Alan had ever known it in the dry season, and most of the tracks had been rutted deeply. Whole regions, a few square miles in extent, were just sodden with water a foot deep. Through these we whirled with all four wheels in low gear, and through most of them we got safely to the other side. When we did not, it was a matter of pushing the slime away from the tyres, putting some wood beneath them, and then sledge-hammering a steel spike into the ground. To this we attached our winch cable and, after one or two tries, the truck emerged from the mud before the spike did. It was all a matter of keeping up the momentum and of not driving into the same tracks that anyone else had made.

We had not met any other trucks that day, but back at camp beneath the fig-tree an African arrived with the tale that his party were firmly stuck. He described their position —a good 9 miles away—and as they must already have been in the mud for four hours, we finished our tea in leisurely fashion before driving off to pull them out. The African said they were Americans, and were angry even when he had left. Being stuck in the mud is part of African travel; it should not be resented because some firm schedule has gone off balance. On the way we decided, with infinite conceit, to extract them with the utmost aplomb. They had no right to be angry in a place like the crater, particularly if their clothes showed they had left the business of extraction solely to their driver. So we planned to humiliate them as best we could, to whistle quietly as we worked, and to pull them out within a single minute.

On our arrival we swung round with casual ease, and pulled up with our truck facing theirs. There were three Americans, quite untarnished by mud, extremely furious with everything, and just as we had imagined. There was also a driver, caked from head to toe. We said "Hello", and the plan went into action. With nothing more than a little whistling, albeit of independent tunes, we stepped out into the grassy water and went to work. One of us wound the wire round the winch, another put the hook round their axle, and a third looked after the running of the engine. It was aplomb at its most evil. It is hard whistling or looking nonchalant for ever, and occasionally a sort of laugh would come from someone. Anyway, they were out in less than the one minute, and we drove off to watch them get stuck again. Sure enough, for the poor driver had lost his nerve, his wheels were soon whining themselves deeper and deeper.

"Don't worry," we said, in between whistling and looking indifferent, "you'll be soon out again." And soon they were. And then they were in. And finally they were out just as the sun set and the night was not far off.

"I think you had better follow behind us," we said.

"Please, please," said one. "We were due at the Crater Lodge three hours ago. Can you put us on the right track?"

Faced with such abnegation, we rubbed it in mercilessly. When driving along a good section, with apparently more of it to come, we swerved rapidly to the right and went through a hideous bog lying to one side. Faithfully, the second truck followed suit. Later on we regained the good section, as if to point out that the bog had been chosen instead of some far more treacherous obstacle. The other truck came alongside.

"You certainly know this place like the back of your hand," shouted an American voice.

"Well, it's tricky here and there."

"Yeah, it must be difficult for strangers."

"It's quite easy, really." The three of us shouted back at him, making it quite certain he understood nothing.

Anyway, we then swerved off the track and drove straight for the lake. Their truck followed us, and was soon wallowing along more than axle deep in the water while flamingoes scattered to each side. In this fashion we carried on, disregarding the dry land, until we emerged to join the main route through the crater. The quite unnecessary detours were over.

"You won't get stuck again from here. But come and have a beer at our camp first."

"No," said the same voice as before. "That's a swell idea, but we should have been up at the top nearly four hours ago. We'd better get going."

So they did, and we watched their red tail light going off to meet the schedule as best it could. They were not the last of many tourists we met who were frantically and fearfully trying to meet deadlines. It is all very well working out time-tables in Hamburg or Denver, but Africa treats them carelessly. The remark "This must be Verona, because it's Tuesday" does not apply when bridges collapse, and roads become rivers, and mud just stays as mud. That evening we felt slightly humble about our treatment of the truckload. It was only that our own personal delight at being in a place like the Ngorongoro persuaded us that everyone else should feel the same, whatsoever timings had gone awry.

Certainly we did not let these minor tremblings of conscience spoil the warming effect of a perfect day. Moreover, nothing upset our hyrax. With ear-splitting precision, as if it could not bear the sight of people eating cheese biscuits, that notable creature shook the world around him with his unearthly cries. Nothing else could have exceeded that monstrous finale. It was a fitting conclusion to a perfect day. I felt enormously privileged, as we turned in later that night, to have seen what I had seen during the day, and to have heard what I had heard ever since those zebras had woken us up in the mistiness of dawn.

CHAPTER SEVENTEEN

THE SALEH SITE

BY the end of a week we had thoroughly explored the crater, from the particular point of view of a balloon safari. All the time we had borne those hydrogen cylinders in mind. In theory we wanted to begin the flight a few miles to the windward of the crater. The wind would then take us up the crater slope, over the rim, down into the crater, across its varied floor, up the other side, over the rim again, and finally down to a landing spot somewhere to the leeward of the Ngorongoro region. In practice, we discovered there would have to be compromises to this basic idea. Part of the trouble was the wetness of the season, and part was that Africa is extremely full of inaccessible areas.

The intention to fly over impenetrable portions of the continent, and to see what could be seen of swamps and jungle and marsh, was a built-in feature of the main plain. This kind of aerial survey had to be investigated for its possible usefulness. On the Manyara flight, for instance, roughly 50 miles of the journey had been over land and water and the various mixtures of the two that no one had been able to penetrate for many months. Four-wheeled drive trucks are fairly ubiquitous, and they have opened up the continent remarkably in a short time, but there is much that is more than a match for them. Normally they cannot cope with water more than a couple of feet deep and, of course, they resent rocks, or gradients steeper than their wheels can grip. Yet there are other equally restrictive obstacles, and the type of vegetative soil known as black-cotton is high on the list. It is widely distributed, and so is the silt deposited after flooding. This sandy substance looks good, but has no body to it. Other snags, apart from the countless variations of swamp and bog and morass, are formed by areas where the grass grows high enough to hide the stones and tree-trunks lying amongst it. Like reefs beneath the surface of the sea, they can carve their pattern on a tender sump in no time.

I agree that men can walk over most of these areas, but it takes time to walk, and occasionally it is dangerous. Moreover, the jungle walker, or the high-reed walker, may get through to the other side, but he might witness nothing in the process. All he will see is the next twig to hit him in the face, or the next clump to stride over. Of the animals he may well see nothing. It was over this sort of territory that an aerial platform would have notable advantages.

In good times the road round Ngorongoro's rim is usable for two-thirds of its circumference. Part of it is always satisfactory. This all-weather section runs from Wilkie's Point where we had first looked down into the crater and were blind to the animals living there, round past the turn-off to the cliff road, past the village of Ngorongoro, past the Crater Lodge (which is a log-cabin type of motel, superbly placed), and on to a spot known as Windy Gap. The road then leaves the crater rim and saunters down towards the huge plains of the Serengeti a couple of thousand feet below. The other portion of the rim road is by no means as reliable. From the junction at Wilkie's Point it travels north around the eastern side of the crater, and it eventually joins up with a minor village called Nainokanoka.

This perimeter system we surveyed, in so far as it was possible to do so. The wind had been blowing initially from the north-east, and therefore we paid most regard to that section up to Nainokanoka. The nearer we could get to that village, the longer the flight would be over the crater region. Unfortunately, no one had reached that village with a light lorry, let alone a heavy one, for several months, and the last heavy lorry to do the journey had left fearful ruts a foot or two deep along the track. We found these could normally be circumvented by driving into the surrounding jungle to make a detour round them; but 8 miles from Wilkie's Point a misguided river had been meandering along the route. This was of no great depth, but it had deposited far too much silt for us to negotiate and the ways round it were too steep. It formed the end of the line.

With effort the Land-Rover or the Gipsy could have been forced through, but not those cylinders. Due to the slightly lower pressure being pumped into them at Nairobi than existed in the original consignment, we needed sixty for the Ngorongoro flight. This meant two well-laden 5-ton lorries. It could not mean sixty trips by Land-Rover, for the cylinders were 9 feet long. They jutted out too far from the tail-board. There was no possibility of persuading two heavy lorries to wallow through that stream. There was also no chance of getting them down the cliff road, then past our camp and across the crater floor itself. And there was not enough labour available to contemplate plans for carrying the cylinders, with perhaps five men beneath each load, to a suitable point upwind of the crater.

These investigations, despite their depressing features, at least demonstrated what was feasible and which of the various London-born schemes would have to perish forthwith. Only two launch sites were now practicable. One was at a point 4 miles north of Wilkie's Point, an open space known as Saleh, and at 3 o'clock, if the crater can be imagined with 12 o'clock towards the north. The other site was at 9 o'clock, a couple of miles to the west of Windy Gap. Both were accessible by road. Both served the purposes of a balloon's demands. It may seem contrary having them in juxtaposition to one another, but the crater winds at that time were blowing either from the west or from a point slightly to the north of east. On the day that the cylinders arrived, it was coming most determinedly from the west. Therefore, with a team of Wambulu hired locally, the lorry was despatched to off-load its cargo at the chosen spot beyond Windy Gap.

During the preliminary and exploratory excursions, we had not been entirely single-minded about the balloon's requirements. We had also carried on with making the film. There were 11 miles of black and white 16 mm. to be exposed, and the crater is full of photogenic material. This was Alan's particular métier, and he was supreme at it. A trademark of much of his filming was a shot that lingered on one animal and then, merely by a gentle tilt of the camera, revealed another of quite a different calibre. The crater's intermingling, with plovers darting about near the feet of lions, with a jackal family surrounded by wildebeest, was very ripe for this manoeuvre.

He was also excellent at making the right noises. If one squeals, and in a manner not too different from that of a baby rhino, an adult rhino can be brought up to investigate. He, or she, will be suspicious, but will advance cautiously, with lips twitching and eyes peering, to reach the source of the sound. In this way it is possible not only to bring a rhino within a few yards and see every wrinkle of its horny skin but to put the animal in a position that if it did decide to charge it would undoubtedly succeed in achieving an impact. Alan once pulled the noise trick off to perfection with a jackal. Two pups were sitting stiffly outside their hole, bravely hesitant, and staring at the truck which had now stopped before them. Any extra noise, such as that of a camera's motor, would have sent them pell-mell to safety. In any case, their obvious concern made them a dull picture. So Alan looked around, saw the mother, trained the camera on her, and then made a noise. As she got up, the camera whirred, and she then trotted back to the hole. At that spot, before descending, and having the retreat within easy reach, she paused and regained confidence. So did the young ones. With their mother at hand they both leapt from the hole, started pulling her around, biting her ears, and boxing at each other, without caring at all for the camera which was easily recording the lot.

This type of shot, like many others, came under the photographers' heading of lyrical. In animal photography, we became increasingly concerned with quite another type, and one for which no name exists. If two zebras are happily chewing each other's stiff mane, or are pressing their noses together, the camera is kept running to capture this faunal devotion. But if one zebra then urinates, or defaecates, or, worse still, mounts the other, the camera is stopped with an exclamation of despair from the photographer. He is not against such practices, but the convention is that they do not appear in films for general consumption. This is a fairly ridiculous state of affairs.

Consequently, one evening after supper, we planned a company devoted to greater reality. Suitable names, we felt, were either Sick Productions or Twentieth-Century Hyena. Instead of that well-known lion roaring in the centre of the opening frame, there would be a hyena, laughing quietly to himself and crunching someone's bone. In tune with the new idea, and as a revolution against the sentimental gush which has oozed from the commentators of animal films for far too long, our man would have a different approach, and preferably an American accent.

"Well, here's Harry the Hyena. Poor little chap, he looks hungry. Those furry features are sore in need of some little morsel to keep him going. Now what has he seen with those cute little black eyes, and why is he dribbling from his mouth? Why! he has seen a baby wildebeest being born, and that's his favourite dish. Well, now we see him trotting over to the treat in store. Poor chap, he's having to pant so. Will he get there before that wild wildebeest can run away? Will he? Yes, he does, and did you hear that snap of his jaws? Well, there's Harry, happy at last. Snap, crackle, pop go those dreamy bones. And down they go, as we say farewell, into Harry's now fat little tum.'

The reason for this particular theme was that we had been filming it that very day. Naturally, in any nature reserve, man is not allowed to interfere just to prevent one carnivore from feeding, and we had been filming the birth of a wildebeest when the hyenas had started to take an interest. To begin with, and while the mother had kept on walking with the calf's two front feet sticking out on either side of her tail, first for an inch and then for a foot or more, the hyenas had been watchful, but at a respectful distance. Some jackals had come nearer, but there was no danger from them, and they only wanted the placental after-birth. When the calf's body had fallen on to the ground, and the mother had turned round to inspect this new-born thing, the hyenas had got to their feet. Within one minute the baby was making efforts to stand. Within two it had succeeded. Within three it was making little hops. Within four it was going round its mother. And on the fifth minute the hyenas attacked. Mother and calf ran off, but there were four hyenas and the mother was the sole defender of her offspring. The herd carried on with its own business of grazing and doing nothing in particular. The mother did what she could.

Even after the calf had been knocked down three times it still ran on, and the end came only when two hyenas just picked it up. Its feet stabbed jerkily into the air. At this point, with the whole terrifying episode miraculously on film, Alan took a panga and went to kill the calf. The hyenas dragged it into the water away from him, and there they dropped it. He picked it up and hacked twice. Some seven minutes of life had been mercifully ended. The hyenas moved in again as Alan left, and they fought over the little carcase. They whooped, and snarled, and soon ran off with independent portions. Within ten minutes of that pathetic birth there was nothing to be seen. The mother had moved inconspicuously amongst the herd again, and the life of her calf might never have been. Presumably, feeling all the better for it, a small group of hyenas had returned to their burrows and were settling down to digest the tender meals inside them.

By no means was such an episode an integral part of Sick Productions, but nature had been rather too natural for most palates. On my return to England—to jump ahead in this particular story—I met film representatives. The British ones said the death was too painful for many people. The Americans saw nothing wrong with the death, but said it would be impossible to put that birth on their screens. I think the trouble stems predominantly from the fact that nature, so far as films are concerned, has been glossed over to excess in the past. Slush Productions have been in charge. The sentimental commentator has called the tune.

On the following day we all drove up the cliff road again, and then round to Windy Gap. The sixty cylinders were all neatly stacked. Their sixty caps had been unscrewed and laid in front of them. A space for the inflation had been cleared. There was only one trouble, and this we proved by sending off a pilot balloon. The wind was wrong. It was not blowing from the site towards the crater. Instead it was moving almost due south, and the balloonist would merely have been given a good all-round and distant view of the Ngorongoro herds.

This was a depressing discovery. We talked the matter over, and decided to move the cylinders round the other side to the Saleh site. We could have waited for the wind to blow correctly at Windy Gap, but we might have had a long wait. At least the wind had now reverted to its proper direction for the time of year and there was a fair chance of it staying there. Hence the decision to move, a decision not taken lightly, for the available local transport meant four journeys were necessary. Moreover, the circumference of a circle being what it is, the trip round half the crater's rim meant a journey of nearly 40 miles. There and back four times multiplied the distance to 310 miles, and over roads extremely poor in parts. In fact, that decision to move meant two days' work for everybody, including the recruited Wambulu.

The trips were made less tedious, if such a word is valid in that sort of countryside, by a certain rhinoceros. He had grown partial to a mud wallow right in the middle of the track some two miles north of Wilkie's Point, and about as far south of the Saleh site. On our first pass, surprised as both parties were by the sudden meeting, he decided to biff. The lorry stopped, and the driver blew on his horn. At the last minute the rhino thought better of a physical encounter and sheered off into the grass. Not only did the lorry have seven more passes to make, but the Gipsy kept going by that point on various errands. Many charges were made and many last-minute changes of mind; but the animal did once collide with the Gipsy. His first horn became wedged beneath the steel bumper, and during the animal's extrication of this aphrodisiacal possession the mudguard became much mauled. Thereafter he watched the traffic from a distance.

A biff had been effected. Damage had been done. Pliocene honour has been assuaged.

At the new launch site the ground crew cut down all small bushes in the way, and took great delight in destroying every nettle in the area. An extremely vicious pair of species lived there. One was a foot high, packed with venom and as evil as they come. The other, with leaves like soup-plates and standing 8 feet above the ground, also produced a powerful punch, as well as a tingling that lasted for 48 hours. We discovered them when prospecting the site, but were to meet them considerably more intimately at the conclusion of the flight.

Once again we laid out the balloon fabric before an exciting piece of country. Down there on the crater floor were the 15,000 animals. In the woods leading up the slope towards us there were elephants and buffaloes. On the gradient behind us, and where the wind was coming from, the fall down to the Karatu plain was much less steep, but far more thickly covered with the lush tropical forest growth one expects to find in a hot country at seven and eight thousand feet. What we hoped to do was to push off from the rim, with as little lift as possible, and then sink down quickly to the crater floor. "More like tobogganing than ballooning," said Douglas, and stared down at the crater 2,000 feet below.

Perhaps it was, but the intention was that the toboggan should cover those 12 miles and then climb up again over the other side to disappear in the general direction of the Serengeti. Anyway, we thoroughly prepared the balloon, attached the ropes inside it, put on the valve, put the net over it, and then loosely rolled it all up in case hyenas felt like chewing it experimentally during the night. We also linked up the cylinders so that, once again, it would just be a matter of turning on the gas in the morning. Most of the Wambulu went off, carrying many complex instructions about bringing more people early the next day as additional ground crew. At this stage John Newbould, pasture research officer for the Ngorongoro district, who had been acting as "our man" in the area, became firmly sucked into the expedition, and had been offered a place in the basket instead of Alan Root, who had had to go off temporarily to Nairobi. Also Bill Moore-Gilbert, local game warden and sudden balloon enthusiast, was co-operating in every way possible, and most effectively. In short, about twenty-five people would be on hand at the take-off. I did not consider this an excess by any means.

That night Douglas and I stayed at the site together with half a dozen Africans to help with the earliest stages. The eight of us had erected a couple of tents, and we sat around a fire eating some semi-roasted wildebeest meat. (I forget quite why the animal had been shot or who had shot it.) The Southern Cross was high in the sky, and the two pointers of the Plough indicated some distant spot well below the horizon. The wind, both at our level and slightly higher up where some cloudy wisps were moving, was blowing over the crater correctly. It stood fair for the Ngorongoro.

My apprehension of travel by balloon was as great as ever, if not more so after the Manyara flight. Once again we were to commit ourselves to the element of air. It was wonderful to contemplate taking off from that crater edge, and flying with the wind over the world's most fantastic arena; but each such thought was hard pressed by others. How had we escaped that Manyara cloud? What about those which settle above the rim each day? As for the landing, that clearly required luck as well as judgment. Would luck always hold?

It was fairly cold up there, and Douglas sat before the fire well wrapped up in war surplus. Every now and then he took another burning twig to light another cigarette, while he also kept his apprehensions to himself. I remembered our supreme confidence that night in the dripping Highland cottage, as we digested the cockles and planned with the joyful ease of those who cannot be bothered to think of difficulties. Now, high up on a moist piece of Africa, with a balloon all ready, and our stomachs digesting wildebeest instead, the confidence waned as the night grew more chilly. It would be so easy to come down too fast, hit a rock, break someone's leg, or worse. I wondered what on earth was going to happen. Where would we go? Would it be forest or swamp or something better that would receive us? Where was the unknown destination we would journey to?

"Looks a nice night," I said, fishing slightly for Douglas's thoughts.

"Yup," he said, and gave it a look.

"Ah well, I think I'll get some sleep then."

"Yup. Sleep," said Douglas, and that was the end of the day.

CHAPTER EIGHTEEN

THE FOREST LANDING

It was not a good night, mainly because it was cold. There was also a firm wind, blowing comfortingly from the right direction, but with no great warmth to it. The tent panels slapped back and forth, jerkily. Douglas, with an Army cap-comforter down over his ears, slept noiselessly. A hyena whooped into the night, and I listened to hear it again. A few months previously a man had had his foot chewed off by one of that breed, and I retracted mine still further on remembering his story. His error had been to camp out beneath neither tent nor mosquito net, and to have a large hole in his sleeping-bag. A passing hyena had seen a whitish piece of flesh pointing into the air. He then took a grab at it, and ran away. There was, of course, a man attached, and after a while he had had to relinquish his hold, but not before the foot had been well chewed in the process. The only other recent such story came from the Serengeti. Again it was a case of no mosquito nets, and it is quite strange how deterring these are to the largest of carnivores, as well as the whining Anopheles, which are their prime concern. It was a three-man party, and they had had a tent, but they slept head to toe with the central man's head at the entrance. They did not tie the flaps together. A lion grapped hold of this exposed head, and ran off with it. The two other men woke up and gave chase. The lion had also relinquished its grip, but there is a great difference between a hyena pulling a foot and a lion pulling a head. In the second case the victim is dead.

A game warden had tracked and then caught up with the lion. He discovered the head-snatcher was a young male desperately trying to find enough food for a lame and helpless male who was dependent upon him. The warden shot them both, for man-eaters must be discouraged as much as the view that lions habitually take this step. It was the first case in the Serengeti for several decades. Even so, it had happened, and when the tent sides bulge in and out with the wind, it is easy to imagine it happening again.

There is one big trouble about being cold, and a trifle anxious, and staying awake in the middle of the night. One's bladder likes to make its presence felt. I got up awkwardly, undid the tent flaps, and left the tent for the moonlight outside. I stepped a decent distance away, and stood there nakedly feeling as white and useless as some grub exposed to the light for the very first time. A man may look a confident piece of machinery as he strides along in the day-time, but take him out of his clothes and his shoes and put him in a moonlit jungle clearing, and very quickly the twentieth-century individual is a pathetically gawky sight. Nettles sting him. Stones make him wince. Cold wind puts goose pimples on his whitest bits of flesh, and something like an unobserved gorse bush forms a barrier with insuperable ease. He cuts a ridiculous figure as he stands there, relieving himself, shivering silently, virtually incapable of smelling any danger, certainly incapable of hearing an approaching footstep as the wind plays over his ears, and not even being able to see anything if it stands in the shadows. As for feeling, he knows that his right foot is resting on a lumpy twig, and his left calf is smarting painfully from another nettle encounter. He makes his way, cautiously, back to the tent, and then goes through the complex manoeuvre with knees and elbows of fitting himself inside a sleeping-bag. There, within that chrysalis, he is safe again. Douglas woke up, and stared concentratedly before speaking.

"I thought you were a lion," he said, and then went back to sleep. So, shortly, did I.

A few minutes later, or so it seemed, Bill Moore-Gilbert and the contingents of helpers began to arrive. Then John Newbould came, having been mildly hit by the rhino on the way, and his Land-Rover was similarly packed with men. So, without more ado, and with no desire for a wildebeest breakfast, Douglas turned on the gas. I and most of the others looked after the balloon. The wind was calm and gave little indication of its intentions. The crater floor was filled with a mist, making it look like a gargantuan bowl of pale-white porridge; but everyone assured me this was frequently the case at dawn. The sun would banish the effect before very long.

The orange bulk of the balloon steadily grew, and became a larger and larger thing in all that greenness on the crater edge. It was doing splendidly, but the half-way point was reached when Douglas had consumed more than half of the cylinders. Someone had miscalculated the pressures, or the cubic footage they represented. Anyway, we went on, with Douglas extracting the last puff from every cylinder. Finally, he could produce no more and the balloon swayed gently above its restraining sandbags. It was approximately 95 per cent full, and that would have to do.

In the meantime, and during the three hours of the inflation, the wind had only imperfectly made up its mind. Two cubic feet of the precious gas were used to fill a couple of pilot balloons. These were released within minutes of each other. One went east and the other flew slightly west. The day was changeable, to say the least. However, whatever the actual direction, I wanted to get off as quickly as possible, because I wished to make the most of the stillness of dawn and avoid the worst of the afternoon's turbulence. So Douglas and John Newbould and I climbed into the basket and set about the process of finding equilibrium. At 8,000 feet there is roughly three-quarters of the lift at sea-level. Also a balloon only 95 per cent full is less efficient. Therefore we had to cut our equipment and accessories to the minimum. Consequently, it was with only five sacks aboard that the balloon started to disregard the ground.

"Hands on again," I said, and Bill shouted the necessary Swahili.

As I had no wish to rise higher than, say, a hundred feet above the tree tops, and not to disappear upwards a thousand feet or more as had been our habit, the trail rope was attached to the ring, but then laid out along the ground. There was nothing near by it could damage, and I hoped our initial lift to clear the surrounding trees would then be sufficiently impeded as more and more of the rope's weight was taken up by the balloon. With luck the 45 lb. of rope would stop Jambo's customarily rocket-like tendencies.

"Hands off once more."

The wind carried us, but parallel to the ground.

"On again," and fifteen pairs of Wambulu hands brought the basket to a stop, which is more than happened to the Wambulu talk. The chatter, about whether or not, and why and how, the balloon would rise was no momentary curiosity. It had continued unceasingly since Douglas had turned on the gas, and was now reaching a fanatic crescendo. One man stopped, for a second or two, as I poured 5 lb. of sand on to his feet, and then Bill shouted again.

"Toa mkono. Hands off."

The 5 lb. had been enough. We rose, almost vertically to begin with, and the trail rope uncoiled as we went. I remember seeing Bill's small child catching hold of a still dormant section of it. I shouted something, and then watched that same section flick mercifully out of his hands. By then we were out of shouting distance, and another flight had begun. It was at this sort of stage that Douglas would push whatsoever cap he had on further to the back of his head and make some general observational point, like: "Well, we made it."

Indeed, we had made it, but away from the crater. At the end of ten minutes we were about a mile from the crater's lip, and 400 feet up, and quite motionless. This slight rise meant that the balloon was no longer floppy at the bottom. The gas inside had expanded, and Jambo was the perfect shape she should have been. However, there was room for perfection in the flight itself. It was strange to see the small cumulus above scudding along in traditional fashion, to hear a wind rustling the trees below, and yet to be poised unmovingly between the two. Douglas took panoramic shots of the enormous expanse laid out beneath us, and John examined its botany. He took pleasure in observing the rigidity with which various ecological zones met each other. The lines were like those curious slicks at sea which form long streaky patterns over its surface. So it was in the forest and the clearings beneath us. The short grassy areas stayed stubbornly short, despite the mountainous profusion of growth bordering upon them. The nettle zones were compact areas. There was either a dense mass of them or, quite suddenly, there was not. The *Acacia lahai*, about the most shapely of the whole range of well-proportioned acacia trees, almost looked as if its plantations had been put there by man, so orderly were the areas in which they grew.

Despite that manoeuvre with the trail-rope and our initial stabilization at only 400 feet, we next began to rise quite steadily, though keeping station over one huge pillar tree all the while. Douglas was vexed at seeing the land recede further and further from him, and screwed longer and longer lenses to his cameras; but there was nothing else that could be done. Anyway, those clouds above us were moving in the right direction, crater-wards, and we would surely go that way once we had risen to their height. As I had no intention of going higher than need be and of making certain that we caught the very bottom of that air-stream, I threw out no sand. The present tendency to rise would get us there in the end. This was inevitable, for the more we climbed that day, the more the sun shone upon us. There must have been a mist down there above the trees, or at least a greater and invisible humidity of the air, for as we rose the sun grew hotter and the air became brighter. The hydrogen responded to this increased radiation and expanded accordingly. So, with the launch site still in view, but becoming increasingly fuzzy as time ticked by, we rose with all the simplicity in the world above that incredible view.

To one side, now appearing small for the first time in our experience, was the Ngorongoro Crater. North of it were the steep rolling areas of the Crater Highlands, pocked with volcanoes like Embagai, and rising to 10,000 feet or more. Appearing still higher even than our basket was the active L'Engai, not smoking but flecked with white at the summit as if it were the conical roosting place of some monstrous and productive form of bird. Some 40 miles to the east of us was the big cliff drop to the Rift Valley, the Manyara lake, and the wide traverse of our previous endeavour. To the south were just hills and a lake and more hills, and a promise of at least 3,000 more miles before the massive continent comes to an end at the Cape. I do not fully understand the desires involved and of wishing to be levitated above the face of the Earth, but up in that basket at 10,500 feet above sea-level I felt supremely content. I shifted my feet, gazed fondly at Loolmalasin and Oldeani and then looked round at the others.

"Good view," said Douglas.

Down below, our dot of a shadow then began moving towards the crater. It danced over the big forest trees; it went more gently over the open grassy zones. Then it crossed that rugged rim road and took no time to cover the remaining stretch before the wall began. Down it slid, over trees, and rocky buttresses, and steep slopes. Down to the gentler gradients, and then more slowly over the crater floor itself. Without so much as a puff of wind on our faces, we had in ten minutes made in the air a journey that would have taken a mere pedestrian on the ground many hours. We had arrived over Ngorongoro.

It may have been like tobogganing for our shadow, but for us it was nothing of the sort. Our shadow had leapt down to the crater floor and had become even more of a pin-head in doing so, but we had continued at the same old height where we had met the airstream from the east. We were still 10,500 feet above sea-level, while the shadow was now over a mile below.

This was aerial observation of animals to some degree, but not the one we wanted. It was like examining pond water before the days of the microscope. We had to take a rather closer look. Allowing for the direction of the sun, I waited until the shadow indicated we were some 3 miles within the crater. Then I pulled for three seconds on the valve line, and almost at once a breeze pushed past our faces. At 500 feet a minute we made our descent. It was fast, and roughly the speed of a parachutist, but we had plenty of time to watch the changing shapes of that remarkable piece of geography. The flatness beneath us became steadily less so, and the distant hills sank like so many setting suns behind the crater wall. After nearly 10 minutes, and when 1,000 feet above the ground, I threw out two hands of sand to break the fall. Later I threw out two more, and once again we were poised a mere 400 feet above the world.

We hovered momentarily over the general swampy area around the Goitokitok spring, and had a look at some hippos walking through the reeds. Over to the west and south were the main herds of animals, but over to the west and south we did not go. We stayed over those reeds for a very short time, and then returned in the general direction from whence we had come. The only difference was our height. This time the crater wall was not a diminutive thing thousands of feet below, but a huge tree-covered mountain coming our way. It seemed that the arena all around us was being heated by the sun, and the air was expanding up its sides. We were certainly in an airstream that was moving up the wall for shortly afterwards, with no sand-throwing by me, we were ascending that face like a funicular. The huge mossy trees were 50 feet below, and less than 50 feet to one side. John rattled off their names whenever the bigger ones bulged up towards us, and Douglas did what he could with a countryside that had suddenly stood on edge. I was not flying the balloon in any active sense. I was just bemused by watching a 2,000-foot wall disappear beneath us.

At the top, with the trail rope still searing at the trees which had just passed by, we slid over the rim and the rim road at a casual 20 miles an hour. Thereafter, never more than a hundred feet above the ground, we descended still eastwards over the gentler slope that led away from the crater's edge. We were too low to see anything of the ground party, and so looked out instead for animal life. I think all of us saw the buffaloes at the same time, and all said "Look!" together. I heard the camera click while they were still lolling on their backs, and then every one of them leapt to its feet. With a great crashing of the undergrowth and of everything standing in their way, they set off at a mild gallop.

For some reason, possibly because it was downhill, they ran directly beneath us. They were head to tail and, like so many express trains, moved through the tangle below. Each file of animals, each set of carriages, took its own independent path, but frequently the files converged upon each other. Fresh files formed, with nothing more than a rending and a breaking as bushes were swept before the charge.

"Keep after them," said Douglas, "this is excellent stuff," and we did, miraculously, keep after them for a full two minutes. Then they verged away, and we were left in silence once again.

It was while we were thinking we would go directly over three elephants standing by a pool, and while still at 100 feet, that a powerful thermal took hold of the balloon with all its might. Instantly, the trail rope was flicked up beneath us as we soared into the sky. This was no gentle rise, as we had known over Manyara. This was far more drastic. In perhaps a minute we were 3,000 feet above those trees and those now invisible elephants. Above us was the familiar base of a thunder-cloud, and this time there would be no dallying beneath it. This time we would be in it, if strong counter-measures were not taken.

I pulled for five seconds on the valve line. We still went up. I pulled for another five, and once again we heard the slight sucking sound as the gas went out. The balloon was now distinctly pouchy at the bottom, but we were still rising, and over 9,000 feet above sea-level. I pulled for another five, and watched the bottom panels withdraw inwards again as the gas rushed out of the top. At last the altimeter showed we were rising no more, but the air of the thermal still blew past us. I remember John taking some silver paper off a piece of chocolate, and then having that paper blown vertically out of his hand. All the time, for we were stationary in a strong current, we rocked about like any dinghy in a choppy sea.

"What happens when we get out of this thermal?" asked John, who hit nails on heads with disarming ease.

"We shall go down, fast," I replied.

"Very fast," I added, a few seconds later as the bucketing increased.

"Uh-huh," said Douglas.

Sure enough, the thermal did move itself elsewhere. Then, dropping like any stone, we achieved a speed of descent I had never known before. There was no time to read an instrument. What did it matter if it were two or three thousand feet per minute? To hit the ground at either speed would be equally fatal. John and I bailed out sand in great dollops at a time. Then half sackfuls. Then more dollops, and more fumbling around in the bottom of the basket for more sacks. Our speed slackened slightly, but we couldn't just throw everything overboard. To have been excessive with that sand would surely have sent us up towards the thundercloud again, with every opportunity of repeating the episode, and with far less chance of having enough sand afterwards, to break the second plummet-like fall. Yet to be parsimonious with the sand was equally uncalled for.

"I think this will have to be the landing," I said.

"Right," said Douglas, and went on filming.

"More sand, John. Yes, that's right. Now more, yes the rest of that sack. Get up another. Now wait with it. Hold it ready. Yes, tip out half, and now the rest. Yes, this is the landing. Douglas, this is it."

And down we went. This was no occasion for choosing a spot. The trail rope must have touched the ground just as we were reaching the tallest trees. I do not know how we missed them. We seemed to be going where a tree had fallen. I could see its long trunk lying there. And its upturned roots. And then it was time to rip. But there wasn't time. Because we hit the ground, and stayed there.

The balloon had not toppled over, and the three of us were standing there quite over-towered by plants. I pulled at the rip, but the rope just came down in my hands. Soon its end came, showing where it had torn free from the rubber fabric. Why, I had no idea. It meant we had a three-quarters full balloon, swaying back and forth at the branches above us.

"John, what's that tree? Is it spiky?"

"Oh, that! Good Lord, no! Not a spike on it. That's *Cassipourea elliottii*. Certainly no spikes."

Puncture material or not, that tree was not doing the balloon any good as the two of them were blown at each other. So I attached a rope from the basket to the fallen tree beside it, and then felt everything was sufficiently safe for me to climb out. The other two stayed in as ballast while I had a look at the situation from somewhere better than the neck-creaking angle of the basket's viewpoint. A soup plate leaf touched my arm, and thousands of vegetative ampules injected their contents into me. It was a nettle patch of immense size in which we had landed. It was also a major highway for ants, and their formic acid produced its own even sharper sensation when they rammed it home. Consequently, John and Douglas did not see a man coolly taking stock of an awkward situation. Instead, they caught glimpses of flailing limbs which lashed out from the green depths of that poisonous neighbourhood.

At least I had seen that there was nothing else to be done except pull on the valve line. It was the only way of losing the gas. I had thought it might be possible to reach the valve itself from higher up the bank, but the ant-nettle combination had reduced enthusiasm for that plan. So we pulled on it steadily, and gradually Jambo began to sink towards the earth.

We were, when everything had been collapsed, spread out on one steep slope with an audible but invisible stream somewhere at the bottom. The three of us cut down clubs with which to clout those nettles, and folded up the balloon and net as best we could while suffering the various slings and arrows of the environment. It was a very real piece of forest. There were no animal tracks, and even the buffaloes had let it be. It was impossible to move without thwacking down everything that stood in the way. It was also fairly difficult even to stand up, for the earth that supported all this growth was a rich, humus-laden mud. In short, our cavortings in the air were as nothing compared with those manoeuvres on the ground. However, in the end, everything did get stacked inside the basket, and we were ready to leave. We had only a vague idea of our position, but we knew that the rim road was somewhere up the slope.

What we most certainly did not know was an event taking place at Karatu. Fifteen miles away an African clerk from a treasury office had solitarily witnessed our descent. He had considered, with remarkable accuracy, that not everything had been under control. In his opinion, and he had cause for it, the landing could best be defined as a crash. So, with all haste, he had rushed into the Karatu Police Station to tell his story. He had told it pungently, but he had garnished it to excess. It was all very well to call a landing a crash, for only the expert balloonist's eye could tell the difference—particularly at 15 miles, but it was utterly wrong of him to add that we had exploded. The Police Officer then set the various wires humming and reported the matter to Arusha and the capital. "Safari Balloon Crashed. Loud Bang Reported. Balloon Seen To Explode. Fate of Crew Unknown."

The message went out shortly after I had failed to get at the valve, from the bank, and had been more interested in the fate of the ants still alive within my trousers than in our own. By the time the balloon had been folded up, three lorry loads of "Special Force" constables were on their way to the area from the provincial headquarters. A room had been prepared at the Arusha hospital for three. The Civil Aviation authorities had advised pilots flying over the district to keep a look-out for wreckage. In brief, that one African observer, that one teller of a very tall tale, had had his message flashed to every relevant corner of the administration, and many more besides. After all, "exploded" is a powerful word, and he had used it convincingly.

The broadcasting units helped to spread his story, and soon it was common knowledge. However, there were three people who were most gloriously ignorant of it. They were just bashing away, in turn, at nettles and thorns and shrubs and creepers, while trying to carve a path up the slope. When they did stop to wonder, they never dreamed for a moment of what in fact was occurring. Instead, they reserved all their curiosity for wondering where on earth they were.

CHAPTER NINETEEN

THE RETRIEVAL

THE amount of destruction we caused, in the shape of broken nettle trunks and well thrashed plants, not only enabled us to make progress but also, or so we thought, made it obvious there would be no difficulty in rediscovering the balloon. There was no need, we considered, to blaze this particular trail. After all, it did not exist before we had laboriously passed by. So we hit and thwacked and fell over and got stung and yelped and thwacked again as we made our way up the slope. The vegetation towered above us, except in the narrow crooked path we left behind.

After climbing 400 feet by the altimeter, we met the first of the buffalo tracks. The cloven hoof prints, and their size, proved how they had been made, and we talked and generally created noise so that any possibility of a meeting in those buffalo-size confines might be reduced. At times they were like dark tunnels, and we saw them much as a mole must see his mole-run. At other times they were more open, more like a shrew's track through a grassy field, and the sun dappled the ground. Occasionally, when at the base of some gigantic forest tree, we had to step over the wedge-shaped roots which ran up to the trunk like so many buttresses. Eventually, after 1,000 feet of climbing, and nearly three hours of walking, we suddenly found ourselves on that narrow rim road.

Naturally enough, there was not a soul in sight, nor any sound of one. The ground party, not Joan this time but two sets of Africans, had been told of our plan to land well beyond the far side of the crater. Our Gipsy and John's Land-Rover had intended to divide up the landing zone and search accordingly. Presumably, in dashing round the crater road, they had seen our contrary movements, and had then dashed back. Yet they could not have attempted to look for us in that jungle, even if they had seen roughly the point where, hawk-like, we had hurtled from the air. There was only one thing they could do, and that was to go back and forth from Wilkie's Point both along the rim road and along the better track leading up to the crater. In this way, and by covering two sides of the triangle in which we had landed, they would meet up with us wherever we chose to emerge.

However, they had quite a mileage to cover. As the temporary take-off site camp had been dismantled and abandoned, we set off instead for Wilkie's Point on foot to meet them there, or somewhere in between. This meant walking past that rhino's favourite wallow. Our approach was made most gingerly, for there is all the difference in the world between being biffed in a car—where one tends to laugh, and being biffed on foot when one would have less opportunity. Our steps suddenly took on more confidence when John caught sight of him sniffing the air half a mile away. All was well, and it was round the next bend that we met the Land-Rover. The distinctive kind of conversational bedlam to be heard everywhere in Africa broke loose with its customary joyful confusion.

Briefly, they said they were amazed we were not dead. We said we were delighted they had continued to patrol the area, despite their imaginings. Then, with conversation quite undiminished, with the same accounts being told over and over again, the three of us levered ourselves into the Land-Rover and went off to find the Gipsy. This did not take long, but the ensuing conversation did while everybody swapped everything they knew with an opposite number from the other truck. The delighted babel only hesitated when a police truck stopped on its way towards Karatu. We were in a part of the world where all trucks stop on meeting another, balloon flights or not, and the three policemen received a multifarious description of the day's events. They knew the flight had been about to take place, but had heard no more. They had certainly not heard any message from headquarters about it, although we did not ask them about this; and John concluded the conversation by asking them to tell their officer in charge that the flight had been concluded, and all occupants were safe.

Had we known of the alleged explosion, in fact had we known anything beyond what had happened, our message to those three policemen would have been different. As it was, they returned to Karatu to be peppered with questions about the balloon, and were asked about the explosion. Of this they knew nothing, for we had told them nothing. They could only say that we three were well. Therefore, the police sent out an addendum to the earlier message. "Balloon party rescued by ground crew. No one injured." People were later perplexed how 26,000 cubic feet of hydrogen could explode with a loud bang, and not succeed in injuring at least somebody; but the second report only seemed to emphasize the veracity of the first. Consequently, countless newspapers printed that a British balloon making an aerial safari over the big game herds of Africa had exploded and crashed near the world's largest crater, and the crew had been rescued uninjured. The message bore the stamp of the Reuters' News Agency.

However, while it was being freely circulated, the three of us were still blissfully unaware of the tidings. Ngorongoro has no telephone, and the solitary two-way radio to Arusha is only switched on twice a day, once at mid-morning, and once in the afternoon. That evening, with the "Special Force" lorries still grinding their way up country, with the Karatu treasury clerk presumably contentedly asleep, John opened a roughish bottle of dark red wine, and he, Douglas and I drank to a remarkable day. Our legs glowed from the nettle stings, and soon our systems were lulled by the coarse embrace of that crusty drink. The drive down the crater road, with its 2,000 feet of lethal possibilities, seemed less and less of a good idea; and so the day ended with three bodies lying, so to speak, where they dropped. Nevertheless, for ballooning seems to have this effect, not one of them stirred until the sun was high in the sky.

It was 11 o'clock when I drove round to the Crater Lodge to send off the weekly message to the *Sunday Telegraph*. Mr Dodds, the manager, was sitting with his head cocked towards the radio loudspeaker's shrieks and chatterings when I strolled in. He dropped his pencil, slapped his head, and shouted something into the room. Unfortunately, due to the radio, the space was already saturated with noise, and I learnt nothing. He then became rather speechless, not knowing where to begin; but eventually I learnt the story about our crash. Would I, therefore, speak to the Director of Civil Aviation, and the newspaper stringer in Arusha, and East African Industries (who had been asked why their gas had exploded), and Peter Champney (who had been asked practically everything else), and the Arusha Hospital, who were still uncertain how many beds were required.

It was a strange morning. Anyone who has ever worked a two-way radio link which is shared by fifty other subscribers will know quite how tenuous the connection can be. An engineer is explaining about a chamfered nut to some moron who cannot understand the message, but you chip in the moment he ends, and then someone barges in the instant you hesitate, and he talks at length about a fan-belt and a prop-shaft and a cam-shaft and a half-shaft while some nit-wit at the other end tries to take it down. Then you chip in again, but someone on roughly the same frequency in the Congo roars in with a combination of French and atmospherics that makes Arusha unintelligible to you, and you quite inaudible to Arusha. However, one way or another, I did speak to everyone, and managed to send 1,500 words to the paper. Then, stepping out of that asylum of a radio room, and breathing the air of insects and bird-song once again, I left the Crater Lodge and drove off to see how John and Douglas were getting on with the balloon.

The short answer is that they were not getting on with it. They had not been able to find it. This may seem ludicrous, and is indeed a fatuous state of affairs; but hundreds of buffaloes had been through the area during the night. John had a Masai tracker with him, as well as his normal retinue of drivers, assistants and clerks; but the tracker could naturally see no mere human footprints when herds of buffalo hooves had later passed that way. The day had ended without success.

This time Douglas and I returned to our camp beneath the fig-tree down in the crater. Kiari was there, and bountifully

191

pleased to see us again. As we had spent two nights on the top, one before the flight, and one after, he had had almost three days to himself in the crater. Having been born, and then brought up, in Nairobi, he was not entirely at ease with the wealth of fauna circling round that camp. At all times there was a good fire going, and at night he zipped himself into his tent with an airtight thoroughness. Once, later on in the trip, after he had unzipped it in the morning —although how he knew it was morning I never quite understood—he looked straight into the face of a lion looking straight at him. A couple of feet separated the two. There was a roar from the lion, and then the shriek of a zip from Kiari. At this the rest of us woke up, and saw from our own tents one lion walking slowly round Kiari's. There was no more noise from either of them. After a minute or so the lion walked off. After thirty minutes Kiari was persuaded to emerge, doubtless a very much older man, although no wiser, for he had always suspected all lions of having the worst of intentions towards him. In the three days of our absence at Ngorongoro, he had not even been approached; but his enthusiasm for seeing us again was intense, and he produced the best supper of his career in return. The tree-hyrax also screeched a welcome later on, in its own throat-rending fashion. We vowed not to leave them alone for so long in the future.

The next morning Douglas and I left camp early. The plan was to get to the top of the cliff road before anyone started coming down it. The narrowness of the road had enforced a regulation that times for going up and for going down should be distinct and separate. From dawn until 11 a.m. the track was for the sole use of those who wished to enter the crater. Therefore, Douglas and I set off as soon as possible after first light to reach the top before anyone should wish to come down. By this time we were fairly familiar with the road and did not mind unduly having to back down some particularly rough piece of it when need be, until reaching a place where two trucks could pass; but those who were in their rights, and travelling in the correct direction at the proper time, usually pointed out this fact

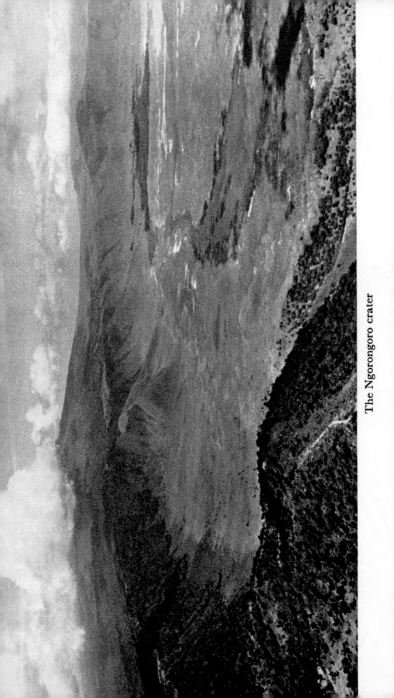

The Ngorongoro crater

Masai bowman with an irresistible urge

Burchell's zebra in the crater

with a certain vigour. Perhaps it would be a German truck-load, fresh from Frankfurt. "Vot are you at? This time, men go down, not come up."

The best plan, and to avoid this kind of conversation, was to drive up fast, and then to stop once in a while with the engine off. In this way a truck coming down could frequently be heard before it was seen, and it was possible to drive into some niche before the righteous ones actually arrived.

"Good morning," one would say, casually.

"Good mornink," they would say, in return.

On the day Douglas and I left camp early to look for the balloon we managed to get to the top before anyone had started on their way down. We then drove round to Wilkie's Point and on to our place of exit from the landing. John arrived at the rendezvous later on with a remarkable collection of people, plus a black labrador who loathed nettles, and a rifle. Two special police trackers had been borrowed, and they set off in front. The rest of us, with the heavily limping dog, followed them. It was a wearisome business. The trackers, examining bent blades of grass and slightly flattened earth, or any signs of our route, went slowly on their way. At every junction there were at least four separate paths to be inspected before the men could decide on one of them. Those of us following behind sat around while they made up their minds, and we took turns to comfort that miserable labrador.

Eventually the trackers admitted their defeat. They could find no more traces, and Douglas, John and I argued our own respective hunches. It was not a place for certainty of any sort. No tree seemed memorable. Every soup-plate nettle looked, and felt, just like its neighbour. We should have blazed our course, but had not foreseen the difficulty. Besides, it is not easy marking a route thwacked out from the undergrowth, and we had thought our very thwackings would be sufficient. The buffaloes had proved us wrong. While the three of us argued, it became clear that Douglas and I, for no reason we could put into words, had an idea it was the valley on the right. John and his trackers were plumping for the left-hand one. So we split up, with each party occasionally sending back envoys to report the lack of success. Finally, when Douglas and I were both convinced we were wrong, when we had climbed every climbable tree within reach, when the air was sweetly heavy with the sap of downtrodden nettles, we found it. An African shout from the middle of an ivy-wrapped perch somewhere above us was unmistakably the shout of success. Sure enough, 15 yards away, and quite untouched, was the basket and the balloon.

We all crowded round it, and fingered it, and laughed, and laughed even more when it began to rain. There was no question of carrying it back then, for the sun was low and the day was running out. Therefore, with our party making the point of our superior skill time and time again to the rival group when we met it, the whole contingent walked puffily up those 1,000 feet to the road, while the dog limped on all four legs behind it. The balloon was not one yard distant from its abrupt point of arrival, but we were a contented lot. The shame of having mislaid such a vast thing had been absolved. At least, we now knew where it was.

The next day, with twenty people to help us, we returned to the now well-trodden point of exit. The rhino, whose wallow lay slightly to the south, was on this occasion nowhere to be seen. With at least two trucks a day passing that spot, it had lost its former abandoned appeal, and he had left it. Our vast party had no difficulty in retracing the previous day's steps to the balloon, and once again the air was filled with African astonishment as everyone retold the story of our landing. There was no question of just a few men being able to handle the balloon fabric, for the going was much too severe. Therefore we laid it out in a straight line up the slope, and then put loops around it, such as a sausage-maker used to divide his meat. Under this great snake of balloon then stood ten men, who were on alternate sides, and they carried it on their shoulders. The basket, which formed the next most tricky item, had two poles strapped to its flanks. Thereafter, suspended from the shoulders of four men, it resembled the more traditional kind of African load. The net was carried by one pole and two men. Everybody else took pangas, and carved a larger way through the bush so that the main body of the caravan could get through. Next time, I said to myself, even though it had not been possible on this occasion, I will surely have to land in rather better country. It was Monday when we had flown. It was Thursday when the balloon was safely delivered out of the jungle.

Despite the considerable energies expended thus far, and the fantastic luck in having no one injured, we were still short of our goal. We still wished, and with a greater determination than ever, to fly quietly and gently over big groups of animals. We would have proved nothing until this had been done. All we had shown to date was that Africa's atmosphere had a hundred and one tricks up its voluminous sleeve. It probably had a few more, and we were likely to learn about them; but we had to discover more about the animals in the meantime. However, we had most definitely acquired great respect for the balloon. What else but a basket could have survived the indignities we had inflicted on ours? What else but a balloon could have landed three men travelling at 20 m.p.h. horizontally, and some 500 feet a minute vertically, right in the middle of primaeval forest, and left them standing there without a bruise to show?

As we lurched and skidded and jolted down the crater road that night, I decided that we had had enough of the rough country. Scenically, it was magnificent. Aerodynamically, it was treacherous. The crater was a superb thing to look at, and live in; but the contrary vortices and airflows caused by this piece of geological activity had been too much for a free-flying balloon. From now on we would stick to the plains. The great open areas would surely be more dependable, and the air above them less tortuous in its behaviour.

"I think we'll go to the Athi Plains next," I said.

"Uh-huh," said Douglas.

"Should be a good flight," he said, five minutes later.

I waited another five minutes, so as to be in phase.

"Should be," I replied.

"Yup," he said, somewhat hastily.

CHAPTER TWENTY

THE AFRICAN FILMS

On the following day a passing truck brought us our mail. Also a party travelling under the auspices of Ker and Downey, the safari firm, camped under the very next tree, scarcely 50 yards away. Civilization was catching up with us. One by one, and like inquisitive neighbours in any suburban area, the three of us thought of excuses for visiting their camp, and each brought back accounts of their furnishings. "Did you see that they had two refrigerators?" "Did you see how their iron works, and the table they've got for it?" "Look at that pile of tins already!" However, they were to leave after two days, and the envy, such as it was, had no time to manifest itself.

The letters were far more disturbing. That one treasury clerk had a lot to answer for. The story of the crash, and then the customary newspaper practice of printing minute denials, had caused many repercussions. People wanted to know what had happened, why the gas had exploded, whether the balloon had been at fault, whether it was true that we were uninjured, and if this was some form of cover story to conceal the real one. There was also news from Nairobi that the compressor situation was not as well as it should be, and from Arusha that the transport firm would not be able to collect our cylinders from the Saleh site, now that rain had fallen there. In short, it was time that I paid another visit to town. It is excellent living under a fig-tree but, administratively, it has its drawbacks.

Alan and Joan were due back any day, but they had not arrived when I set off. Douglas took me to the crater top, and from there I got a ride into Arusha. The driver was in a hurry, and there was no time for stopping. We hurtled round the Wilkie's Point bend, neglecting the road to the rhino and the take-off site, and then twisted down the curves leading to the Karatu plain. On going through the scattered and drawn-out village of Karatu itself, I longed to know who it was that had reported our explosion. Was it that man wearing the bright blue track suit with a tie round the neck? Or that one wearing a sort of mustard-coloured jacket with purple trousers, or him with a white toga, or that one just in a ragged pair of shorts? I longed to know. I swivelled round to have a last look at an exceedingly gaily dressed lot, but they gave me no clue. In the dim distance, half hidden in the haze, was a thin blue line of hills cut out against the sky. How that man had picked out our balloon among those Crater Highlands I do not understand. Perhaps he imagined the whole thing! Perhaps a blob swam across his vision, as blobs sometimes do. Whatever it was, he had told his tale and, what is more, he had been believed. So good luck to him, whether his clothes are mustard or purple, white or ragged grey; I, at least, shall not forget him.

Back in Arusha I visited the police, the hospital, the information department, the bank, the garage, the post office, the Parks office, the camera shop, the travel agency, and much else without having more than a short walk between each of them. Arusha is a most compact little town, with everything in easy reach of the visitor from out-of-town who wishes to arrange his affairs in a morning. Over the whole place is Mount Meru. This great, grey slab of a volcanic mountain is frequently not there, when the clouds are low everywhere, or when its own steep sides cause a mist around them. Every now and then, always surprisingly, it is suddenly there. Without any warning, as if it had erupted silently from the earth, a 14,979-foot mountain stands against the sky. Instead of the town's streets tapering away vaguely into the distance, they then abut most effectively against it.

That evening I met Hugh Lamprey again, game biologist, fellow Oxford zoology student, and pilot. He was flying a light aircraft to Nairobi the following morning, and I gladly accepted a lift. The trip began early, and the air was still calm when we took off from the Arusha strip. Flying again in this kind of machine was a strange experience. I had forgotten quite how deafening flight could be. I leant forward from the back seat whenever wishing to hear Hugh speak, and then shouted in return. Very soon we lapsed into the mime and dumb-show that is almost as effective, and less painful to the epiglottis. I was also intrigued by the savage buffeting, even at that hour of the day, as the propeller carved its way through the air. It was a very crude business, relative to the balloon. It was like square wheels as opposed to round ones. The machine was not part of the atmosphere, as we had been. It merely exploited it.

For the first part of the flight, and at the maximum angle, Hugh steered for the low-lying foot-hills to the west of Mount Meru, and thereby skirted the mountain. The machine was a perfectly competent type, but its rate of climb was pathetic beside that of a balloon. Steadily, and noisily, we were achieving two or three hundred feet a minute. Back over the Ngorongoro, even though I had been fighting against it, we had leapt up 3,000 feet in a single minute, and would probably have accelerated still more had I not been releasing gas as fast as I had dared. I think that a balloon could have competed favourably, over a limited course, with the fastest jet fighters of a few years ago in a straight struggle for the greatest number of feet climbed in any given minute from level flight.

Once over the saddle of foot-hills we dropped down, and then flew at 1,000 feet over much of the so-called marginal land lying in that area to the south-east of Nairobi. It was well populated with giraffe, and the long-necked antelope or gerenuk also live there. These animals live in many parts, and in regions where the countryside is much less barren; but when they and giraffe are the dominant species it is a depressing state of affairs. It is nice enough seeing them, but they both—together with the minute dik-dik—have an ability to survive in exceptionally arid bush conditions. Where they alone exist in reasonable numbers, the area is called marginal. It is a borderland between the support of life, and the lack of it. It is the half-way stage between desert and fertility.

We plopped down at Wilson Airport, Nairobi, narrowly

missing a blundering kite when doing so, and then went our separate ways. We were to meet the next day to fly back to the crater. I went straightway to the Director of Civil Aviation. He was the man in charge of flying through East African air, and I had been going through some curious aerobatics in his domain. One way and another, although mainly due to that long-sighted Karatu observer, I felt apologetic when I knocked on his door. My fears were dismissed, instantly. Instead I was invited to take part in the Nairobi air rally in ten days' time. The prevailing wind was from the north-east, and a flight from that city would take me straight over the Athi Plains. I accepted gratefully. A launching with all the assistance of an airport at hand had agreeable sides to it. Our various benefactors and helpers in that capital would see the balloon, and would be given captive ascents. Moreover, at the conclusion of all this, there would be those flat plains to the leeward, and they were what we now desired.

That evening I took John Bridgman, our active man in Nairobi, and his wife Margaret out to dinner at the Pagoda. There was a certain difficulty in doing so. In the afternoon I had seen East African Industries, and had worked out our gas needs for the Nairobi flight. I had also arranged some insurance, tardily, and despite the accounts of our trips. I had then paid many bills, and had generally rushed around; but I had been temporarily floored by the necessities for an evening out. When living in a crater, much goes by the board. On being transported abruptly to a different world, I had to borrow socks and a tie from John, a respectable shirt from one neighbour, and a jacket from another, before being able even to get inside the restaurant. Nairobi may be superbly placed right in the middle of a huge under-developed continent, and there are certainly wild lions within six miles of the centre; but there are few features within the city reminding you of such facts. However, it was a most excellent meal. Chinese waiters were serving Europeans in an American style mostly with eastern food in Africa.

Hugh and I took off at 1 p.m. on the following day, and

flew first over that Athi area. It was generally flat, but frequently there came deeply eroded gullies, exciting to look at, but depressing in their destruction. There was such a tenuous relationship between man, the animals and the rest of nature when nineteenth- and twentieth-century man moved in to the area that disruption of the old order was inevitable. The great scars beneath us were the wounds of over-grazing. The red rivers were flowing with soil, and making this particular circle as vicious as any other.

Beyond the plains was the Rift Valley. There is nothing else like it on the surface of the Earth, but this section near Nairobi was different to the Manyara bit now indelibly engraved on at least three minds. Instead of one big cliff wall, there were many cliffs, each perpendicular, and each dropping the level of the land down another couple of hundred feet. Down in the bottom there was Lake Magadi, and then Lake Natron. Both are soda lakes, with the Magadi one being exploited. A special railway carries the soda away, and has a difficult time among those cliffs. No child ever takes his model railway up the stairs, but the Magadi track does just that, and must cover ten times the distance, from beginning to end, that actually separates the two points. It cannot emulate the crow, as we did, and as we began the long climb towards the Crater Highlands.

It was a most fantastic journey, for after the geological contortions of the Rift Valley, there came the 9,443 feet peak of L'Engai, the area's active volcano. We edged noisily by its silent summit. The top looked something like the old glass type of orange squeezer, with a smaller pointed cone coming from the middle. Its sloping sides are as steep as its rocky lava will allow, and the way up is difficult. The mountain can be climbed but, like Mount Kilimanjaro which is not so far away, any climber has to take advantage of the chilliest hours when the loose and difficult scree is held together by frost. I think it important to see active volcanoes from time to time. They are most blatant reminders that we live our days on the thin crust of a planet which has by no means settled down from its fiery birth.

Shortly after nudging past L'Engai's cone, the Mountain

of God according to the Masai, we were over the wide sweeps of the Crater Highlands. These link together several dead volcanoes, with Ngorongoro being one of them. Embagai is another, perhaps the most beautiful for it is well proportioned, with its woody sides leading down to a deep and permanent lake. And then we were over the final wall, and swooping about above Ngorongoro. We could see no sign of the others and, after buzzing the empty camp beneath the tree, landed near by. The animals had scattered on our first pass over the chosen area, and did not run in the way of the final touch down.

Hugh switched off the engine, and we climbed out into that remarkable place. I do not think one could ever cease to be amazed at it, but arriving in one hour and thirty minutes from Nairobi heightens its qualities most dramatically. Animals are all around, and beyond are the dots of countless more, and beyond them are those towering walls. At no time of the day does the crater look the same as at any other moment. Huge shadows retreat as the day advances, and then slink down again when the sun loses its power. It has all the symmetry of a perfect shape, and all the wonder of an untouched world. Like a ruin it combines the merits of having been created, and then having reverted to something finer still. It is a place of fabulous beauty.

After a while Alan turned up having been given a lift in a passing Land-Rover because his own had become partially engulfed in the mud over by the landmark known as Figtree Kopje. Hugh took off, circled like any pelican to gain height, and then disappeared over the crater wall while we collected the Gipsy from camp. Afterwards, in the most magnificent brown light of the evening, Alan and I drove out to the beleaguered vehicle. On the way, apart from the normal hazards of driving through the place, we had been delayed by a family of lions. A scraggy old male looks scarcely more interesting than a scraggy old animal of any species, but a lioness in good condition is a seemingly perfect piece of creation. As she walks about, being nudged by some cub, being moved by an unknown impulse just to get up and plump down five yards away, her muscles work with exquisite finesse. As a piece of engineering, and of colouring, and of grace, a lioness can scarcely be matched. Perhaps her rhythm and power tend to be high-lighted by the fact that, in almost any group of lions, one or two of them are not in such excellent condition. In a system of predators and prey, particularly when the carnivores exist communally, it is possible for some of them to survive in a weakened state for far longer than the prey on which they feed. A visibly sick wildebeest or gazelle has only a few more hours to live, unless some remarkable recovery is effected rapidly. An aged lion can survive for years provided he is with a community prepared to kill for him.

It took quite a time to extract the truck. On arriving there I had removed my Nairobi-polished shoes, and my new socks, but my Nairobi-pressed trousers had to suffer as I stepped out into a foot and a half of water. It seemed difficult adjusting the two lives. Despite the fact that we had two winches, and one unstuck truck, all of us splashed around for a couple of hours before the mud gave way. A vital bit of equipment on these occasions is the Tanganyika jack. This is no ordinary jack, as its name implies, but a barely liftable contraption of wood and iron that has only one role to play. Under almost any conditions, provided it has another block of wood to stand on, it can lift any bit of a truck. Its hook is strong, and the method is to lift up each wheel in turn. In the cavity these wheels have dug for themselves almost anything other than mud should be interred, and they will then have something on which to grip, even momentarily. Without the invention of the Tanganyika jack the number of man-hours stuck in the mud would increase immeasurably. Without ours on that occasion we would have been sucked dry by insects. I have never known the air so thick with six-legged forms as it was at dusk that day. They flew everywhere, into mouths and into eyes, and those with a suitable proboscis drank well. Fortunately they were a local manifestation. On driving back towards camp we left them behind.

Instead we encountered hundreds of spring hares. They danced about in front of the head-lights, with their big hind legs prancing them along, and in an area where nothing of them could be seen in the daytime. These nocturnal creatures, about the size of rabbits, and with the limb proportions of a jerboa, almost ask one to leap from the truck and try to catch them. There are three reasons against this idea. One; the crater is well equipped with lions and others who extend no similar invitations. Two; the spring hares browse near their holes, and these pitfalls are large enough to contain one ankle. Three; even if you do not break a leg, you will not catch a spring hare. At least, we never did, and we tried hard enough.

When in Nairobi I had despatched a large quantity of the film we had already exposed. For some reason, that first night after my return, we argued about the ethics involved in photography, particularly of animals. Alan told tales of the old days when the film men had first brought their cameras to the continent. Then, or so the stories said, Africa had been painted as savage and raw as possible. Human clothes had been stuffed full of zebra meat, tucked into sleeping-bags and placed in tents. With the cameras clicking, the celluloid had captured the frightening spectacle of a lion removing and then eating a man. Such tricks, and others, are now forbidden by the game authorities, for lions must not think of tents or sleeping-bags as food containers. The film men thought it proper to portray an Africa that people wished to see, rather than one which existed.

Alan said this wish to see "the real Africa" was still considerable. It was also difficult to achieve. "What's the good of going to film pygmies who've seen you before? They wear vests, and you can see they do by the vest-patterns sunburnt on their bodies. They come running up, asking for money, and practically telling you what exposure to use."

"But they're Africa whether they wear vests or dinner-jackets."

"Sure," he replied. "But that's an altogether different type of film you're making. Most people don't want that. You must get pygmies the same colour all over, if you're going for pygmies. You must get your animals without roads or cars in the background. If there's going to be a house anywhere, it's got to be a thing of mud and straw. It can't have tiles on it, or a gravel path."

"But suppose a real lion in a real bit of Africa does really walk past a car," I said.

"Well, that's too bad," Alan continued. "Things should be organized better. Get the other side of the lion, or something. I agree it's difficult knowing where to draw the line. Some people organize everything, and practically bring the animals to Africa. They stack up their car somewhere in Nairobi, and say how they're going to search the Northern Frontier District for a rare beast. Five miles later, having found an empty bit of country, they get out looking suitably weary. Five miles later on they look wearier still, and the tension mounts. Finally, having secreted the animal in something looking like its customary lair, they get out of their car and proceed to find it. All very African. All as bogus as hell."

"Surely the whole film business is bogus?" I answered. "When you cut from a long shot to a close-up, and then get round the other side of it, and jerk instantly to an ultra close-up from there with no shot of a camera in view, well, what's supposed to be taking the pictures? There's a great pretence that no one's wielding any camera anywhere. So why worry too much about reality?"

"If people start disbelieving," said Douglas, "and wondering where the cameraman got to, then it's no good.

"You've got to strive for reality of the thing you're actually shooting," Alan went on, "even if it's hard to get. You've got to know what the animal is likely to do next, and prepare yourself accordingly. Animals spend most of their time not being interesting. You've got to be on hand when they do do something that's good for the camera. You can't fake it when it happens, but there's no harm in encouraging it to happen. If bushbabies eat grasshoppers, there's no harm in putting bushbabies near grasshoppers and filming the result. The fact that it's happening in broad daylight, and bushbabies are nocturnal, is too bad. Night-time feeding of that sort just has to go by the board."

And so it went on, with an occasional shriek from the hyrax just to remind us of that particular piece of reality. I myself think most animal photographers jealously guard their reputations, and exert patience and knowledge rather than subterfuge to get their pictures. Even so, they must long at times for a different code.

One day we saw a blind yearling wildebeest from a distance, and then watched four lions have a go at it. The wretched yearling eluded them time after time, for the lions had poor ideas about interception, and it still had quite a turn of speed. The longing to tee everything up, to acquire the rare prize of an actual kill on film was almost irresistible. In fact, a savage downpour made the struggle invisible, and we retreated to camp. Later that evening, when the rain had stopped, we heard the delirious whoopings and near-giggles of a group of hyenas. As we approached with a spotlight, two lions faded away and left their kill to the jackals and hyenas. We looked at the victim, and saw it was the same blind wildebeest. The inevitable had happened without us teeing it up an hour or so before its time. Yet, sympathy for the poor yearling apart, it would have been wrong to engineer the killing. It is wildly frustrating to leave things to chance, and to nature; but then it is nature, after all, that one happens to be filming.

CHAPTER TWENTY-ONE

THE AIR RALLY

Six days later we left that camp beneath the fig-tree on our way to the air rally. In the intervening period we had continued to make the film, for there was nothing to be done about the balloon until another gas consignment was ready, and that had been booked for the Nairobi flight. We had also driven right across to the other side of the crater, up the more inaccessible north wall, and to the lonely village of Nainokanoka. We were the first to go along the track for several months, and it was in poor shape; but the country-side was magnificent with a softness that is rare in Africa. At the rest hut, a comfortable shack kept warm by the hay stuffed into its rafters, we lit a huge log fire, and occasionally made forays into a night of startling clarity for more wood. Earlier inhabitants had even burnt the outhouse lavatory roof, but we were not as desperate as they had been. However, there was something Neronian and intriguing about the thought of a person sitting there in that rondavel of a room with the roof blazing warmly above him.

We spent a second night at that place, having passed the day walking to the crater of Embagai. I had seen it from Hugh's aircraft, and already knew some of its wonders; but the joy of walking over the tussocky grass, with zebras whinneying all around, with solitary wildebeest taking turns to hurtle down the slope, was something I had imagined only inadequately. I had also forgotten quite how exhausting it can be walking at a high altitude, and the crater rim was above 10,000 feet. The effortless ways of the balloon, and the disdain it had shown for the problem of changing height, had not acted as a reminder that mere muscles require more air to feed them when it is rarefied. On the climb my lungs sucked it in and blew it out again offering scarcely any opportunity for the precious oxygen to be absorbed.

They alone worked overtime, while the rest of me slowed down appreciably. I contented myself with putting one foot slowly after the other, and wondering how a more efficient pulmonary system could have been introduced in evolution. After all, the fishes have a through-way method, and do not have to blow the water out through the same small hole by which it has just come in. The fault lay with the air-bladder, that convenient stabilizing device. Had it not acted as a primitive lung for the first mud-based fishes to survive and become creatures of the land, something better might have been adapted from the gills. As it was, that Devonian mistake had led to the general tetrapod employment of a system which most plainly has its drawbacks. At least, that was how I felt as I panted with unceasing fervour to the lip of Embagai.

As with all mountains, the effort was more than worth-while. We did not walk down to the lake at the bottom, but lay about in the soft grass on the rim, savouring the breeze which blew over it. Birds must get a pleasure out of flying, for some kites were also enjoying that same current of air. A few yards above us, with nothing more than an occasional twitch of their tail feathers, they hovered unendingly. Then, with no obvious adjustment of the controls, they would swoop away, and poise themselves over some other identical spot. It was while we were up there that the evening came. This is not an abstract man-made division of the day, at least not so far as tropical latitudes are concerned. Quite suddenly the sun loses its strength. At the same moment, as if the world had been in black and white beforehand, colours break out everywhere. The hills become blue, the water black or silver, and the hard dry dusty earth the most brilliant shades of brown. Evening has arrived, and with it even the air seems to change its substance.

On the evening of the following day we were driving back across the crater floor. It had been a long drive, and at the familiar Figtree Kopje I decided to get out and stretch my legs. They were then nearly stretched for good. The grass around those three isolated trees was about 2 feet high, and I was happily striding through it when a lion suddenly snarled at me. It was a well-maned male, and the last I saw of him was the animal hurriedly getting to his feet. In this type of incident, according to the books and the wardens, it is vital to stand still, and unflinchingly stare back at it. I failed utterly. It was the noise that had most unnerved me, and this had sent me back a pace or two almost before I had seen the lion. So I was already in retreat before I knew what had happened. The moment for an unflinching stare had gone and the lion, according to the others, made a couple of quick steps towards me. It then saw them, and sheered off into the grass. I was back in the truck in no time, laughing idiotically, and amazed by a complete but temporary inability to turn the ignition key. It is easy to forget the power of something like a lion as it lolls casually around in your viewfinder. It is as well to be reminded of the fact from time to time.

Two days later we were in Nairobi. It was so simple, relative to Ngorongoro, making preparations for the flight. A building firm delivered the sand at the airport. East African Industries produced the gas, and Express Transport delivered it. Various air scouts were laid on to act as ground-crew, and flying control offered every assistance with regard to meteorological predictions. A temporary snag was the complete disappearance of part of the wooden valve. In the crater this would have been a disastrous discovery. In Nairobi, with Alan on his home ground, it was just an inconvenience. A man who normally sold Jaguar cars, Peter Walker, effected a perfect repair out of some 7-ply wood and a couple of lengths of rubber. Even so, despite the assistance on every side, despite unparalleled facilities so far as our expedition was concerned, I laid out the balloon at the airport on the afternoon before the flight with something amounting to dread. The African flights had been remarkable and amazing; but they had also been more dangerous than I had ever imagined. No one had been hurt, let alone killed; but luck had been with us disproportionately. Convenient dead trees, unaccountably soft landings, and miraculous events could not be counted on for always. We could not get away with it, or so I constantly felt, for ever. The hazards involved might one day prove extreme.

A couple of boys rode up to help, as they put it. This meant sitting on their bikes, and asking questions. They were both European children.

"Are you the one who's going up in a balloon?"

"Yes, with two others."

"And is this your balloon?"

"Yes."

"What about you taking us?"

"No room."

"Is it dangerous?"

"Sometimes."

"Is there a chance of you being killed?"

"A bit of a chance, I suppose."

"Huh," said the brighter one, "that would make five in two days."

"Why? Who are the other two?" I asked, and stopped doing what I had been doing.

"Oh, haven't you heard? One fell off a lorry this morning in the parade, and the other fell off a rope ladder hanging from an aeroplane. He was practising for the air rally."

"And where did this happen?" I asked, holding a piece of rope limply in one hand.

"Over that way. You could almost have seen it from here. We didn't. We got here too late. You see he was hanging on this ladder, and then he just fell. He had a safety belt on, but it broke or something. Anyway, he fell, and got killed. The other one happened in town. You see he fell off a lorry, and then got run over by another lorry. So he was killed too."

The boys mulled over the story they had just told, and then returning to the questioning.

"Do you really think you might get killed tomorrow? I mean, might it burst or something when you're high up? Or might you fall out, or what?"

I doubted both events, but unconvincingly, for they continued to discuss the chances of another death, or another three, until they abruptly left.

"So long. I hope you don't get killed."

"So long."

We were scheduled, according to the rally programme, to take off during the lunch interval. In this way we would be able to take our time, because balloon launchings have an inborn unpredictability about them, and at that time we would not worry flying control unduly as we sauntered off downwind. It is the law of the air that everything must give way to balloons, but it was wisest to make certain that the minimum number of aircraft should be on the circuit when we took off.

On the Sunday morning of the rally we turned on the gas at 9 a.m. The day looked windy, and I felt the sooner we went at the start of the lunch hour the better. I had no wish to be on the ground when the day's heat was at its most vindictive. To give some protection to the balloon against the wind, the inflation site was to one side of a big hangar. As the balloon grew, so did the wind get up, and scouts running back and forth from flying control brought increasingly alarming measurements of its strength from the man on duty there. I decided to take off even before the allotted lunch-time if this were possible. It would be too humiliating, and wildly expensive, to deflate the balloon just because the wind was strong. "Never fly when the wind is above 15 knots," Jan Boesman had said. "It is now gusting to 25 knots," said the latest boy scout.

Then came a shout from Douglas at the cylinders. The gas had run out. Someone had miscalculated badly. I looked up at the balloon. We needed at least another 3,000 cubic feet. It was a time for fast action, and everything clicked as it rarely does. I looked desperately around, and saw the gas man himself, the man in charge of the electrolysis plant that had been supplying us.

"Have you got any more gas already bottled?"

"Yes. about 3,000 cubic feet."

"Can I have it?"

"Yes, but we have no transport on a Sunday."

Alan pointed out a lorry over by a pub called the Dam Busters. We rushed over there. The vehicle had Sikh Saw

Mills painted on the door. We hurried into the pub. There were two Sikhs at a table.

"Can we borrow your lorry?"

"Yes, but why?"

I explained why on the way. Various people had also clambered aboard, including the gas man.

"Open the gates," he shouted, when we got there.

"Open the gates again," he shouted two minutes later, when we had stowed the cylinders on the lorry as if they were so much thistledown. And we were back at the airfield once more within half an hour of running out of gas. Certainly an inflation at Nairobi had its compensations, even if the hot plain it stood in had its winds.

"It's now gusting to 30 knots," said a boy scout.

We had the gas in the balloon very quickly. Then, with as much haste as possible, I went through the final routine of attaching the basket. It all went well, but this last manoeuvre adds another 15 feet to the height of the balloon. The hangar was no longer much of a windbreak, and we swayed tremendously. The three of us climbed into the basket, while the orange shape above did its best to touch the ground on either side. It was difficult maintaining balance as we stowed everything aboard.

"Could you hand me that camera," said Douglas quietly, at one point, and someone picked it up from the tarmac where it had landed.

"Gusting to 35," said a high-pitched voice from somewhere.

"It's time we went," I said, and heaved bags into the waiting hands of air scouts.

We then gave a great lurch over the ground, covering 25 yards or more, and scattering people wildly. The ground crew rushed up to hang on again. I poured out half a sack, waited until we were nearly upright, pulled open the mouth of the balloon, and cried, "Let go."

They did, and off we went. The swaying stopped immediately, and the wind with it. The calm of a balloon flight was with us instead. We were gaining no height, and so

I threw out the other half of that sack. With customary ease we rose quickly over a Beverley, and the world of turmoil faded rapidly away.

"Well, we made it," said Douglas, as was his custom; but this time the phrase had a different ring to it. On such a blustery take-off anything might have happened, for ropes are being mightily strained, and pressures are very uneven. One sudden gust in an unexpected direction, and things could have started to snap. I remembered Boesman again. "The safest place is the air. It's on the ground that things can break."

Those breathless reports from flying control were being vindicated by the speed we were moving over the earth. Our height was good, 700 feet up, but we were travelling at about 30 miles an hour. Unfortunately, as we quickly realized, we were not going quite right for the Athi Plains. If the wind had backed by 10 degrees, our course would have been right. As it was, we left Wilson Airport, for Karen, and then headed straight for the Ngong Hills. We would have to make do with them. They certainly did not have the flatness I had hoped for, but at least they were a conservation area and stocked with game.

Alan lived at Karen. This means he turned up there once every month or so, dealt with the mail, saw to his menagerie, had a bath, and prepared to move off somewhere else. So he pointed out the features of the area that passed, most rapidly, beneath us. The various overspills from Nairobi then vanished, and we moved instead over primitive farmland. We shouted at the Africans in the fields, and they would look everywhere for the voice except directly above them. Finally, we reached the soft slopes of the Ngongs. These are largely covered with a forest reserve, and we saw buffalo moving among the trees. There were eland, and we stalked quietly up on them at 300 feet above the ground. There was a hacking noise coming from somewhere, and suddenly we saw him. A man was helping himself to wood, and safely deep in the reserve.

"I see you," Alan shouted in Swahili. "And who said you could cut trees in a reserve?"

I have never seen anyone move so fast. He was under a bush in no time.

"I see you under that bush," said Alan. "You might as well give yourself up."

Naturally, this big talk on our part could not be sustained. At 30 miles an hour he and his bush were left rapidly behind, and the first piece of forestry surveillance by balloon was over. As the slope was rising steadily, and we were not moving up with it, I threw out a little sand to make certain that we did. This had no immediate effect, and I threw out some more. The balloon continued horizontally on its way. I threw out more and more, and relentlessly the hill rose up before us. It seemed that the airstream was not undulating over the hill, but going straight into it. It was then, presumably, bouncing over the hill, and we were in for a rough time. I threw out more sand, but with as little effect as before.

"I think we are going to make what is called an intermediate landing," I said.

And, most emphatically, that is what we did. A little farm appeared dead ahead. There were five people grouped by a hut, and they were surrounded by a rather meagre stand of maize. Our trail rope rasped through the field to one side of them as we made our approach.

"Fantastic upward shot of goats," said Alan, as he recorded one of the rarer sequences ever filmed from a balloon.

"Look at those people!" said Douglas. "They're not moving an inch. Heh, Jambo to you! Jambo!"

And with that we hit the ground with a fearful thump. There was a moment while we remained poised on it, and then with a whoosh the balloon lifted us up again to carry us on our way.

"They still haven't moved," said Douglas, sorting himself out from the bottom of the basket. "Kwa heri. Goodbye. It'll be a long time before another balloon lands in your compound. Kwa heri."

As I had suspected, the airstream was ramming the mountain, and not gliding gently over it. Even though I had not been able to prevent the intermediate landing our bounce took us up to 3,000 feet, and we soared over the Ngong Hills with plenty of room to spare. Like fast water meeting a boulder in mid-stream, the airflow leapt over those hills and we went with it.

On the other side of the narrow range, as might be imagined, we started to descend. This was reasonable, and I let it happen. At a quite comfortable 300 feet a minute we dropped down beyond the Ngongs. Then, when we were roughly the same altitude as their highest point, and about a couple of miles from them, the balloon went mad. The basket began to twist back and forth like the balance wheel of a watch. At the same time it swung this way and that, and we all held the edge. Up above us the fabric around the mouth was slapped about by the same contorted wind that had a hold on us. It was an incredibly nasty feeling.

Suddenly it stopped, and we were left as steady as before. We had met something quite unknown in the Holland of my lessons. It was a feature of airflow near mountains that is greatly respected even by pilots of conventional aircraft. It was an aerial wave, and its effects had been most pronounced. Imagine that boulder in midstream again. If the water goes over it smoothly, the surface downstream will also be smooth; but if the stream is too fast, or the boulder too great an obstacle, the smooth flow will be broken up. The subsequent turbulence will not be random, and there will be the undulations of a regular wave going through it. It was precisely such a flow that we had met, and suffered.

"I am afraid we'll meet that again," I said. "It's a wave, and we'll next meet it when twice as far from the mountain as we were the first time."

Sure enough, once again we were going through those ugly motions and at the predicted time. Douglas, who had had an admirably laconic attitude to previous mishaps, looked more frightened than I had ever seen him. Alan gripped tightly on the wicker rim, as we swayed to and fro, and said he didn't like it, he didn't like it at all. Oddly enough, although my stock of courage was running low, I did not mind that particular bit of aerial waltzing. Its very predictability, after the first time, made it less fearful. I remember feeling far more concerned that I might be sick if the pendulum swung much longer.

The third buffeting was much less strong than the second, and we did not even feel the fourth. By that time, just as before the hills, we were once more being taken towards the ground. I threw out sand as before, and yet more sand; but the plummeting went on. Another diving airstream had control of us. Like the previous occasion, I could have thrown out so much sand, perhaps three entire bags, that we would have risen despite the down-flow; but our subsequent ascent would have been rocket-like. As it was I tried to compromise, to soften the fall by handfuls of sand, and then to hit the ground at the sort of speed that would injure no one. On this occasion, the second of our intermediate landings, we hit the ground well and truly, and no one was injured, but the balloon did not rise again as quickly as before.

Instead, and at the same old 30 miles an hour of the wind, we proceeded to career through the thorn bushes that were growing there. All three of us were instinctively well crouched inside the basket as it tore its way through that wilderness of bush. Any arm outside would have had the skin scraped off it in a trice, and so no arms were outside. We just huddled there, aghast at the noise and what might be happening to the supporting ropes; and then were quietly lifted out of the maelstrom of thorn. Not one of us had a scratch, and those manilla ropes from Zanzibar looked as sound as ever.

Once more we soared up high, and once more were looking down from a softly creaking perch 3,000 feet above the land. Another range of hills was looming up, as high as the Ngongs, but with sharp edges to them in place of curves.

"Those are the Ol Esageti Hills," said Alan. "We can't land on them, and there's no track even on the other side. I think we should get down here, somewhere near this road to Olorgasaile."

I agreed. The flight would do damage to something before very long. It should best be curtailed as quickly as possible. We arched gently over at the top of the 3,000-foot bounce, and then began gliding down towards a thorny region lying on the slope leading up to that next range of hills. I threw out sand to keep the descent under reasonable control, and felt liberal with our stocks, for they did not have long to last—or so I thought. I never let the descent build up to more than 200 feet a minute, and we crossed the road about 500 feet up. The downward speed increased slightly, and I threw out two more hands.

Suddenly, I realized this had been a mistake. The descent flattened out more rapidly than I had anticipated. The ground came nearer, with its liberal growth of those vicious thorn bushes, but about 25 feet above them we drew level with the ground, and then rose steeply up. I had misjudged the landing run. The interception of basket and earth had not been made. I thought quickly of releasing gas, but there now was not enough room to land in. A cliff was approaching. To try and land would mean hitting that cliff. There was nothing to do, except let the balloon go on rising. "Sorry about that," I said. "A hand too many. We'll have to come down somewhere else."

The other two looked wistfully back at the road, and then ahead to see what else was coming our way. As was now our custom, it was not long before we were surveying the world again from high above it. In that region of escarpments, and mountain ranges, and cliffs, and all the rest of the shapes that make up the Rift Valley, we were being bounced about like any humble cork. That massive airflow coming over the Nairobi plain had been well churned up since leaving it, and we were following its wild prancings with little opportunity for doing otherwise. A basket is a strange place in which to feel afraid. You stand there, wearing ordinary clothes, and leaning in an ordinary fashion against the edge, and everything in the garden is apparently quite normal. The view is immense. The air is clean. The sun is bright. No one is even scratched or bruised. There is water and food by your feet; but on that day none of us could touch a drop. Our throats were dry, and had also shrivelled unhelpfully. We spoke quite a lot, but tended to make the same point more than once.

"We mustn't land on those hills," said Alan. "You could never get a truck up them."

"We might have to land on them," I replied. "I don't think we should do another bounce. If we come down there we'll have to land."

Douglas said nothing, except to refer every now and then to that twisting from the aerial waves. It, in his opinion, had been unforgettable. After each collision with the ground, it always took a certain time before we became organized once more. I myself used to have the altimeter in one hand and the larger rise-and-fall indicator wedged into a trouser pocket. The other two had their camera equipment, and such things as the field-glasses either in their hands or in pockets. The savage impact with the earth, or just the preparation for the encounter, coupled with some hasty scrabbling for another sack of sand, meant complete disorder afterwards. Has anyone seen the Arri lens hood? Or that film I've just changed? Whose is this? And so forth. The sandbags were the principal nuisance, apart from the jolt itself, for they added to the confusion when brought up, even gently, from the bottom of the basket. The traditional picture of sacks strung round outside is wrong. The rasping thorn bushes had proved that point. Not one of them would have remained on board had we followed the allegedly customary practice.

There were still three sacks left when we started descending again after that abortive attempt at a landing. From our 3,000-foot perch it was only too plain that the current was taking us towards the hills, and not more comfortably beyond them. So I threw out sand, and our descent relaxed.

"Look," said Alan, "you'll never get a truck up there."

He was visibly right. It was going to be hard enough climbing down, without the encumbrance of a balloon as well. I threw out more sand, because the wind seemed adamant in taking us there. By the time we were 500 feet above that exceptionally laval and unpleasant-looking region, I had used up an entire 30-lb. sack and was reaching for another.

Then things began happening very quickly. I saw that the plateau we were heading for ended in a steep cliff down. Should we land on the plateau, or go on? I threw out half another sack. Surely this would make us rise? But it didn't, another collision was imminent.

"Here, Alan, grab this last sack. Throw it out when I say. We'll just have to turn this into a landing. Hell, it's rough. Don't throw it yet. I'll pull the rip. Look out, it's coming. Look out!"

And then we hit, brutally. I saw the edge of a huge rock of lava, and remember fumbling for the rip-panel cord. A bush came, and I ducked. And the others ducked. I was down in the bottom of the basket, trying to see through it how high we were. We were at least 50 feet up, and then the cliff went by. Had I ripped? If so, why were we going up so fast? If the rip had half worked, now we were over the cliff, we had a long way down in which to build up speed. But we still seemed to be going up. That was obvious, even though I had no idea where the altimeter had got to.

"Has anyone seen the altimeter?"

"Oh, I thought you'd gone."

Apparently, both Douglas and Alan assumed, despite the minuteness of that basket, that I had fallen overboard when we had hit the side of the rock. Neither of them had said anything about it to the other. They had both kept the fact to themselves. As we rose up above the world again, the situation showed itself to be distinctly nasty. During that brief intimacy with the land, it was Alan who had been flung out. At least, we gathered so from the fact that there was a cut below his knee. Nothing in the basket could have done the damage, and he remembered hitting something hard. During this manoeuvre, whatever it was, he had dropped the sandbag naturally enough. I, for my part, had used up the last of mine. No wonder we were going up so fast. Every particle of ballast had gone overboard. Not one ounce of it was left to break our fall the next time. Also, due to its loss, we would eventually be coming down from an altitude even greater than before.

As we looked around at our possessions, and made the customary search for lost objects, we gradually realized that much more had gone beyond the one sandbag. A water-bottle was missing. So were a couple of Pepsi-Colas, and Alan's camera battery had gone from his belt. In short, due to this extra loss in weight, we were about to go up even more than we had first imagined. From a far greater height we would be coming down with no sand whatever on board. No one else, no other agency, could help us. We were quite alone in our predicament, alone in a frighteningly large quantity of sky. We all watched the altimeter in a strangely detached sort of way. Its needle moved steadily round and round. Eventually, some ten minutes after that most disastrous touch-down of them all, it stopped. We were well over a mile above the hot, brown dust of the Rift Valley floor. The altimeter had stopped at 9,500 feet.

CHAPTER TWENTY-TWO

THE MANYATTA

A MAN who has taken some tasteless poison, the effects of which will not be apparent for an hour or so, must consider his situation is curiously unreal. On the one hand he feels perfectly fit, and on the other he knows that he will soon be disastrously ill. If he does nothing, and just waits, the poison will get him in time. Even if he does try to do something, but knows there is no antidote, the poison will win in the end. So, for that fatal interregnum, he stands there, feeling perfectly well in body, and wondering what will happen next.

To a certain extent we felt like that man. There was nothing wrong with us, save that we were in a basket poised momentarily well over a mile above the ground. Alan's knee, although it was still bleeding slightly, was the only injury to date. It seemed to emphasize, by its relative triviality, the colossal damage that might be coming our way. He had more blood on his shoulder, but there proved to be no wound beneath it. Somehow it must have been put there by his knee. In any case, what were scratches and cuts when the altimeter read 9,500 feet, and all the sand had gone?

There were two courses of action open to us. The first was to make use of the balloon's parachuting capabilities. It was a practice which had been known to save lives. The method was to cut the rope that held the mouth towards the ring, a rope which normally prevented the bottom of the balloon ever becoming concave. Then the rip-panel had to be pulled open. In theory, if all went well, the gas would rush out and the fabric would stay behind in the net. With good fortune this empty fabric would fashion itself into an umbrella within the net, and this shape would act as a brake. If all did not go well, the gas would leave and the fabric would not form an umbrella above the balloonists' heads. It would end up in an untidy manner somewhere within the net, and would not work well as a brake against the air. In this case the whole device of balloon and crew would hit the ground too hard for them to survive.

The second course was to jettison everything available, and hope this was sufficient to keep the descent within reasonable limits. On board, apart from the lack of sand, we did have a certain amount of stuff which could be thrown away without too much concern, particularly when lives were endangered. Therefore, to assess the situation better, we put on one side all such objects. They included the empty sandbags, the remaining water-bottles, a packet of unknown and unopened food Joan had given us at the last moment, the cine film stock, both exposed and unexposed, and one or two containers used for parts of the camera equipment. In all, I suppose the weight of this motley lot was about 30 lb. In a second heap, which we did not bother to create physically, there were the articles of rather more worth. These included all the cameras, their lenses, the instruments, our shoes, and the field-glasses. If the first batch proved inadequate, we would quickly have to start upon the second. An Arriflex with a 400-foot magazine clamped to it, and three long-focus lenses screwed to the front, is a costly and beautiful piece of work; but it is heavy. I foresaw no hesitation in throwing it out if the need came.

As there seemed quite a lot to get rid of, either expensively or less so, I decided to abandon the parachute idea and rely on the jettisoning. Certainly, the choice was easier to take, even had we been less well equipped with available flotsam. The courage required to pull the rip in mid-air, to be rid of all that supporting gas, must be immense. I, for one, doubted if I possessed a sufficient stock of it, and was heartily relieved when it did appear that the second course was feasible.

Up at 9,500 feet we had plenty of time to talk over the situation, to check our inventory, and plan ahead. Alan and Douglas took charge of the first pile to be thrown out, and mentally noted the position of the more valuable second consignment. I was to read the altimeter, check our speed of descent, and tell them when to throw. I even explained the various last-ditch measures, such as cutting away the trail-rope or scrambling up into the ring and cutting away the basket. Both acts are possible, and have been used; but I had little intention of doing either over the harshness of Africa. Admittedly, the basket weighed 94 lb. and was therefore equal to three sandbags; but I felt our chances of survival inside it, although at a greater downward speed, were better in a countryside of thorn and lava than without it, however slowly downwards we might then be travelling. Descent might be minimal, but there was still the horizontal speed of 30 miles an hour. Our shadow showed that the wind had not abated, and the thought of three bodies arriving at that sort of velocity, when sitting unprotectedly on the trapeze of a ring, was sufficient to banish the idea of losing our precious wicker basket. For the same sort of reasons I was against cutting away the trail-rope. It is invaluable in lessening both horizontal and vertical speeds just at the right time before the landing. People have cut it away, but usually to gain extra mileage, to be given the grace of a little more flying time, to reach the other side of a town or a lake when there was no other way of doing so. On our flight from Nairobi there was no virtue in achieving this. We wished to end the trip as quickly, and safely, as possible.

At 9,500 feet, when in such a predicament, there is almost a desire to step over the edge and to have done with the flight. Anything seems better than just being held there, being kept waiting while other forces make up their minds what next to do. We stood in the basket, not saying much, not even thinking much, and certainly not looking at the view all around us. Suddenly, the wind touched our faces, and we knew we were going down. It was frightening, but at least the end had begun.

I had decided, as against the normal practice of dribbling out sand all the way down which prevents the speed building up, to let ourselves accelerate, and then to start throwing things out 1,000 feet above the ground. I wanted to make use of the inevitable heating of the balloon as it rushed through the air, for the more the gas inside our canopy was heated up the more lift it would impart. Travelling through the air fast naturally causes friction, and this heat is passed on to the gas. In ballooning this procedure has even been given a name. It is called the Montgolfier effect, and I wished to take every advantage of it. So, from our pin-point in the sky, we dropped steadily faster towards the earth. First it was 200 feet a minute, then 500 feet, then 1,000 feet, and finally 1,500 feet a minute. At this speed we seemed to achieve a kind of terminal velocity, for the acceleration hesitated. Anyway, there was no occasion to worry about that. The time had come to start jettisoning.

"Right, start throwing it out," I said, and the other two got going at once.

"All gone," said Alan, and we listened to the various thuds and cracks as the objects hit the rocks and earth below. I watched the descent slacken off and the ground coming fast towards us.

"Something more," I said, and the spare 400-foot magazine went over the edge.

"That's enough. O.K., prepare for the landing. Doug, hang on to the cameras. Alan, you pull the valve when I pull the rip. I might miss it again. Right, it's coming."

And it was, very fast. The nearer we approached, the faster the ground slipped away beneath us. A dry river-bed rushed by. Good, the place had banks we were well away from. Now it was coming. The trail-rope was jerking us about. Just a second or two more. Now.

And Alan and I pulled on our ropes just before hitting. I felt mine give. Then we hit the tree. And something cracked. We left it. But we were only 20 feet up. I pulled, and went on pulling. We twisted a bit, and then came down again. Another tree. More cracking. And a bump as we hit. I went on pulling. Yes, we had stopped. The basket leant over and fell on its side. We all fell with it. We all lay there. The flight was over. Ahead of us the balloon was still collapsing, and soon it too was still. Jambo had come to rest.

At that moment, when our senses were coming to once again, a great roaring went overhead.

"What on earth?" said someone.

Alan scrambled out. I saw his other knee was cut, and then he was shouting and waving. It was a small plane, and we all scrambled out to show that everything was well. I slapped my legs and skipped about to prove the point. The others went through similarly ridiculous antics. In truth, we were telling ourselves more than any passing pilot that we had survived. We were all right. The flight was over. We were not dead. Also, not that this seemed particularly important, we were not even injured. So we slapped, and skipped, and laughed, and waved, and soon the plane flew off, leaving us none the wiser.

I do not know why, but my first impulse was to leave the place. With the strong wind flapping my clothes about me, I walked back along the line of the trail-rope. It was draped over the thorn bushes and slightly to one side of the shattered specimen which had taken the first impact of our landing. It then trailed across that dry river-bed and up the other bank. Alan came along, and together we looked for some of the things we had thrown overboard. Most of them were fairly conspicuous, a sandbag caught up in a tree, a shattered bottle on a rock; but we never found the film we had taken, or any water which had survived the fall. Only when we had searched the area thoroughly did I feel like returning to the basket and the point of our final arrival.

The three of us leant on the wicker and discussed what had to be done. The light plane had seen us come down. It had zoomed over the area a couple of times and had then departed in the Nairobi direction. Its pilot would certainly pass the word around that we were all right, although a trifle remote. The nearest road, so Alan guessed, was the one to Magadi. He thought it might be 9 miles to the east of us. There were three sandwiches, but there was no water. However, there was a possibility that someone from the air rally might come over and have another look. So we tore up

Anthony Smith and the bogged-down truck

The expedition's well-padded instrument panel.
The various legends were added in the light of experience

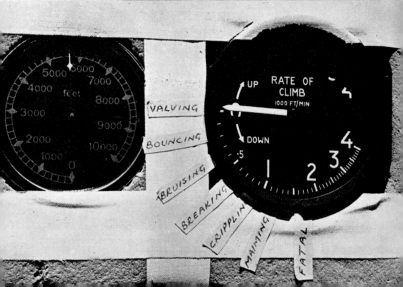

Three Masai and the first balloon ever to come their way

a rally programme and stuck its pages on the thorn trees which bordered a reasonably open square of land. Should a helicopter arrive, this place provided room for it to be landed. Should another light aircraft fly over, the marked-out square would at least be conspicuous.

It was while we were debating about thirst that some Masai turned up. We had seen some of their manyattas from the air, but had not known whether their inhabitants had seen us. Their arrival meant that water must be somewhere near, and so we set about packing up the balloon. Thirsts could be slaked later on. Extracting the balloon from that wilderness of thorn was no simple matter, for every mesh of the net seemed to have its own personal attachment. The fabric of the balloon was easier to pull and to lift, but every now and then there came a popping noise as another thorn broke through it. The Masai men, normally loath to work, stuck their spears in the ground and pulled with us. They had no idea how we had flown through the air, and were intrigued by our sudden descent in their midst. More important, with their help we finally got everything put inside the basket, and then everybody sat beneath a tree to recuperate. Idly we looked at the shattered prismatic compass, a casualty of the landing, that had been inside my pocket, and were more amazed than ever at our fortune.

Thirty minutes later, with the white pages still fluttering in the wind, it became plain that we had been left to fend for ourselves. This was perfectly reasonable and we were accustomed to doing so; but the buzzing of that aircraft had made us imagine differently. Anyway, we finally gave up such wishful thoughts—which had even led to a discussion on whether a small beer barrel would have broken had it been dropped from the air—and turned to the Masai. Alan did the talking.

"How far is the road from here?"

"It would be dark before you reached half-way."

"And where is water?"

"Come with us. We will give you milk."

The prospect of stumbling over that lava in the dark was not a good one. The offer of milk was, and we got up to follow them back to their home. They also said we could spend the night there, and this too we happily accepted. It was a curious way to spend the evening of an air rally, strolling along towards a manyatta for drink and a night's lodging; but most welcome.

A few hours later, when the thorn doors had all been fitted in place, we settled down for the night. A Masai encampment is a simple and archaic arrangement. It is circular, and the outer rim is a tall wall of thorn branches wedged tightly against each other. Leopards and the occasional lion have been known to jump them, but they are a formidable barrier. Inside these spiny corrals the cattle and goats are driven at night, and these move around the few dung huts in which the people live. No one, except the children, can stand up inside them, for they are nowhere more than $4\frac{1}{2}$ feet high. Looking like rectangular igloos, they have a narrow archway of a door, and through one of these we crawled to inspect the accommodation. I am aware that a squat dome made of sticks and manure in the middle of a cattle yard has obvious drawbacks, but inside it did look most cosy. There was a pretty girl sitting by a little fire, and a podgy baby was sitting on her knee. There were some logs on which to squat, and we sat there while our section of the room was made ready. This meant clearing a space the size of a normal single bed, and then putting a dry and crackly cow's hide on the earth. Our host indicated that we could lie down. The space was not large, but it could just contain the three of us. Douglas lay in the middle, with Alan and I on either side of him.

I still felt ridiculously thirsty. When we had arrived at the place we had been given mugful after mugful of warm milk from a salami-shaped calabash. There was only the one mug, and the three of us had sat in a row against a hut passing it around, much as those three old women did whom Perseus had seen sharing their one tooth and their one eye. To begin with, that milk had been ambrosia, delicious to feel and then to swallow. By the third mugful the taste had definitely palled. Alan explained that charcoal was always used by the Masai to clean out and, incidentally, sterilize their containers. However, milk flavoured with scouring

226

charcoal or not, we continued to drink it, and successfully finished the calabash. The Masai also drink blood, but neither it nor milk was forthcoming. According to them, we had drunk quite enough. It would have been ungracious to have asked for more.

This concern over hurting other people's feelings did not embrace the three of us on that rock of a cow-hide with regard to each other. There was not room for three shoulders if three backs were flat on the ground. Therefore it was necessary to sleep sideways and just forget about a complaining hip-bone. Douglas, as usual, with his innate ability to go to sleep by the elementary procedure of shutting his eyes, behaved in his customary fashion, and breathed deeply of that smoky air. I did not know what was happening to Alan on the other side, but I knew perfectly well, and most convincingly, that I was becoming more awake as the night wore on. I got up, found my shoes, crawled to the doorway, listened to the wind outside, and said: "I may be a little time." But both were sound asleep.

Outside there was plenty of life. The cows were contentedly chewing, and the goats were within their own special enclosure. I lay down in the lee of the hut and tried to emulate Douglas's excellent method of going to sleep. I shut my eyes. I composed myself comfortably. I put a sort of grin on my face and breathed the night air heavily. A cow loomed up inquisitively and breathed much that was certainly not night air straight into my face. I blew back, effectively; for she stabbed at the ground with her hooves and disappeared. Then a goat started up on the other side of the thorny thicket just by my head. I do not know what was wrong with that goat, save that it was something dire. It put its whole heart into making that desperate bleat. It was a ghastly noise, full of all the agony on this Earth. It was deep-pitched and the sort of sound a man might make were he ever to give birth. Had a beggar taken that goat with him, as some do with monkeys, and had he persuaded the animal to bleat, I think he could have wrung the charitable heart of the most miserly, tight-fisted, mean-minded usurer the world has even known. It was not fulfilling its rightful role.

that goat. Its talent was being wasted. Of what use was it merely to keep one traveller awake for a night?

The next morning, despite their dark dung encasements, everybody woke up with the sun. The women shoved the cows around to milk them, and I lay dozing for a while until a violent tingling of my feet woke me up. The two children, still holding feathers in their hands, had plainly been the culprits, and I lobbed a convenient clod of dung over in their direction. They ran round it easily, and helped me wake up the other two. Douglas and Alan admitted having heard a goat during the night and assumed carelessly in their sleep that the animal was probably being strangled. Anyway, with little more ado, they arose, crawled out, and smelt the morning air. Our male hosts were there as well, and the three of us started offering our thanks. The women kept well away and carried on with their milking. The men suggested one of their number should go with us and point out the easiest way to the road. This offer we most happily accepted. Just as we were leaving with our guide, a big cow mooed straight at me. Not to be outdone, and having a moo among my repertoire, I mooed back. The effect on the cow was negligible, but on all those silent women it was instantaneous. They rocked about on their haunches, they held their hips, they laughed with big wide mouths.

"Well, you can't improve on that exit line," said Douglas, and so, with that, we left the place.

On the way we checked briefly that all was still well with the balloon. Then we set out on that three-hour walk to the road. It was pleasant enough, striding along on the rocks, jumping down to the dusty river-beds, and edging a way between the thorn bushes; but we were all possessed of mounting thirst. The Masai, like so many people living near the subsistence level, were unaware of the excesses to which we were accustomed. Our guide, for instance, had certainly neither drunk nor eaten anything before we had set out. It would be well past midday, and after an 18-mile walk, before he would be back again at the manyatta.

By the time we did arrive at the road, a thin streak of stone and dust winding through the countryside, we had stopped talking about drink. The subject was too pressing. The Masai guide left us and we settled down under a tree to wait for a lift. Within the hour a Consul came along, laden with people and an appalling sick-looking child. We three squeezed in, and then levered ourselves out a couple of hours later when on the Nairobi outskirts. The air trip, and the subsequent night, had left us looking a shaggy trio outwardly; but within we were joyfully happy. I think each one of us was still amazed that all three could be walking along, on six perfectly serviceable legs, with nothing more serious to show for the flight than Alan's two cut knees and that mysterious patch of blood on his shoulder. Our clothes were torn, but they only served to remind us of our most commendable luck. So it was with a very jaunty step indeed that we strode uphill towards Alan's house, and then turned into his lane before banging on the door.

Ten minutes later, having heard messages from the two servants, having read messages inside the house, and having telephoned for more, we realized precisely what had been happening while we had been away. In a sense, it was that Karatu story-teller all over again, only this time the man with a tale to tell had kept it to himself. Neither that pilot who had seen us come down, nor his passenger who had decided belatedly to try and film us from the air, had mentioned our safe landing to the authorities. They had flown back to Wilson Airport, the point of our departure, and had not said a word. Consequently, without a single final report to go on, and with only some stories about our trampoline antics both this side and that of the Ngong Hills, it had been decided that a search should be mounted. A police plane had taken off. Another had been made ready with supplies. And all sorts of cars had gone to various likely areas to look for us. It was therefore necessary to call off this search with the minimum of delay.

CHAPTER TWENTY-THREE

THE SERENGETI

IT was not for another two days that we could leave Nairobi and drive to the Serengeti. It took us some time, and much apologizing, to clear up that mistaken search. Alan and I went to see the Police Air Wing. The pilot of the search plane bore no grudge, but had, nevertheless, been put to a lot of trouble. The Army had prepared a Beaver aircraft with parachute supplies, and so we saw the Army. The Directorate of Civil Aviation had ordered the search, in the absence of any evidence that such a move was unnecessary; and so we explained the matter fully to them. The Soda Works at Magadi, which were fairly near the area where we came down, had prepared an ambulance; and to them an apology went by radio. A Nairobi newspaper felt it had a point to make about public funds, and made it. Therefore I went on the apologetic rounds again, and was much relieved to discover that no one involved agreed with the newspaper. In short, there is more to a balloon flight than a little sand here and a release of gas when necessary.

It transpired that three points had encouraged the initiation of the search. In the first place, many of those at the airfield knew we had lost part of the valve. They also knew that a piece of plywood and a couple of bits of rubber had acted as a replacement. In fact, it proved perfectly adequate, but the makeshift repair had unnerved the authorities on our behalf. Secondly, and on this there was complete agreement, the day had not been ideal. A few of those intermediate landings had been reported, and it was judged— with reason—that they had been contrary to our general intentions. However, I suspect that the third point was more telling. A Tiger Moth pilot, running out of fuel not so long before in the same area as we had landed, had died of thirst. Instead of staying by his plane, he had gone to look for water and help. He had found neither. The searchers had found the crash very quickly, but they did not find him until too late. The memory of that unnecessary death had been at the back of everyone's mind, and no time had been wasted in preparing to rescue us.

Apart from these administrative worries, there was also the balloon. The three of us walked through all the waiting Africans to the Labour Office and signed on as a temporary employer. We wanted sixteen men to retrieve one basket, one balloon and associated equipment from a spot 9 miles west of the Magadi road. Soon we were given sixteen identity cards and, together with their owners, we drove out of town.

"What's the work?" said one.

"Getting that balloon out of the bush—the one that flew yesterday."

"Ah-hah! Eeeh! Ah-hah!" they variously exclaimed. "We knew it would be hard work from your clothes and shoes as soon as we saw you walk into the Labour."

On the Nairobi side of the Ngongs the country was fertile, and farmed. Beyond it, and having dropped a thousand feet, the situation was different. It was dry, and hot, and nothing much grew apart from the thorn we knew so well. Our labour force was from Nairobi, and had probably been born there.

"Look at all this land," said one. "Man, we could get rich here. Grow coffee. Grow corn."

"It looks pretty dry," said another. "You've got to have water."

"Just bore a hole. That's how you get water. That's how you get rich. We should do something about this place. It needs people."

Just then Alan's truck got a flat tyre. While he was changing it the Africans climbed out and walked around. They kicked at the spiky plants. They scooped at the dust of an empty river. They leapt from one lump of lava to the next. And they fanned themselves in the scorching heat of that useless arid valley. The puncture was then mended, and everybody climbed back on board.

"Maybe it won't grow coffee," said one.

"Maybe it won't grow anything. Maybe we'll have to find some other place."

With that remark a giraffe suddenly cantered across the road, gawkily and wildly. Those of the Africans who had not seen one before uttered amazement that such a curious creature could exist. They forgot about the coffee and wondered instead whether there was any point in hunting giraffes. What was the meat like? Or was it all bone?

Soon we came to the particular spot where we had emerged so thirstily from the bush. We drove as far as we could, a jolting business which certainly stopped any more conversation, and then got out to walk the rest of the way. There was no inherent difficulty either in finding the balloon this time or in retrieving it; but it was exhausting work all the same. We passed three Masai women, who were astonished at so much male activity; but for the most part the country was barren of anything except that endless triumvirate of thorn and lava and dust. We had another two punctures on the way back, for the thorns were having their say, and then paid off the men in Delamere Avenue with a shilling more each than had been their stipulated due.

At last, exactly 54 hours after we had taken off, that air rally flight was finally concluded. It had provided much, rather too much; but it had not enabled us to fly lowly and easily over great herds. This desire is becoming something of a reiteration, but it was our dominant aim and it had eluded us. The Serengeti, flat, wide, well stocked, and huge, would surely give us what we wanted. We would take off on the right day at the right time and not according to a programme's time-table. Our launching site on that vast plain could be anywhere, so long as there was plenty of game downwind. This time we would make certain of success. This time we would take off how we liked, where we liked, and when we liked.

Normally there is a road leading fairly directly from Nairobi to the Serengeti via Narok. Unfortunately, for several months it had been out of action, and so we had to take the long way round via our old haunts. The first leg was from Nairobi to Arusha. A big locust swarm spattered itself against our windscreens, and we scraped them clean when it had gone by. From Arusha we travelled south on the Great North Road, had trouble with a broken fan belt, and then turned right at Makayuni for Manyara. At Mto-wa-Mbu we had the ritual drink of cold Cokes from those two Indians, and discussed ballooning with those of our ground crew who wandered up. On the escarpment we had trouble with a trailer shackle, and got it fixed at the Manyara hotel. Then on to Ngorongoro, and to pick up all the camping kit we had left there. Finally, having driven past Windy Gap, and the spot originally chosen for the crater flight, we started on the long twisting descent towards the Serengeti Plains.

There are first impressions that can never be forgotten. I had never dreamed that the Serengeti could be so beautiful. At first the country was still fairly broken, and at one point we crossed the Olduvai Gorge, but when we met the great plain itself I was astounded. We were in three trucks, for Alan had brought another of his, and so I was alone in the Gipsy. This meant that I could give full rein to every sort of expression of amazement, and wonder; and meaningless jumbles of words could pour out without trespassing on the nerve-endings of someone else. I love to shout, especially above the drone of an engine, at magical sights that are passing by. I love letting this instant happiness flow out as I sing the praises of the world in view. So I sat in that noisy cab, bouncing up and down from the hummocks on the track, talking and singing and shouting, and trying to grasp that such a place was real while our three trucks drove through it, and the thousands of animals bounded along by our side.

Of course there had been much wild-life in the crater, but driving in it had been quite different. It had not been a matter of going anywhere, or of going fast; the rocks and the bogs and the nature of the ground had seen to that. Out on the Serengeti, with the whole flat plain ahead, and with a horizon to reach, driving became a carefree occupation. It assumed something of the animals' own disregard for the ground they were running over. It was in harmony with their own enthusiasm and zest. They pounded along by the side. They kicked at the ground, and we helped to turn its earth into flailing dust.

The three of us kept apart from each other, for there is no fun in breathing the gritty air chucked up by another, and so each man had his own thundering world to himself. Some instinctive reason meant that the animals hated a truck driving in front of them. They had to pass in front of the truck. Therefore, if they saw an interception coming, the wildebeest and zebras and gazelles would double their pace at once. They had to pass in front. They had to win. And they stepped up their speed accordingly. They would rarely change their course to prevent that possible interception, once it had been foreseen; and they put all they had into getting there first. It was this competitive urge that hammered the ground at every angle. Our horse-power and their leaping limbs raced along side by side. The Serengeti Plains were giving their traditional welcome.

It was not just the big wildebeest and zebras who had this fervour, but the Grants and Tommies as well. Instead of hurtling heavily by, they would leap and dance in their own enchanting manner. However long they kept up the chase, it never seemed to tire them. A gazelle, even after a lot running, still seems as light upon its feet, and nothing like a pant or puff was ever visible. Before they started to run, and after getting to their feet, a sort of shudder would twitch through their little bodies, and at the same moment they would be off, leaping, swerving, and then hopping over the ground.

Many days later, and at the spot where I first saw the Serengeti, I met a small party of Germans. Most of them were talking among themselves, but there was a very old man apart from the others looking back at the great plains through which he had just been driven. The jolting could have been none too easy for him, but he was ecstatic. It took him time to find words. Most of his mind was still back where he had been, but he did eventually speak. "I am an old man. I have seen much. But never before have I had such a day. It was a miraculous day." He underlined that last adjective with a cracked kind of power, and shook his fuzzy head from side to side in amazement at it all. "Jetzt, noch ein Loewe," said the others, and bundled him back into his seat; but his head was still moving slowly from side to side in incredulous wonder as they drove him off to look for another lion.

Before I met this man, and on that first drive into the Serengeti, I too had shaken my head in wonder. Every now and then we had stopped when someone's absence showed he must be behind with a puncture. The Magadi thorns were leaving a long legacy, but they did spin out the fascination of that drive. Once Alan suddenly leapt out of his truck after a fierce bit of braking, and when it was still moving slightly. He took off his shirt as he ran towards a spot, and then danced around holding the shirt in front of him. Douglas and I also slewed to a halt, ran up to Alan, and watched him play a cobra.

"Not the spitting sort," he said, rather breathlessly, and continued to leap around the hooded thing. It stared at him, and every so often made a pass at his shirt. Soon Douglas was leaping about as well, trying to get the two of them in the same viewfinder, while the 5-foot snake either writhed its way to a new position or reared up to defend the existing one. I remembered Kipling's story of a cobra firing itself like an arrow at the mongoose, and possessed an innate belief that everything Kipling had said was correct.

"Suppose it decides to strike, and comes at us really fast?"

"It won't," panted Alan. "Look, it's striking all the time. Can't do it any faster."

And with that not only did the spell of an old story vanish for good but the cobra suddenly disappeared down a hole. Douglas looked resentfully at the ground. The animal had no right to leave before it had been duly recorded.

We spent that night at Seronera. This is a beautiful settlement of a handful of houses right in the middle of the 5,000 square miles of park. It has the vast, smooth, granite blocks near by, so much a feature of Africa, and there is plenty of shade from acacia trees. Most of the beds are in round huts with steeply thatched roofs on top, a sort of rondavel which looks most apt. The following morning we borrowed two 40-gallon drums, filled them with water, and took as much petrol as we could carry. Then, having explained our intentions to the wardens in charge, we left to find a camping spot.

About 30 miles from Seronera, and back in the direction of Ngorongoro, we settled down at Naabi. This is a diminutive hill, certainly less than 100 feet at its summit above the surrounding ground-level, but it does command magnificent views. The land around is so flat, and so wide, that anyone on Naabi can see for miles and miles. We put up the tents on its eastern side beneath a convenient couple of trees, and then set about surveying the area. The hydrogen was not due for another five days, and we had plenty of time to prepare for the flight. Apart from noting the wind, we wanted to find out what animals were where, and when they were likely to move.

On the first morning in our new camp some animals decided instead to inspect us. I had vaguely heard noises in my sleep, and then woke up to see Alan looking in the tent. "Be very quiet," he said. "There's a lion five yards away." Douglas and I moved quietly out of bed and then had a look. Sure enough a young female lion was amusing herself with one of the camp blankets. She was pulling it about, much as any kitten dismembers a ball of wool. Soon another young lioness came up to join in the game. She emerged from the bushes without a blemish of noise and caught hold of the blanket's other end. Great holes appeared in it, and the object of their play began to resemble more and more the kitten's woollen ball. The blanket had not been taken off anyone's bed, for it had been left spread out by the side of Kiari's tent. A bad piece of packing by me before the drive to the Serengeti had meant that one blanket had arrived saturated with paraffin, and one paraffin tin had arrived empty. The blanket had been spread out to rid it of the smell, and the lions had instead taken a fancy to it, thus ridding it of value for ever.

While this tug-of-war was going on, a pair of male lions, full-maned and in their prime, appeared on the other side of the camp. In fact, as we looked around, the heads of yet more lions were among the bushes and the trees. There was even the scrabbling from somewhere as a lion climbed one of them. Our camp was right in the middle of this activity, and no animal seemed to mind. The male lions were intent only upon those females, and the females cared only for the final destruction of the blanket. The tree-climbing individual was happy on his branch, and those that were squatting on their invisible haunches in the grass stayed there, and sniffed the morning air.

Unfortunately, the five of us within the camp could not remain immobile and peering stiffly round a guy-rope for ever. Kiari began, with infinite quietness, the routine of the day, and we started to get dressed. The lions then deigned to realize there were others about, and slowly shifted their ground. The skeins of blanket they took with them, and we settled down to breakfast. Our first day in the Serengeti National Park had begun.

Its 5,000 square miles are flat, generally speaking, because at many times in the past the waters of Lake Victoria have encompassed this area. The eroded gorge of Olduvai shows, for the palaeontologist, how the lake has advanced and retreated, how it has laid down sediment over the centuries, and how the people living on its banks kept themselves alive. The animals of those early times were not quite the same as the species of today, for some have become extinct and others have altered their form, but the place gives the impression of being quite unchanged. The most ancient human remains from that mine of a gorge are said to be one and three-quarter million years old. The men were hunters, living mainly on the animals that fell into their traps or those they managed to kill in the open.

The expanse of Lake Victoria is now far from the gorge, but the Serengeti has the lake for its western border and almost meets the gorge on the east. It used to embrace it; but, when the Ngorongoro reserve was abstracted from the park, the Olduvai Gorge went with it. The present border between park and reserve follows no natural line of demarcation, and certainly it pays no respect to the migratory habits of the animals. They can move in and out of the park as they choose, and they do so constantly. This is all very well, but the laws affecting their security and well-being in the park are nothing like so stringently applied in the reserve, and still less so when they wander either north or south into territory where no strict brief is held for their safety. An intermittent line of earth-filled drums marks the borders of the park. On one side of it the wardens have authority over the animals, and exercise it diligently. On the other side, and where there is not even a reserve, laws of a sort do exist for the protection of wild-life, but there is little that can be done on its behalf. The Africans living outside the park quite rightly look upon the game as meat, and hunt it accordingly. The wardens could therefore despair of a system whereby their charges wander, so frequently, and so disastrously, beyond their control. Yet there is more than enough for them to do within that huge expanse of park to occupy every moment of their time.

In the old days wardens were principally game exterminators. They shot the lions which had turned into man-eaters. They destroyed the elephants which had become rogues, and they accompanied the slaughterers who had come out to turn a lot of money into truck-loads of trophies. In the middle period the wardens were content just to try and keep the animals alive. They attacked disease, so far as they could. They chased the poachers, and caught thousands. They pulled up the snares and the bow traps, and destroyed them. They fought the drought, and the floods, and the storms, and the ivory gangs, and the rhino horn gangs, and they desperately tried to keep a wild situation under control.

Nowadays every problem is too well known to take anyone by surprise. The old battles still exist, and the situation is still perilous; but the present plans do give hope. In every attack there must come a time when, after years of a frontal assault on the problem, someone thinks of going round the back. With limited means in the past the wardens have been attacking the poachers. Now there are many schemes for raising those means, for making the parks produce protein as well as beauty, for turning the poachers into herdsmen, for using the excess stock profitably, for welcoming tourists and using their money, and for turning the game areas of

Africa into the assets they should be rather than the despairing liabilities they have frequently become.

However, this is never going to be easy. All attempts to control nature are vigorously defended by nature herself. Permanent water was given in Kenya to some elephants dying of thirst. They recovered and then, not having to keep up the eternal search for more to drink, laid waste to the area. Even now some unknown impulse is causing hundreds of elephants to bark and then kill the boabab tree. They are helping to destroy the habitat that permits them to survive.

One big trouble is ignorance. No one can go round the back of any problem until he knows all about it. Why should elephants attack baobabs? How often should water be made to dry up to help keep animals on the move? What makes the wildebeest migrate? They often leave good water and good grass to go to an area where both are inferior. Why? How much do lions eat a day, and how often do they wish to eat, and why do their numbers fluctuate when meat is so abundant? What is the so-called yearling disease of the wildebeest? Most of the game diseases are given the simple names that man himself used to give to his own ailments in the days when he knew nothing about their cause, but knew only too well what their effects looked like. Science and medicine must come to the aid of the game problem. The first full-time scientist in the Serengeti only started work in 1961. A small laboratory was only opened there at the beginning of 1962. The scope of its future work is colossal. So little is known that it must be harder for the scientists—there are now four—to know where to begin than how to do the work.

It is not even known with any great accuracy how many large game animals live in the Serengeti. The present estimations may be wrong by 100,000, or more. Counts have been made from light planes flying up and down pre-planned routes, by circling over every herd until it has been assessed, by taking photographs and examining them at leisure, by using a high-flying Canberra and counting the specks and dots its cameras have recorded, or just by driving thoroughly over every area on the ground. The assessors have been diligent, but every census result has been notably different from the others.

For instance, Pearsall in 1956 reckoned "at a rough estimate" there were 101,000 wildebeest in the Serengeti. Swynnerton in 1957 thought there were 180,000 to 200,000 "very approximately". The two Grzimeks, father and son, counted 99,481 from the air in 1958. Talbot and Stewart saw 221,699 during their aerial survey three years later. The zebra story was similar for the two surveys from the air. The Grzimeks counted 57,199, while the other team counted 151,006. The Grzimeks saw 5,172 topi, but Talbot and Stewart claim 15,766. There are plenty of reasons for these discrepancies, for it is difficult counting such huge animal concentrations; but it is important to try and fix the actual numbers as accurately as possible.

We had particular interest in the problem of population survey, for we felt a balloon might have a part to play in it. A kite balloon that could be put up from any spot, to give its tethered passengers an unhurried view of the world, say, 1,000 feet beneath them, might have marked advantages over both aircraft and ground-based vehicles. It was up to us to measure its feasibility. Yet this was not the main thought that bubbled so urgently to the surface after each day's outing. Instead, and having seen unforgettable things, the sole desire was that anything and everything should be done to conserve the Serengeti. Perhaps it had been 30,000 wildebeest thundering past a spot that had sparked it off, or a pack of hunting dogs, or a baby zebra with the light and the world behind it, or a solitary topi standing sentinel on a mound; wherever we went in the Serengeti, and whatever happened, there were sights to be seen that were immemorial and wonderful. We came back each evening heady with enchantment and longing for more. Like anyone who goes there, we were immediate converts to its cause. The Serengeti is a legacy that must always be. Whatever the difficulties, it must survive: its destruction is unthinkable. For anyone who imagines otherwise, let him go there, and let him be enriched by it.

Flying at 30 m.p.h. over the plains of Kenya

Farewell to Jambo

CHAPTER TWENTY-FOUR

THE HERD

BY this stage of the expedition I knew my companions fairly well. I felt constantly grateful for their existence, and equally relieved that the normal kind of expedition bickering had never even begun to gain a foothold. It is so customary that I wondered why it had not arise in this instance. I think the combination of extreme danger and then more than enough to do had kept it at bay. Anger of the sort that creeps pettily into small groups takes time to accumulate. Such irritation that has accumulated is entirely dissipated by encountering some major hazard, such as the Rift Valley thermals, and surviving. Petulance cannot exist in such circumstances. It had no place any more.

On the other hand, this may be maligning my companions. I have a feeling that Douglas would be good at diverting the fruitless energies involved in a squabble, and Alan would leave such an argument so that he could do something else. In any case, it never came to the test. I was constantly being amazed by Douglas's phlegm. After all, his life was being jeopardized by my antics with the balloon, and yet he never interfered. That side of things, he considered, was my responsibility. His concern was with the photographs. Moreover, he seemed incapable of building up resentment in the way most people find only too easy. I remember leaving him once in a hot, shadeless place at midday while I went off for five minutes to pick up a bolt. On the way I got a puncture, and I then discovered the spare was flat. It also took time to find the bolt, and over two hours later I eventually returned to that hot, shadeless place—and Douglas. So far as I can recollect it, the conversation went like this:

Douglas: Hi!

Me: I hope you didn't get too thirsty. Here's some water.

Douglas: Thanks.

Me: Sorry I'm late.

Douglas: That's all right. Do you realize a man walked by here a while back with a couple of big safety pins in his ears?

Me: Well, that's one place to keep them.

Douglas: Yeah, I suppose it is.

Me: Look, I'm sorry I took such a time.

Douglas: That's all right. I wonder really why he used safety pins in his ears.

Me: Don't you want to know why I'm late?

Douglas: I expect you got held up.

Me: Well, yes, I did.

Douglas: Uh-huh.

Alan was quite different. He was incapable of sitting still and musing about a man with safety pins. He was just incapable of sitting still. He had left school early, a place where a lot of quiet sitting is expected, and had first taken a job in a meat factory. Very quickly he had realized that natural history was more in his line, and he decided to learn it. For weeks and months at a time he lived alone in the bush of East Africa, examining and then filming the life around him. His camp was a sleeping-bag, a veteran and much-loved object which managed to pour forth feathers eternally, and which was even banned from the Serengeti when the wardens thought the decaying thing too unwholesome to be admitted into a decent park. He bought another just as the last feather left its ancient predecessor.

His mother works in a bank; partly, one imagines, to get away from the zoo into which her home was turned. A bongo, which weighed 350 lb. at the end, was too precious for a cage and lived for 11 months in the spare bedroom. A young baboon lived with the family for 6 years, and enforced its authority more and more as the years went by. To begin with it respected everyone. Then, as is the nature of baboons and various other community species, this male tried to achieve dominance. It quickly won over his sister and his mother, but Alan resisted its attempts to overcome him. The animal and Alan would both make the same noise, the deep loud ugh-huh ugh-huh of the baboons, and for 6 years Alan could shout it down. Then it disregarded even him, and emerged in its own eyes as boss. Unfortunately, this meant indiscipline, biting whom he chose, and raiding the neighbourhood. The baboon's tribal triumph led to his end, and he was put down.

Alan's first earnings, apart from the meat factory, came from snakes. He collected a large number and put them on show at a local fête. With "Root's Reptiles" over the door, he charged an entrance fee and began to prosper. Now, when only twenty-four, he is doing even better. He filmed much of the Grzimek production *Serengeti Shall Not Die*, and still spends the greater part of his time filming animals. He had married Joan a year before the balloon safari, an exceedingly competent girl with a face of eighteen who is just as much at home in the bush as Alan. Her family took tourists around East Africa, and as soon as she was old enough to hold a dish-cloth she went with them.

Then there was Kiari, their Kikuyu cook. He had highly arched eyebrows, and so he looked at his Africa with a face of perpetual surprise. He was never very happy in the company of lions or rhinos, and preferred Nairobi to the world surrounding it; but he was diligent, and friendly, and obliging, and once we even managed to put him in the basket for a short, silent, captive flight into the air. I am certain he loathed each second, but he had been shamed into it by every one of the ground crew having a ride before him. His eyebrows had practically disappeared into the black, fuzzy tangle of his hair.

Kiari completed our camp complement. Every day we would leave camp and drive about the Serengeti. There was always so much to see. A cheetah, perhaps, slinking through the grass, and then bounding away with great greyhound leaps. A leopard, crouching well down, and then moving along as if, like the snakes, its legs had atrophied and its ribs were doing the job of locomotion. Once, during heavy rain, we watched three lionesses rush in turn at a sick zebra. They all missed it, for not one of them started the attack until the terrified creature was at its nearest point to them. Lions normally stalk their prey, and the galloping zebra showed up their lack of skill in the encounter.

Alan could also produce animal stories to supplement those going on before us. The one I liked best concerned a large troop of baboons and one leopard. It should be remembered that the favourite food of the leopard is a baboon, and that nothing has quite such a terrifying effect upon a baboon as the scent of a leopard. One day Alan saw a leopard walk quickly across an open space and climb up a tree. Shortly afterwards a group of baboons came swaggering along towards the same area. There were about fifty of them, rolling their shoulders as they moved, looking boastful, proud, arrogant and mighty pleased with themselves. One of the biggest, a leader, was out in front, and his shoulders swayed more than any of them. He was boss. He was king. Every muscle testified to his dignity. Suddenly he met that scent. With one loud squeal he leapt vertically into the air. Then, like any Disney hound, his legs starting running before he hit the ground and, rocket-like, he left the place. Moments later there was nothing to be seen but the long tail of the leopard hanging down from the tree.

Leopards have various ways of catching their favourite dish. A simple method is by the use of terror. The predator approaches, and his squealing, jostling prey make for the nearest tree. The leopard sits below, while the tension gradually mounts in the branches above him. Every so often the spotted shape lets out a snarl, and the nudging and the squealing and the shoving for better positions reaches a new peak. Five minutes more, and it snarls again. The fear above becomes frantic: the jockeying for safety yet more intense. Another snarl. More squeals. More shoving. One more snarl, and then a baboon's nerve breaks. With one bound the wretched ape leaps from the tree to make for another, but with one bigger bound the leopard secures its feast. Up in the tree the tension immediately vanishes. The arrogance returns. Life can go on until the next time.

Because the Serengeti is on such a huge scale, the numbers of all species follow suit. It is not one dragon-fly that wings its way through the evening air but suddenly several thousand. Every tree is then clicking with them, as they flutter about, and squadrons more are flying in from every quarter.

Similarly, when out driving, the front wheels almost run over a pair of quail which get up, hurry along for a short distance, and then flop down in the grass again. This is the signal for countless other quails to do the same, to wait until the wheels are upon them, to fly and then to flop. For mile after mile an apparently identical pair are going through the same performance. Then, suddenly, they stop. There is a slight variation in the grass, and a new species takes over. Driving through the Serengeti is something like flying. It is almost necessary to move by compass, or by fixing on a very distant cloud, if some area is to be reached in the shortest possible time along the most direct route. A pilot when lost tends to fly more and more towards the sun. I found a similar tendency on the Serengeti, and had to be constantly on the alert if I did not wish to drive in an arc rather than a straight line.

The evenings were always a rare experience. It was sad when the light went from the sky, but the noises were an equal compensation. Seeing a lion moving slowly past camp is one thing; suddenly hearing a roar not 50 yards away out of the darkness is an adequate substitute. We sat there over the fire, talking quietly, wondering what was going on around us and listening for any sound. One night there was no mistaking what had happened. Some lions had been roaring fairly steadily earlier on, and quite close by, but the noise had gradually changed to the hysterical scuffling of hyenas as more and more of them came near. Then there was fighting, and the occasional yelp as a bite went home.

"That must be a kill," said Alan, and we drove out to have a look. With a spotlight to help us, we soon came upon the cause. Two lions moved away as we approached, but there were at least fifteen jackals and some ten hyenas moving round a dead wildebeest. We drove right up to it, switched off the engine, and kept the single beam of light on the half-eaten animal. In the silence of the night there was something operatic about the scene. It was straight before us; but detached, as if on a stage. The whoopings had stopped with our arrival, and there was then nothing like enough noise for all the activity. The animals darted in and out, but their feet made no sound. They tore at the meat, and even that tearing was quietly done. All the time fresh eyes were looming up, one colour when looking at us, another colour when looking away. We stayed, fascinated, until every scrap of that wildebeest had been removed. The act had been played out. The stage, a small and open bit of ground, was emptied, and all the characters had gone their separate ways into the night.

On the fifth day, and right on schedule, the gas arrived. The two 5-tonners from Nairobi came whining along that Seronera road, and we diverted them to our camp. The time for filming and watching the animals from the ground had come to an end. Another flight was due. However, no risks were to be taken on this occasion, no taking off before the time was absolutely ripe. We would leave when we, the wind, the prospects, and the animals were all in order; and not a moment before. This load of gas, this consignment of sixty cylinders, was not to be squandered on more aerobatics. This time we would achieve our aim and fly as near ground-level as possible over as large a body of animals as could be contrived.

On the day the lorries arrived the wind was blowing freshly from the north-east, and everything looked too unsettled for a flight on the following morning. Therefore we told the lorry crews to make themselves comfortable. In the meantime we continued with the final preparations. I had neglected the balloon since our arrival at Naabi, and a casual inspection showed it to be in a poor state. That landing near the Masai had been more damaging than I had assumed. The normal practice with punctures is to mend as the balloon is inflated. Each layer of balloon successively reaches eye-level during the inflation, and its contingent of punctures is then seen and patched. The pressure of the gas inside such a partially filled balloon is so low that the leakage through its punctures is extremely small before they have been satisfactorily observed and mended. However, my casual inspection at Naabi showed rents rather than small holes, and a big mending session before the inflation was clearly necessary.

The technique was simple, but hot. I climbed inside the balloon, walked or crawled through its folds, and easily saw all the holes as the bright light pierced through them. Joan marked the places outside with a cross, and Douglas followed with the glue and the patches. If anyone wishes to lose a stone or two in a morning's work, I can recommend being the inside man on a balloon repair job. The sweat can evaporate nowhere. It clings. It pours rivulets. It smarts into the eyes. In the meantime, and like anyone caught in a maze, the sweat-loser himself tries to remember if he has been that way before, if the flabby fold in front of him has already been inspected. Eventually we considered the job finished, and then drank enthusiastically to put the lost liquid back again.

In the afternoon we drove over to the shifting sands and took the sandbags with us. These crescent-shaped mounds are a remarkable phenomenon. Technically they are known as barkan, and they result if there is sufficient dust on the ground and a unidirectional wind to blow it. The dust collects around a stone, and this collection accumulates more. The process continues, with the mound growing all the time, and then it begins to move. The crescents have their two sharp arms pointing the way the wind is going, and the whole shape is beautifully symmetrical. As it moves— perhaps an inch a day if the wind is strong—the mound moans, for the sandy earth is very dry, and the grains rub complainingly against each other. We drove up to this thing, and fooled around with it for the entire afternoon. It was high and steep, and we flung ourselves over its edge to slide rapidly down to the bottom. Any child who ever encountered a barkan would never look at a sand-pit again. There is no comparison between the two. Certainly that is how we felt as we swam and rolled and leapt about on that noisy tummock. We also, belatedly, filled the sandbags.

The next day Douglas and Alan went off to check the movements of the large herd we had been watching, the one over which we wished to fly. It was vital for us to predict its intentions accurately. This was not easy, for the herd had been stationary some days, and on others had travelled

20 miles or more. The annual migration is a wild and impulsive affair. No one knows what causes it, and certainly no one has any idea why the desire to move on fluctuates so markedly. We had watched the lightning on the horizon at dusk, and the big clouds during the day; but neither seemed to act as a lure. The theory that the migration always moves towards rain, or the signs of it, was not borne out by our observation of the selected herd. It was a big group of animals, about 15 miles long, but it would be easy to miss it with a free-flying balloon. A little veering of the wind, a change of impulse among the animals, and the chosen take-off spot would be proved quite wrong. We had to leave the choice to the very last minute. There was always a risk of missing the herd, but we wished to lengthen the odds against doing so as much as could be managed.

Briefly, the plan was to go just beyond the Serengeti boundary, near the Loliondo road and beneath the hill range known as Ol Doinyo Gol. All five vehicles would move there in the evening, and would select a site 10 miles upwind of the herd for the inflation. In choosing this place we would have to allow for the herd's movement when we were sleeping, and then take off in the early morning aiming to go right across the middle of it. This meant inflating the balloon during the latter part of the night. It would be foolhardy blowing it up the day before and then tethering it while we slept. We had often been woken to sudden squalls that had hit the plain from nowhere, and we wished to reduce the time to the minimum between inflation and departure. After all, the Manyara storm had warned us of this peril. The idea was to turn on the gas at 4 a.m., to reach the tricky stage of the basket's attachment by first light, and then to take off with the earliest hint of the morning breeze. For the flight itself, there was the whole wide plain of the Serengeti to be traversed.

Alan and Douglas came back after midday bewildered by the herd's behaviour. The animals had been thundering through the country near Lake Lagaja and moving very fast. The 30,000 of them were still together, but much more closely, and there was now nothing like 15 miles between the front and the back. Admittedly, any transect across the Serengeti would mean flying over animals, but it was imperative to go over a packed herd as well. We ate a meal, and then left camp with the essentials for one night's stop and with the balloon in its customary trailer. The two 5-tonners trundled along behind.

Alan made a detour on the way, to look for the herd again and was no less perplexed. It had entirely left Lake Lagaja. However, it was still moving in the same direction, and we chose a camp site 10 miles south of that Ol Doinyo Gol range. Four lions slunk away from the spot as we approached, and they did not wait to watch us start the preparations. We laid out the balloon on its tarpaulin, arranged it correctly, and attached the cords. The net was then draped over the fabric, pulled symmetrically, and finally anchored with one sandbag to every four meshes. We removed the cylinders from the trucks, unscrewed their caps, joined ten of them to the ten-way filler, and attached that to the inlet pipe. The balloon's valve was put in place, the basket was made ready, and for the last time it was only a matter of turning on the gas.

Conditions were ideal, but that made them seem all the more slender and tenuous. Any change would make them less ideal and the flight more chancy. Any puff of wind was to be dreaded. Anything and everything was suspect. Kiari laid out a meal. My stomach, as disloyal as ever, accepted only some of it. Later, even that was rejected. One's body is a mixture of extremely independent parts, each voicing discontent or abnegation in its own particular fashion. I decided that sleep was the least I could do for the constricted bits of me, and joined the others in their cocoons of sleeping-bags. The alarm clock, an anomalous thing in that desolate spot, had been set for 4 a.m.

CHAPTER TWENTY-FIVE

THE FINAL FLIGHT

THE alarm went off with punctilious accuracy. I looked up at the sky. The light layer of stratus had encroached slightly, but there was nothing sinister to be seen. The flight was on. We climbed into clothes sticky with dew, and set silently about the inflation. The trucks had all been parked facing towards the balloon, and we switched on their headlights shortly before Alan switched on the first of the cylinders. That weird noise of expanding gas reverberated through the night, and Jambo began to assume her shape. Douglas and I looked after the sandbags, and lowered them one mesh at a time as it became necessary. We said little, and grunted at each other rather as sentries must have done when they met on the darkened battlements. Even if there are two people looking after the same balloon, the thing is soon so big that they rarely do meet if each one has taken a particular semi-circle as his beat. He sees only that the other sandbags are being lowered, and he hears the net jerk up as it is relieved of the weights holding it down. Alan maintained a steady flow through the pipe, and his hammerings sounded much like some busy smithy as he connected up fresh cylinders and unscrewed those that were empty. All the while the huge thing rose darkly into the sky, and more and more of the stars disappeared behind it.

When dawn came, at 6.15, we were almost through with the inflation. Someone switched off the headlights, and gradually the colours of the earth reappeared with another day. In particular, of course, there was the great big orange egg of the balloon, perfectly immobile with not a breath of wind to touch it. Mick Tippett then turned up right on schedule. He was working on the excavations in the Olduvai Gorge, and had promised a team of men to help with the tricky basket attachment. They emerged from his Land-

Rover, and joined the Nairobi lorry team in general talk. Everything was in order. It was time for coffee and something to eat.

Sitting there in that most welcome sun of early morning, sipping the hot drink, feeling it seep down, and casting happy glances towards the secure balloon was extremely pleasant. The fear of what might happen still existed, but everything was safe for the time being. The sky was clear. The day was calmer than any we had known on those plains. The coffee produced a sense of well-being that only coffee can.

It was at 7.30 that we attached the basket. This was done with a simplicity not equalled before on the trip, and soon the whole balloon was towering high above us. I have said before that it ended up 55 feet tall, but the repetition may be necessary because each time its dimensions took me by surprise. Between every flight, when its entire substance was packed into that diminutive basket, memory of the balloon shrank with it. The subsequent inflation was always a thing of wonder.

Even when everything was ready, the air was still so calm that I decided to try some captive flights. These had only been barely possible on the previous African trips, and quite impossible at Nairobi; but on the Serengeti the ground crew attached the trail rope to a car for safety, and then let the balloon rise to 200 feet. I had a selection of the helpers on board, and together we looked for and pointed out animals in sight. It was indeed a superb lookout point. It was also not a problem going up and down. One man on the ground could have done it; but everyone in fact pulled on the rope to bring us back to earth, mainly I think to try and sharpen the bump. I took on fresh passenger batches, and each time tried to spot more animals from that 360-degree viewpoint. Eventually the day began to stir as the sun warmed it up. It was time to go. The breeze had come to carry us over the herd.

When at Zanzibar, and to a varying extent on the subsequent flights, we had been ready to depart, we had just departed. Without so much as a handshake, we had taken off as soon as we could, while the necessary civilities were forgotten in the general anxiety. Zanzibar had been the most ill mannered, for hundreds of people had helped us there, and thousands had turned up to watch; but all they got was an abrupt wave from a couple of hundred feet. So, on the Serengeti, and with a slender handful of observers, we at last managed to effect a leave-taking that was polite. A balloon's departure should, at the very least, not affront the people on the ground. Douglas and Alan and I shook hands with Joan and Kiari. We then did the same with the lorry teams, and with the gang from Olduvai. No one else knew it, but justice was at last being done to Zanzibar, Jambo could now take off.

It was also the best departure of the series, and so it should have been. It was not Etten, with its churches, poplars and chimneys. It was not Manyara, with its yellow thorn trees, nor Birmingham, nor the lip of Ngorongoro, nor Nairobi, nor any hazardous spot; but the Serengeti, with its eternity of open land leading away downwind. Up we went, with the tail rope on the ground, and then stabilized at 300 feet— another record. The wind up there was about 5 knots, and very nice it was. I decided to fly as I had never flown before, by giving 100 per cent attention to the instruments. I saw no reason for any repetition, however small by comparison, of that leapfrogging over the Ngongs and beyond. As soon as either the altimeter or the variometer gave a flicker of a movement downwards, I would trickle out a little sand. I would let no momentum build up. I would fly on as even a keel as could possibly be arranged. Admittedly, this should always be the aim, but from Nairobi it had been impossible. Very quickly we had been forced into the relatively crude business of throwing out half sacks at a time, and then of cannoning into the ground.

On that early Serengeti morning things were different. When sand went overboard it was in half handfuls or less, and the flight started off with a finesse never achieved before. The first animals below us were Thomson's gazelles, slightly frightened initially, but soon quite calm. They stopped their trotting and turned to have a look at us. A rhino, 50 yards away, next saw us, but did not raise his tail. Then a hyena, sitting by its hole, moved off straight beneath us and trotted along at our speed. We could hear the grass rustling as its furry body brushed past, and I scattered some sand on its back as we started coming too near. The intention was to travel no lower than 200 feet and no higher than 300: the range in between was optimum.

As the flight progressed a measure of confidence in ballooning began to return. There was no ocean span to cross, no jungle ahead, no distraught airstream; and it was still the calm of the morning. Well to the east of us were the Ngorongoro Highlands, now shrouded in cloud, and obviously a place where trouble could be expected. A few miles in their direction was the great crack of the Olduvai Gorge, a dry and arid scar across the ground. Beneath were the animals and the moon-shaped barkan, those shifting sands where we had spent that infantile afternoon. They had zebras cropping the grass near them, and a herd of eland farther away. These big antelopes are the most timid of the lot, allegedly because they know their meat is prized. Some are being husbanded in captivity as an alternative to beef, and even from our height we could see the heavy folds of flesh. Those below us were wild, but every member of the species, whether being fattened or not, always seems to have plenty of meat on board. Their long twisted horns reaching back over their necks must have saved them again and again. I looked down for too long and had to throw out sand hastily, for a descent had begun to build up.

After an hour of travelling, and a mounting concern about the big herd which lay ahead, we first caught glimpses of it. The sight was astounding. I had never imagined the world could be quite so full of animals. To begin with, they appeared as a kind of blur, with dust rising above them all. Then the blur changed to specks, and the dust columns rose higher into the air. Then the specks changed into individual forms, some galloping, some quite still, until the whole horizon in our path was full of them. Our point of aim had been perfect. We were due, sudden contrary winds permitting, to go over the very centre of that vast animal concourse.

Alan and Douglas made everything ready with their cameras. I arranged the remaining sacks conveniently at my feet, and promised a stable run over the herd. We were much too involved to be particularly happy, or rather to show that we were; but everything was going exceptionally well. I dropped the height down to less than 200 feet, and the tip of the trail rope began to touch the ground. There was an occasional brief tugging as it went straight over a solitary tree, but the trees were rare and becoming rarer. The herd was in an open place, and there was nothing but a few drying water-holes, the slender traces of dust, and those thousands upon thousands of animals. Meanwhile, for the sun was in the east behind the balloon, our shadow moved steadily ahead of us, and showed the way. It moved over the ground like some giant amoeba, undulating slightly at the edges with the unevenness of the earth, and then pushing out a pseudopodium as it climbed up one side of an isolated rise in the ground. It became an exceedingly sensitive form of altimeter, for the eye is good at appreciating whether something is growing or shrinking before it. So I stared at that shadow leading us towards the herd, and threw out sand accordingly.

At last we came near, and as we did so an immensity of noise came up towards us. I had listened to that congregation on the ground, but when heard from the air it was far more deafening. The nasal grunts of the wildebeest were strung together so continuously that it sounded as if a swarm of buzzing bees had dropped their note an octave or two. It was a raucous vibration coming from everywhere. It was the real noise of a migration on the move, not the half-hearted imitation of it we had heard when on the ground. It was one mighty impulse. It was a herd, and it was careering, walking, eating, and galloping on its way. It was magnificent.

The shadow cut clean through animals, so to speak, and they disregarded it. The zebras, Tommies, Grants, and wildebeest were all the same. The sudden blotting out of the sun by the sharpness of our form caused no reaction. We might as well not have been there, but for the fact that we spoke. This made them aware of us. It seemed silly to us, assuming stealth when so blatantly visible, and assuming quiet when the whole earth is pulsing with a remarkable din. So we spoke, more out of enthusiasm than with any intent to say a message; but we did speak, and the animals heard us. The group immediately below frisked up their tails and cantered off in the idiotic heel-kicking manner of the wildebeest. We experimented with other groups. If we were quiet, all was well; but if we talked, we were instantly overheard, despite the din.

Having learnt this lesson, we respected its findings and remained silent. This was easy, for there was plenty to observe and too much to say. The whole sight was so magical. To both sides there were ten miles of animals. To the front of us, and to the back, there were thousands of them. And above them all we floated with the simplicity that only a balloon can possess, provided the air is calm and the African day is young. Of course, it was growing older all the time, and we were soon beginning to realize it. My job was becoming steadily more difficult, and that nice constant height of 200 feet was becoming exceptional rather than the rule. However, to begin with, this meant only more attention by me, and the general photography and observation was still well under control.

Towards the end of the herd, when its flanks were behind us to the left and right, and when only a few animals remained in front, we were pleased to note that a water-hole was certain to pass directly beneath us. It was nearly dry, but some wildebeest were standing in the mud by its edge, and some others were on the hard, dry, down-trodden earth around it.

"I'll go over this at 200 feet. You just wait and see."

"Fine," said Alan. "It looks well. I'll use up the rest of this magazine on the approach."

Alan did in fact use up the film, and the approach was at the right height; but then we hit the air above that hot patch. Alan had disappeared into the basket to fix the camera, but Douglas and I watched the ground sink rapidly below, and knew that the gentle hours were over. I read the altimeter casually, knowing only too well the sort of thing it would say, and saw the needle rise from 200 to 1,500 feet. The hot patch's thermal was having its effect. During this rise Alan had been down in the wicker bowels of our vehicle, and he rose at the end of it to see a world transformed. He clutched suddenly on to the rim, and his shoulders shrunk from vertigo. Neither Douglas nor I had bothered to point out the obvious to each other, but Alan had been unaware of it and had suffered accordingly. The world had no right to vanish like that. He had left it a mere 200 feet below. It was a third of a mile away when next he looked at it.

From then on the flight did not have its previous serenity. Intermediate landings were frequent, and sand was thrown out several pounds at a time rather than the gentle and occasional trickle of before. However, there was plenty of Serengeti still to come, even after the herd had gone, and we continued the flight, although more erratically. I remember a dead zebra down below, with the vultures swooping in from our height. In a sense we were only seeing things as the vultures had seen them over the centuries. They have watched life on the plains, and they have always been ready to scavenge them free from death. The vultures used outstretched wings on their effortless way down to the zebra, and only flapped them at the very end. We watched, and then prepared for another intermediate jolt of our own.

Eventually, despite the yearnings to go on, the flight had to come to a stop. Our path through the air had become more and more distorted, and the turbulence increasingly did what it liked with us. I achieved the best I could, but it was plainly not good enough and at the twentieth unintentional bounce I decided it was time to land. There was no hazard in the way, and the bounces were injuring nothing and no one; but they were extremely tangible tokens of the disturbances to come, and each was harder than the last. Besides, the herd was now behind us and we could imagine no rival that would compete with it. We hit the ground again, having dropped from 300 feet despite volumes of sand, and this time it hurt. The next occasion would definitely have to be the landing.

Douglas and Alan sorted out who would film it, because the man holding the cine needed both hands for that job, and the other man had to hang on to both the operator and the basket so that no one would leave it prematurely. I, meanwhile, prepared the valve and rip lines, blue for valve and red for rip. Instead of waiting for a downstream to take us earthwards. I valved a little and down we went in our own time.

"It's coming. Hang on. I'm about to rip. Ripping now." And it came. The basket creaked, but did not even bounce. Slowly it tipped on its side, and slowly we went with it. The coarse grass of the Serengeti brushed against our faces, and the flight was over. Jambo deflated herself in the proper manner, and all was finished. There were three shapes inside a basket, a lot of orange fabric, some netting—and nothing more. Traditionally, safely, beautifully, a balloon had expired. It was no longer a part of that most excellent canopy, the air. It had flown, but its journey was now ended. Its African days were over.

So, too, were mine. There was, of course, plenty still to be done. We had to pack up our equipment, have it sent home, see who should be seen, and thank all those in whose debt we were. I was to fly back by freight-plane as before, but on this occasion the machinery being exported to Africa had been replaced by animals travelling to Europe. There were monkeys, such as the proud Colobus; there were baboons, and there were hundreds of Vervets. I and the steward fed them when need be, and tried to prevent the thousands of lovebirds from belying their name. The dogs we exercised at Khartoum and Malta, and time after time I clattered down the steps towed by some urgent hound in need of grass. It was a most satisfactory journey, and gave me strength for the encounter with the Customs.

"A balloon, sir? I don't think you can import a balloon just like that. We've got regulations, you know. And we've got to abide by them. Let me see. Ah, yes, here it is. Balloons and airships—20 per cent. I am afraid you'll have to pay 20 per cent of its registered value in import duty. You see it was made in Belgium, and now you're importing it. That's the regulations, seeing as how it's not a British-made balloon. Now, if you'd had a British-made balloon, that would be different."

"But . . ." I said, and then petered out.

Later I summoned up arguments about antediluvian laws, and the need for reform, and common sense; and I asked them how many airships they inspected in a year, or in the past three decades, or in this century, or why airships and balloons had a higher duty than ordinary aircraft, and I suggested they looked beyond the narrow confines of their regulations, for I had no wish to be penalized by their pettiness. I asked for the import figure on crossbows, and flint-locks, and abacuses, and Belgian-made coracles, and how much my balloon was worth if no one but me was entitled to fly it, and how many honest watch-girt, scent-bedecked smugglers they thought were getting through while they argued with me. I continued, and so did they. "But . . ." I said again, and petered out once more.

As we extracted ourselves from the basket on the Serengeti, all this was still to come. Not for one minute did I think of Customs men as we packed up the balloon that day; my mind was still back over the herd. And I certainly did not do so that evening when the weather broke, and the steadiness of the downpour coupled with the even grey of the sky showed that the rains had come. The flight across the plain had been only just in time.

For the last few days of our stay in the Serengeti, and while completing the arrangements amongst ourselves, we camped by the edge of Lake Lagaja. It was probably the most beautiful camp-site of them all, and certainly the hardest to leave. The plan was that I should go ahead, while the others tidied up some loose Serengeti ends. So I drove out of camp alone and began the journey back to London. As was the custom, the zebras galloped alongside, the gazelles danced over the ground, and the front wheels unerringly sought out the hyena holes. I drove and drove past the animals, past a slovenly group of lions, and some hartebeest, and more big herds, and a cheetah, and the largest group of eland that I had ever seen. I then met the track that leads through the Serengeti. Resenting its forthright purposefulness, its clear indication of the way to go, I swerved on meeting it and turned round to have a last look at the world I was leaving.

I switched off the engine and walked a few yards away from the truck. The haze was beginning to dance over the ground and some of the farthest animals were shimmering in this heat. Suddenly, I saw that one was apparently coming my way. It was by itself, and moving fast. It was a baby wildebeest, quite apart from the others, and running as swiftly as its spindly legs could carry it. It continued to come towards me; and then, when a mere ten yards away, stopped in bewilderment. Its instincts had played it utterly wrong, and only now did it realize it was as lost as before. Its wild impulse to go for an unattached shape had been a drastic move. It stayed there, staring at me, having no idea what to do next, and looking wretchedly confounded by its few hours' experience of life. It was doomed, that poor young calf, for the Serengeti is no place in which to be both weak and isolated. Even the great herds themselves could well be jeopardized if things go wrong. The calf, full of distrust, yet desperately in need, so much on its own, yet symbolic of them all, just stood there and did not even bleat. I got back into the truck and drove the calf towards the likeliest looking wildebeest herd. Then, almost deliberately, I lost sight of it among the others of its kind. This time, when I reached the track, I did not turn round, but drove away as fast as I could.

BALLOON PHOTOGRAPHY

By Douglas Botting

1. THE PROBLEMS

A. *Photographing a balloon from the ground*

Balloon photography, especially in Africa, presents special problems. For the cameraman on the ground trying to photograph the balloon in free flight, the main problem is to be able to follow the balloon overland sufficiently closely to get any sort of picture at all. It is a measure of the magnitude of this problem that, as far as is known, no cameraman has even been able to manoeuvre close enough to that unpredictable event, a balloon landing, to take a photograph of it—although once in Holland I found myself only 400 yards from where a balloon came down but failed to get a shot because (a) I hadn't expected it to come down then, and (b) I had run out of film. I thus missed a unique photograph, especially as the passenger was thrown out of the basket on the first impact and the cameraman in the balloon broke his 35 mm. Arriflex movie camera on the second impact.

Alan Root and myself have now followed balloons by car, motor launch and aircraft, but none of these pursuit craft is entirely satisfactory. In Africa there are few motorable tracks and it proved impossible to follow Jambo by car across Lake Manyara, or into the largest crater in the world, or over the violent Ngong Hills. It was difficult enough coaxing Jambo over these enormous topographical features, let alone an Austin Gipsy. Alan followed us by motor-boat from Zanzibar, but since we were moving at twice his speed we soon became a minute speck which even his longest lens could not magnify. I have photographed a balloon from a light heavier-than-air craft, but in this case the balloon is travelling past at the airspeed of the aircraft. This is all right for a still shot, but it is absurd to see a balloon travelling at 80 m.p.h. across a television screen.

The only really satisfactory way of photographing a balloon in free flight is from a helicopter. Jambo was photographed in this way at the commencement of its ill-augured flight from Nairobi. A helicopter must, however, be used with caution. I have heard that a retired Spanish admiral was once forced down by the downdraught of a helicopter. And when he hit the ground, his balloon burst.

Ideally, a balloon photograph should set the balloon in context, so to speak. A balloon simply pictured in a blank sky soon becomes dull. It is better if the country over which the balloon is flying is included in the shot—whether from the ground or a helicopter. Jan Boesman, our instructor, always demanded that every balloon photograph should be "romantic", and he had photos of his own balloons reflected in the mirror surface of some Italian lake, or floating over the Pyramids across the Nile. A balloon is nothing if not romantic; its floating free is entirely magical.

To capture this romance and magic the balloon photographer needs lenses ranging from 24 mm. wide-angle on 35 mm. cameras (or wider, since a balloon is over 50 feet high and at take off towers over the cameraman) and 12·5 or wider on 16 mm. cameras—up to 400 mm. telephoto for capturing a hopelessly distant balloon or getting some sort of close shot of the basket and its occupants in flight. And he should obviously have colour film.

B. *Photographing the ground from a balloon*
This is a much bigger problem. For one thing, the basket of Jambo measured only 3 feet by 4 feet and contained three persons, sandbags, and miscellaneous equipment such as telescopes, megaphones, bunches of bananas and a bushbaby. There was thus no room in which to move to get a better picture; nowhere to put the movie camera when changing film; nowhere safe to put the photographic equipment—any hard box with square edges would be a danger to the crew

during landing—so that lenses jangled in trouser pockets and cameras not in use hung casually down from basket toggles; and when filming activity in the basket it was rarely possible to have one or other of the crew members farther than 2 feet away from the lens. Photographing in a balloon is like photographing in a strait-jacket.

A second problem, probably peculiar to ballooning in Africa, was that Jambo flew at anything from 3 feet to 6,000 feet above ground-level. A balloon photographer needs a range of lenses to cope with such a range of altitudes. Our intention was to photograph game from the unique view-point of a balloon. For this our optimum height should have been 200–300 feet above ground-level, but in Africa it was rarely possible to maintain such a height, and we photographed animals on anything from 12·5mm.wide-angle on the 16 mm. Arriflex movie camera to 400 mm. long-focus on a 35 mm. still camera, at heights varying from below the level of the subject of the picture (what Alan described as his "unique upward shot of goats" on Ngong Hills) to 1,500 feet above ground-level (what Alan described as his "unique downward shot of vultures" flying over the Serengeti).

It was never possible to fix up a tripod-head mounting on the balloon basket (too cumbersome, too slow to use, too dangerous to the crew on landing), but compared with a normal aircraft the balloon is so stable and the balloon itself so slow moving that it was possible to make hand-held movie shots (using pistol-grip or shoulder pod) with lenses of longer focus than usual. I shot an elephant 1,000 feet below us on the edge of Lake Manyara with a 150 mm. lens; and made a prolonged tracking shot of a herd of buffalo on a 90 mm. lens when the balloon pursued them as they went crashing through the Saleh Forest, Ngorongoro. Using a 400 mm. Novoflex lens on my 35 mm. Edixamat Reflex still camera presented no problems at all.

A third problem—one which in time became our *idée fixe* —was to find a way of making pictures from a balloon that fully conveyed the unique experience of ballooning over Africa; the sensation of floating like a bubble over wonders, of peering at the world of lake and forest and great animals as if from a magic carpet. We had to make pictures that could not be mistaken for those taken from, say, a helicopter. Primarily this was an artistic problem, a problem of presentation—but for technical reasons it became almost insuperable. In brief, it demanded that a shot of the ground from a balloon also included a foreground actually in the balloon. In a shot, say, of the coral reefs of Zanzibar unrolling beneath us, "us" were as important a part of the picture as the coral reefs, otherwise the sensation of floating would not come over fully. This demanded a remote-controlled camera fitted somewhere above the balloon ring, pointing downwards so that the crew members were clearly visible in the foreground and the reefs or whatever were equally clear in the background. This was our ideal, and it would have been nice to have had shots of us drinking champagne over the Zanzibar Straits while beneath us was revealed the wide panorama of blue ocean, yellow reefs and green Tanganyika shore. But we never succeeded in mounting a movie camera in this way.

For remote control one needed an electrically driven camera, and the Arriflex was too heavy, and too precious, to risk on some tenuous system of ropes and scaffolding, out of our reach, floating high and dangerously over Africa. How would we recover the camera easily for reloading? How would we accurately control the composition in the viewfinder? What would we do in a surprise intermediate landing, when the heavy camera would descend into the basket at the risk of our coxcombs? And how could we ever get round the hard technical fact that the perspective distortion of the wide-angle lens we would be bound to use would reduce even an elephant on the ground to the size of an aphis? We never used a remote-controlled movie camera, but on our last flight we did successfully take remote-controlled stills by means of a 35 mm. camera held high up on the end of an aluminium pole and the shutter released by a Rondo air-release (the lens was a 24 mm. Isco Westrogon). But even then the pole was dangerous to us on that flight. It seems the only way round this problem is to shoot the balloon basket and ground with a telephoto lens mounted in another, accompanying balloon. Which is near enough impossible.

There is a fourth problem, not peculiar to balloon photography but to all photography on an adventurous enterprise in which the cameraman is not simply the aloof, hidden eye, but an integral member of the team. This problem is that whenever anything very dramatic or dangerous happens the photographer usually drops his cameras and helps the others, and so there are no photographs at all of the most exciting moments. This happened to us. When the basket ropes snapped at Zanzibar, when the balloon was nearly destroyed on the ground in the sudden storm at Manyara, when the trail rope got tangled just as we were floating over a vast herd of buffalo, and when we repeatedly bounced among the Ngong Hills, photography was forgotten and we all pulled ropes, or prayed. The answer is simple. You take a photographer who continues to press the button even while the legs and heads are broken all around him. He is the ideal, amoral, detached operator with only one function. But an expedition with such a man among its members would not be a happy one. He would have his own grandmother strangled to get a good shot.

The one assured dramatic moment of every balloon flight —the haphazard business called landing—we did sometimes manage to photograph (once at Manyara in entirety, elsewhere partially). This depended on the cameraman's nerves and common sense. It meant he had to resign himself to hitting the ground at about 20 m.p.h. in a sort of laundry basket, not holding on to anything but his camera. It is not recommended to beginners. Viewing the rushes of our film it was fascinating to see the moment at which the cameraman's nerves broke (wisely)—a snippet of a dead tree rapidly approaching, a few frames showing wild forest trees engulfing the basket, then blankness. We never filmed the landing after our Nairobi flight because we had thrown our film out of the basket in lieu of ballast. I do not think balloon photography, to sum up, is very easy, but it is most interesting.

A. *Cine*

We required a 16 mm. camera that was tough, had reflex viewfinding, was electrically driven, could take lenses of any focal length, and had provision for both 100-foot rolls of film and 400-foot magazines. The only suitable camera fulfilling all these specifications was the Arriflex. Alan Root had one, and the other we hired from B. Bennett & Sons Ltd, of Oxford Street, London. We were worried at one stage that an electric-drive camera might be dangerous in a hydrogen balloon, but both balloon and wild-life movie shots often require longer uninterrupted running times than is possible with a clockwork drive. The 8-volt Varley batteries driving the Arriflex proved spillable and heavy and they got in the way—we were not sorry when we had to throw one of them out of the balloon as ballast. Alan Root had constructed his own battery—electronic flash unit cells, each with three floating balls to show the state of charge, the whole embedded in foam rubber and encased in a small metal box which clipped neatly on to the waistband of one's trousers. This battery was non-spillable, light and tucked out of the way. Both sorts were chargeable from the Land-Rover battery via a step-down 12-volt built in series—this was necessary when we were in the bush, away from an electric mains.

We had two tripods—an Arri tripod with a gyro head, and a Miller tripod with a fully fluid head. I can't think why the Australian-made Miller head is not in universal use. It is beautiful to operate, giving smooth, controlled pans and tilts even with extreme long-focus lenses. The Arri gyro head will only pan in this way; it tilts like any ordinary head, and the whole apparatus is rather heavy for the sort of work we had to do.

We had a range of eleven lenses for the Arriflex. The 12·5 mm. was excellent for shots in the balloon basket and with black and white film had an enormous depth of focus. The 40 mm. and 90 mm. Kilar lenses were excellent for close-up natural history work, since they could be rapidly focused down to a very short distance and obviated the need for awkward extension tubes. The 150 mm. and 300 mm. Kilfitt Kilar lenses were mostly in use for big-game photography from the ground—the 240 mm. and 400 mm. Novoflex lenses, with their follow-focus grip, were used mainly with the Edixamat Reflex still camera, since their focus tended to "creep" too much for movie work.

The following is a list of the major items of cine equipment we had with us on our balloon safari:

2 16 mm. Arriflex cameras
2 400-foot film magazines
3 8-volt camera batteries
1 Arri tripod with gyro head
1 Miller tripod with fully fluid head
Filters for Arri matte-box—yellow, orange, red, green, neutral, density, polarizing
Pistol grip
Shoulder pod
Extension tubes
Lenses—12·5 mm., 16 mm., 25 mm. (all Taylor Hobson); 40 mm. (Kilfitt Kilar); 75 mm. (Taylor Hobson); 90 mm. (Kilfitt Kilar); 150 mm (Taylor Hobson); 150 mm., 300 mm. (Kilfitt Kilar); 240 mm., 400 mm. Novoflex.
Battery charger
2 metal Arri carrying cases
1 Norwood Director exposure meter

B. *Still*

35 mm. single-lens reflex cameras proved the only satisfactory still cameras for use in the confined space of a balloon basket. They were suitably small, light and quick to use, could take lenses of any focal length and did not require reloading too often, since each cassette provided thirty-six exposures. Most of the pictures in this book were taken on an Edixamat Reflex (Model D), or on a Voigtländer Bessamatic which, together with its three lenses, was kindly loaned to us by Voigtländer's British agents, Johnsons of Hendon. The Edixamat proved entirely satisfactory in operation, and much tougher than most cameras of this type. It survived six more or less violent balloon landings (on one training flight

it had ended up underneath the basket); it had been stolen and thrown into the bush by a hard-pressed thief; and it had been dropped from a Land-Rover moving at speed. The Bessamatic had the advantage of superb quality lenses, with bayonet mounting which made them rapidly interchangeable, plus a built-in exposure meter. The camera was thus very quick to operate. The Edixamat was used mainly for colour photography, the Bessamatic for black and white.

Of the other cameras, we used the Bronica and the Polaroid occasionally—the Alpa and the Linhof never. The Bronica we took with us on the Serengeti flight but it was awkward to use in the basket, especially because of its waist-level finder. The Polaroid was kindly given to us by the manufacturer's British agents, Johnsons of Hendon. It was intended as a kind of *laissez-passer* among the Africans in the areas we travelled through; the trouble was that the Masai had such little use for white man's toys that, vain though they were, the Polaroid 10-second prints of themselves failed to impress them.

The lenses most commonly used on still cameras were the extreme wide-angle and the extreme long-focus. The 24 mm. Isco Westrogon continued to serve well in spite of being filled with rain like a champagne cup during the nefarious Manyara storm; its perspective distortion was far less than I had expected. The 240 mm. and 400 mm. Novoflex lenses were adapted to the Edixamat and were excellent—good definition, easy to hand-hold and quick to focus.

The following still photographic equipment was taken with us on the balloon safari:

1 35 mm. Edixamat Reflex Model D
1 Voigtländer Bessamatic 35 mm. reflex
1 Alpa V 35 mm. reflex
1 Zenza Bronica reflex
1 Linhof Technika camera
1 Polaroid camera Model 110B
Lenses—for Edixa: 24 mm. Isco Westrogon, 35 mm. Schneider Curtagon, 50 mm. Isco Iscomat, 135 mm. Schneider Xenar, 240 mm. Novoflex, 400 mm. Novoflex; for Bessamatic: 35 mm. Skoparex, 50 mm. Septon,

135 mm. Super Dynarex; for Alpa: 40 mm. Kilfitt Kilar.
1 Weston Master II exposure meter
1 Weston Master IV
Extension tubes, dual cable release, air release, filters, etc.
2 Braun Mecablitz electronic flash units
2 metal carrying cases

C. *Film stock*

The Travel and Exploration Unit of BBC Television contracted with the balloon safari team for four half-hour
programmes. The first three of these were presented on
television in August and September 1962; the fourth at a
later date. The BBC decided to have these programmes shot
in black and white and gave us the following film stock:

24,000 feet of Eastman Plus-X Pan 16 mm. negative film
in 100-foot rolls

24,000 feet of Plus-X Pan 16 mm. negative film in
400-foot rolls

12,000 feet of Eastman Tri-X 16 mm. negative film in
100-foot rolls

If I had to choose again I would take far fewer 400-foot
rolls, since an Arriflex with magazine attached was very
heavy to hand-hold in a balloon and awkward to use when
filming animals from a Land-Rover. And I would take much
less Tri-X high-speed film.

The still film we took with us consisted of:

35 × 35 mm. cassettes of Kodachrome II

5 × 35 mm. cassettes of High Speed Ektachrome

25 × 35 mm. cassettes of Kodak Plus-X

15 × 35 mm. cassettes of Kodak Tri-X

20 × 120 rolls of Kodak Plus-X

10 × 120 rolls of Kodak Tri-X

5 × 120 rolls of Kodak Royal-X ultra high-speed film

D. *Sound Recording*

Ficord midget tape recorder, operating on small, recharge-
able accumulators.

E. *Wild-Life Photography*

A lot of our photography of animals was done from the

ground. This is a specialist technique and requires experience of animal habits, quick shooting and some luck. Most animals are not afraid of man when he is inside a car —his scent is dead, and he can approach very close to lion, rhinoceros and other big game. We mounted the Arriflex on a Miller head attached more or less permanently to a Land-Rover door from which the windows had been removed. This gave the camera great mobility, and it was always ready for shooting and at the right height for animal photography. It is not satisfactory to film from a tripod in the back of a Land-Rover, still less on the top of one.

We got a good many exciting shots of big animals, and missed a number of others. I failed to film Anthony Smith surprising a lion by treading on it in the Ngorongoro Crater, because I was immediately behind him and did not wait to see what happened. And I did not film a lioness which followed me round a tent in the Serengeti because the camera lens was not sufficiently wide-angle! A cameraman should at all times be detached from his subject, whether in a balloon or within spitting distance of a carnivore.

BALLOON LIFT CALCULATIONS

(*a*) Total lift of Jambo at Zanzibar (sea-level; temp. 70 deg. F.).

Payload:

Smith	203 lb.
Botting	181 lb.
Pauw	165 lb.
Cameras and film	38 lb.
Tape recorder	12 lb.
Water, food and champagne	22 lb.

Balloon and Accessories:

Basket	94 lb.
Net	90 lb.
Balloon, valve and ring	484 lb.
Grapnel	12 lb.
Rope ladder	2 lb.
Trail rope	53 lb.
Radio	15 lb.
Sand	336 lb.
	1,707 lb.

Therefore Jambo's actual payload at Zanzibar was 621 lb. In fact, only 60 lb. of sand out of the total were used on the flight. If discretion had also been thrown to the winds, the payload could have been raised to 897 lb. had only 60 lb. of sand been taken. The payload would then have been more than half the all-up weight.

(b) General lifting capacity of different gases:

Gas	Relative weights	Kgs/cu. m.	Lift
Air	1	1·3	0
Hot air (200 deg. C.)	0·6	0·78	0·52 kgs/cu. m.
Coal gas (average)	0·4	0·52	0·78 kgs/cu. m.
Helium	0·14	0·18	1·12 kgs/cu. m.
Hydrogen	0·07	0·09	1·21 kgs/cu. m.

Lift is the weight of air displaced minus the weight of the gas displacing it.

(c) Estimates of the possibilities of hot air:

As can be seen from Appendix 2 (a), the 26,000 cubic foot (about 750 cubic metres) balloon Jambo had a total lift of 1,707 lb. (765 kgs) on a normal day at sea-level in the tropics. To achieve the same lift a balloon filled with hot air at 100 deg. C. above ambient would have to be about three and a half times greater in volume. However, such a hot-air balloon would not be able to raise the same payload as Jambo because its increased volume would mean a greater weight of fabric. The fabric of such a balloon could easily weigh twice as much as Jambo's 450 lb., and once again the size of the hot-air balloon would have to be increased to produce the same lifting abilities. It would not be necessary to carry sand, but fuel for the burner would have to be taken. All in all, Jambo's lifting powers at Zanzibar would only be equalled by a hot-air balloon of about 125,000 cubic feet (3,650 cubic metres) if the air inside it was 100 deg. C. above ambient. Admittedly, the air could be made hotter, and either the lift could be increased thereby or the balloon made smaller, but that temperature of 100 deg. C. is high for many fabrics and their coatings. It seemed to us a reasonable figure on which to base the calculations.

The prospects of having such a large hot-air balloon were intimidating, and the situation became worse as the calculations were repeated for higher altitudes and different temperatures. The greater the height, and the hotter the day, the worse they became. The following four groups of calculations showed how the situation changed.

1. Sea-level, 86 deg. F. ambient, 1·161 kgs/cubic metre air density. (Zanzibar noon.)

>43,000 cubic foot balloon will lift   800 lb.
>53,000 cubic foot balloon will lift 1,000 lb.
>67,000 cubic foot balloon will lift 1,250 lb.
>80,000 cubic foot balloon will lift 1,500 lb.

2. 5,000 feet altitude, 86 deg. F. ambient, 0·970 kgs/cubic metre air density. (Serengeti noon.)

>51,000 cubic foot balloon will lift   800 lb.
>63,000 cubic foot balloon will lift 1,000 lb.
>79,000 cubic foot balloon will lift 1,250 lb.
>95,000 cubic foot balloon will lift 1,500 lb.

3. 5,000 feet altitude, 56 deg. F. ambient, 1·020 kgs/cubic metre air density. (Serengeti dawn.)

>46,500 cubic foot balloon will lift   800 lb.
>58,000 cubic foot balloon will lift 1,000 lb.
>73,000 cubic foot balloon will lift 1,250 lb.
>87,000 cubic foot balloon will lift 1,500 lb.

4. 7,500 feet altitude, 86 deg. F. ambient, 0·890 kgs/cubic metre air density. (Ngorongoro noon.)

>55,000 cubic foot balloon will lift   800 lb.
>69,000 cubic foot balloon will lift 1,000 lb.
>86,500 cubic foot balloon will lift 1,250 lb.

It was in the light of these calculations, and many more, that hydrogen—despite its drawbacks—was adopted as the gas most suitable for a balloon safari in East Africa.